Para-News

By

Richard Thomas

First Published 2012
Copyright © Richard Thomas 2012

Bretwalda Books
Unit 8, Fir Tree Close, Epsom, Surrey KT17 3LD
www.BretwaldaBooks.com

To receive an e-catalogue of our complete range of books
send an email to info@BretwaldaBooks.com

ISBN 978-1-907791-72-7

Bretwalda Books Ltd

Para-News

THE EBOOK PUBLISHING SENSATION
NOW IN PAPERBACK FOR THE FIRST TIME

The best of Richard Thomas –
columnist for Binnall of America
and Blogger for UFOMystic

Interviews, articles, and
columns all fully revised, updated
and expanded

Foreword by

Nick Redfern

When Richard Thomas asked me if I would be willing to write the foreword for his very first book, saying "Yes!" was not a problem at all. Over the last few years, I have followed Richard's work at Binnall of America, and in the pages of Stuart Miller's unfortunately short-lived Alien Worlds magazine. And not only have I followed his writing: I have also seen it grow and develop in scope, depth, subject-matter, and style.

Plus, as is very clear from his written output, Richard has a great passion and enthusiasm for those puzzles, people, and places of the outer-edge variety that he pursues. All of these are (or certainly should be!) essential character traits when it comes to investigating weird phenomena, and/or interviewing Fortean experts in their respective fields.

There's nothing worse than tired, old has-beens, utterly jaded and worn by their time spent chasing the ufological, the cryptozoological, the paranormal, and the supernatural. Thankfully, Richard is none of these! What he is, is someone who is constantly striving to learn more, share his data with others, and to do the latter in an informative, entertaining and thought-provoking fashion.

So, if your interests include (A) strange and ominous beasts of a type that science says cannot, and do not exist, but that cryptozoologists say otherwise; (B) weird and enigmatic outer-space conspiracies; (C) the intricacies of time-travel; (D) spooks and spectres from the other side; (E) the way in which science-fiction and science-fact often cross paths to truly astonishing degrees; and (F) and the ominous Orwellian road that our society seems to be evermore traveling down, then this is most certainly the book for you!

Nick Redfern is the author of many books, including The Real Men in Black *and* Space Girl Dead on Spaghetti Junction.

Contents

82   Chapter 2 – Conspiracy Research

143   Chapter 3 – The Paranormal

Introduction

Interview with Richard Thomas

Henry Baum of henrybaum.com turns the tables on me and asks me some questions about my new book PARA-NEWS – UFOs, Conspiracy Theories, Cryptozoology and much much more published by Bretwalda Books.

Henry Baum: Hey Richard, as I mentioned on Facebook, one of the major things that struck me about your book was the references to Alex Jones, and these are questions that have been gnawing at me, so I hope you don't mind the focus. I get pretty long-winded here, hope that's not a problem...

On with the questions …

In your book, you frequently raise the spectre of Alex Jones and his ideas on eugenics, the New World Order, and so on. Personally, I take some issue with Alex Jones for a few reasons, and I wonder if you could address them. The main thing that leaps out about Alex Jones is that he never raises the UFO issue – you actually interview someone at Infowars who seems pretty disinterested in the whole subject. This seems like a fairly impossible assertion to make – it's pretty clear that there is something going on with the UFO issue, if only because the government explanation for many sightings is so suspiciously stupid. If that's the case, and there is also a conspiracy to bring about a New World Order (NWO), then the two cannot be separated. When you look through at the NWO through the lens of the UFO issue then the NWO makes more sense – not just a way to aimlessly enslave us, but perhaps to make the population more controllable in the event of first contact. Do you think that's a possibility?

Richard Thomas: I've been following Alex Jones off and on since about 2000 when I saw him in an episode of Jon Ronson's "Secret Rulers of the World" series for Channel Four. He's had a big impact on the way I see the world and interpret world events. However, I do agree that he is missing a huge piece of the puzzle by not looking at the UFO topic in more depth. That said, trying to get the average person to accept that the Bilderberg Group really does exist is hard enough ... so I can understand why Alex Jones doesn't cover the topic as much as UFO researchers would like him to.

More recently, however, I have noticed that Alex is talking about UFOs a lot more on his radio show. For instance, I heard him talk about David Icke and Project Blue Beam.

I myself believe that the globalists will use any crisis be it real or manufactured to further their goal of a one world government, be it global warming, terrorism, Colonel Gaddafi, or yes, UFOs.

A lot of UFO researchers tend to romanticise what they call "Disclosure", the day when the world is finally told the truth (whatever that is) about what the US government and others really know about UFOs. I'm more cautious. I think if Disclosure ever really does occur (and that's a big if) we have to be careful that the existence of extraterrestrials or whatever isn't used as a justification to turn the world into a giant police state. Rahm Emanuel (formerly White House Chief of Staff to President Barack Obama) said "You never want a serious crisis to go to waste" and his words sum up the mentality of the globalists perfectly.

Henry Baum: I guess another way of saying this is that what he sees as nefarious might actually have a purpose. Granted, the way they're going about globalization is a total nightmare. I just can't shed the feeling that they have a grander plan than just profit or enslavement. I mean if you have a billion dollars, what's 2 billion? Maybe they're just addicts, I don't know. But I also think all that profit might be going to black projects – sort of like the arks in the "2012" movie. That's not a way of excusing them, but just saying that there's more purpose to this than enslavement for the hell of it. Of course. Hitler had a "purpose" too, so there's a lot to be wary of. In sum: do you think it's possible that a one world government could – in the very long term – potentially be positive?
Richard Thomas: No I don't. Lets say just for the sake of argument that the globalists have a higher purpose of some kind for what they're doing. Maybe they know about a fleet of marauding alien spaceships heading for Earth like in the film "Independence Day" or something like that, and the reason they want a world government and world army is so that the Earth will be able to defend itself against the alien invaders. That doesn't change the fact

that we'll still be living inside a giant dictatorship created in stealth … maybe we would be better off under the aliens, lol.

But seriously even if the globalists were honest and open about what they were doing, and openly said they wanted to create a world government but it's okay because it's going to be a democratic one, I would still be very against the idea. I don't believe something the size of a world government could function as a democracy and it wouldn't be long before it became a dictatorship. Which is why I believe a world government and even the European Union are bad ideas to begin with.

Henry Baum: I'm playing devil's advocate here a bit because the globalists have really tipped their hand about the kind of world they want and it's a bad one. But for the sake of argument – say there was disclosure of an alien that was totally benign. Given the state of the world, releasing this info could be apocalyptic. If people get this upset about sharia law and illegal immigrants, what will the American public – let alone Middle Eastern terrorists – do with a literal alien? Seen through the lens of disclosure, the Patriot Act makes more sense. Not just to stop terrorism in 2011, but to keep an eye on the total global freakout that could be coming. I'm not longing for a police state or anything, but supposing 1% of what we know about the UFO is true – that amounts to a massive amount of world-changing information. Everything that's happened – 9-11, the war in Iraq, and so on – takes on a new meaning. So I wonder if those romantics about disclosure would trade some of their liberty for the big reveal if it meant finally getting some answers to the UFO enigma.

What's always troubled me is that people like Bush Sr. or Dick Cheney are the ones who are more likely to know the story behind UFO secrecy. There's a strange alignment between UFO secrecy and right wing ideology. Do you think it's possible to have disclosure without the world turning into a police state – given the impact it would have on religious ideology and technology?

Richard Thomas: Well it depends what we're told. Not everyone is convinced we're dealing with aliens from outer space. But if we are I suppose if they were "totally benign" and no threat it is possible to have Disclosure without the world turning into a police state. But if they're not. No I don't think it looks good. After 9/11 many people were willing to give up their civil liberties to fight a small group of Islamic terrorists, imagine what they would be willing to do to combat a threat from outer space. But this is all just speculation.

Henry Baum: I also wonder about his ideas on Christianity. In his "Bohemian Grove" video, he points out that the men are sinister because they worship "the occult." He's even targeted Peter Joseph of "Zeitgeist" for being part of the New Age conspiracy, as if Christianity is the one true faith. If you watch "Zeitgeist" or "The God Who Wasn't There" it's pretty clear that the story of Christianity is fabricated. So Alex Jones believes in many conspiracies except one of the biggest: the fabrication of the Jesus story. Personally, I'd rather there be a universal religion than saying this one book (which advocates stoning heretics, among other things) is the be all end all of religious principles. What's your view of spirituality as it pertains to the NWO, or even to UFOs?

Richard Thomas: There's no question that early Christianity was hijacked by the Roman Empire. Christmas is as about as Christian as Halloween, December 25 was an important day to pagans. But I still celebrate it and I believe everyone has the right to believe, think, say, or do as they please as long as they don't knowingly lie or physically try to hurt anybody else.

Henry Baum: Finally, I wonder about things like population control. Studying population growth is not the same thing as advocating genocide, nor is advocating birth control. Planned Parenthood isn't evil – as he says in "Endgame" (which you reference). The Bilderberg conference might be totally sinister, but on the surface a bunch of powerful people all getting together to discuss the state of the world makes sense – why wouldn't they do that? I'm not even going to get into Global Warming science, as that's so loaded. I guess I never see in him any possible solutions – just a lot of paranoia about people who are looking for solutions. Certainly, some of these people are evil, but not all. Plainly our world is disordered, so people looking for a (lowercase) new world order might not all be dangerous.

I'm beginning to sound like a fat-cat apologist. It absolutely pisses me off that Obama and Bush are so identical and the wealthy elite

are profiting off the backs of everyone else and raping the planet.
They really seem to be sowing the seeds of disorder, rather than
sustainability. If you're not paranoid, you're not paying attention.
Jones' answer is to support Ron and Rand Paul – which I don't see
as feasible. Giving corporations even more power via deregulation
isn't the solution – i.e. Big Business isn't any better than Big
Government. So I'm wondering what your ideal system would be,
politically or economically.

Richard Thomas: Well my main problem with the Bilderburg
Group is that most people have never even heard about them. I
don't think that many powerful people should be allowed to meet in
secret once a year and nothing be said about it in the media.
Thankfully because of the hard work of dedicated researchers and
activists around the world that is starting to change.

I get what you're saying about birth control etc, but there's no
question that population reduction seems to be a big part of the
globalist agenda. You just have to look at the comments of people
like Prince Philip or Ted Turner and others.

"In the event that I am reincarnated, I would like to return as a
deadly virus, in order to contribute something to solve
overpopulation."

- Prince Phillip, Duke of Edinburgh, in the foreword to If I Were
an Animal

"A total population of 250-300 million people, a 95% decline
from present levels, would be ideal."

- Ted Turner, founder of CNN

"And I actually think the world will be much better when there's
only 10 or 20 percent of us left."

- Dr. Eric Pianka, University of Texas biologist

What kind of system would I like?

First I think its important to stress I don't believe in Utopia.
There's no such thing, you'll never have a perfect world and every
attempt at creating one has always led to mass slaughter and
tyranny. I think we need to recognise that first.

I think the founders of the United States had some good ideas.
Things like a written constitution that protected the freedom of
speech and other rights of the people, and an educated, informed
public who could understand what that constitution said. Now, of
course, even the early United States had its problems, slavery being

a big one. But I think that's a good place to start. But if readers want to disagree with me ... great ... it's called freedom. Hopefully we can all agree on that.

UFOs

The Sea Devils' Triangle: Is The Bermuda Triangle A Good Place For an 'Alien' Base?

The Bermuda Triangle (sometimes known as the "Devil's Triangle"), of course, is a triangular area of the northwestern Atlantic Ocean bounded by Bermuda, Puerto Rico and a point near Melbourne, Florida, where famously numerous ships and aircraft have mysteriously disappeared over many years. Since records began in 1851, it is estimated that an amazing 8,127 people have been lost in the Bermuda Triangle. With so many missing, it would obviously be impossible to discuss all the mysterious disappearances reported in the Triangle here (as would it be to discuss all the strange phenomena witnessed there), so we're going to concentrate on just some of the most interesting cases – beginning with perhaps the oldest documented account of weird happenings in the triangle.

According to most Triangle researchers, Christopher Columbus was probably the first person to document allegedly strange phenomena in the area. On October 11, 1492, (the eve of discovering the New World) Columbus reports that he and his crew observed a mysterious light moving strangely up and down in the evening sky, appearing and quickly disappearing several times that night. Columbus wrote in his log that:

"The land was first seen by a sailor called Rodrigo de Triana, although the Admiral [Columbus] at ten o'clock that evening standing on the quarter-deck saw a light, but so small a body that he could not affirm it to be land; calling to Pero Gutierrez, Groom of the King's Wardrobe, he told him he saw a light, and bid him look that way, which he did and saw it; he did the same to Rodrigo Sanchez of Segovia, whom the King and Queen had sent with the squadron as comptroller, but he was unable to see it from his situation. The Admiral again perceived it once or twice, appearing like the light of a wax candle moving up and down, which some thought an indication of land. But the Admiral held it for certain that land was near…"

Whatever Columbus and his crew saw that historic night is probably impossible to know for sure now. In that limited sense, at least, the odd light is a true UFO in that it will probably always be unidentified. Perhaps more interesting, though, are the bizarre compass readings Columbus also recorded in the Triangle.

Today, the Triangle is allegedly one of only two places in the world (the other being the Dragon's Triangle in the Pacific) in which there is an unusual level of magnetic interference that can adversely affect compass readings. Whether paranormal or not, this magnetic interference is definitely interesting. Many have speculated that UFOs may be using some form of electromagnetic propulsion. Perhaps there could be a link of some kind between the magnetic interference, UFO sightings and the mysterious disappearances in the Triangle?

The earliest documented case of a US vessel mysteriously disappearing in the Triangle occurred during WWI. Named after the race of one-eyed giants from Greek mythology, the USS Cyclops (AC-4) was one of four Proteus-class colliers built for the US Navy. The ship and crew went missing without a trace sometime after March 4, 1918, after departing from Barbados. The disappearance of the ship and the 306 people on board remains the single largest loss of life in US Naval history not directly involving combat. Amazingly, its sister ship, the USS Nereus (AC-10), also disappeared in the Triangle in similar circumstances during WWII.

However, perhaps the most intriguing (and famous) disappearance of all, occurred just after WWII on December 5, 1945, when an entire squadron of aircraft vanished without trace and no clue as to what happened to them. Of course, this was the infamous Flight 19, which, more than any other case, brought the Triangle into popular consciousness, sparking all kinds of explanations. The strangest and most interesting being the theory that they were abducted by aliens, interesting because it was popularized by Stephen Spielberg in his 1977 film Close Encounters of the Third Kind.

For those wondering about the title of this piece, "The Sea Devils" is the name of a classic 1972 Doctor Who story written by Malcolm Hulke, the plot of which is very reminiscent of the Triangle mystery. The story involves the Doctor investigating the mysterious disappearance of ships off the English South Coast and the discovery that an ancient race of amphibious reptiles, operating from a deep underwater base are responsible.

Doctor Who is one thing but is it possible that there really could be another civilization, of any kind, sharing the planet with us, living beneath the waves in seclusion?

Amazingly, it is true that we actually know more about the surface of the Moon than we do about the bottom of our own oceans. In theory, at least, it is possible that anything could be down there hidden beneath the depths. What's more, making things more interesting, about half of all UFO sightings are said to take place near large bodies of water.

In Invisible Residents: The Reality of Underwater UFOs (1970), renowned zoologist, Ivan T. Sanderson hypothesized that an advanced aquatic non-human civilization may have evolved right here on the Earth. This parallel, aquatic civilization could be twice as old as mankind, Sanderson proposed, and may well have developed space flight long before us. Sanderson even goes as far as suggesting that such a civilization could be behind many of the mysterious disappearances in the Triangle (as well as UFO sightings). Interestingly, more recently Sanderson's ideas have been echoed somewhat in Mac Tonnies's "cryptoterrestrial hypothesis".

Another possibility, of course, could be that the planet has somehow been covertly colonized by an extraterrestrial civilization from another solar system. In Unearthly Disclosure (2000), best selling author Timothy Good disclosed information given to him by "a senior reporter in Washington, DC," who, in turn, received it from "a senior US Air Force officer", about the existence of extraterrestrial bases on the Earth.

Good writes: "According to the officer, aliens have been coming to Earth for a very long time. Following the Second World War, they began to establish permanent bases here, in Australia, the Caribbean, the Pacific Ocean, the Soviet Union and in the United States."

If extraterrestrials are really coming to Earth from another solar system, it would probably make sense that they would establish such bases to save them continually making the long voyage back and forth to home. Also, the reference to the Caribbean is particularly interesting because it shares the same general area as the Triangle.

However, whether from this world or another, where better to build an impenetrable, covert base than beneath the oceans of the world. The Bermuda Triangle, in particular, might also make a good location for such a base because of the volcanic activity there, which could be used to generate geothermal electricity as a power source.

Perhaps the Bermuda Triangle can be explained away by more mundane explanations such as freak weather conditions and human error, but until we more fully explore the bottom of the world's oceans, we have no way of knowing for sure what could be down there.

Is There a Secret US Space Program?

In an article for the May 16, 2010 edition of the Scottish Sunday Express it was reported that the UK UFO hacker Gary McKinnon was – to quote the newspaper article – "set to avoid extradition and be tried in Britain", The 43-year-old, of course, made international headlines back in 2005 after he was accused with various counts of hacking into Pentagon and NASA computers, in search of what the computer wizard described as "free energy technology," which McKinnon believed the US Government had reverse-engineered from recovered UFOs.

To the disappointment of the British UFO community, however, this news that McKinnon was set to face trial in the UK was never confirmed by British Government, and leaves us with more questions than answers. Why have the US Government fought so hard for so long to get McKinnon in the first place? Or, put another way, what might Gary have stumbled upon that warranted such a heavy-handed reaction from the US authorities?

Up to "60 years in prison" seems a bit of an overreaction for someone who was simply searching for something, which according to the US Government isn't even supposed to officially exist anyway. Could McKinnon have really found evidence of UFO crash retrievals, or, did the UFO hacker find something else entirely that the US military-industrial-political complex would rather you didn't find out about?

While the mainstream media largely concentrated on the US Government's dubious claim that McKinnon caused some $700,000 worth of damages to its computers, some truly out-of-this-world comments the supposed "cyber terrorist" made to the author of The Men Who Stare At Goats, Jon Ronson, in an interview printed in the July 9, 2005 edition of The Guardian were all but ignored. In particular, McKinnon's assertions that while probing into the US space command he discovered "lists of officers' names" under the tantalising heading "Non-Terrestrial Officers" as well as records of what McKinnon called "fleet-to-fleet transfers" and even "a list of ship names."

Rather than extraterrestrials, though, McKinnon told The Guardian columnist that he thought he had found evidence of a secret space program of some kind. When Ronson asked McKinnon "The Americans have a secret spaceship?" McKinnon answered, "That's what this trickle of evidence has led me to believe."

McKinnon's suggestion that NASA and its 2004 "vision" to return to the Moon by 2020 (over 50 years after the Apollo 11 landing!) could just be a cover for a much more advanced and deeply clandestine or "black" space program might sound like just another conspiracy theory but McKinnon isn't the first to advocate such a hypothesis. The concept of a secret space program first gaining some prominence in 1977 when the UK's Anglia Television (now ITV Anglia) broadcast the now infamous Orson Welles War of the Worlds-style hoax documentary: Alternative 3. The plot, of which, revolved around a global conspiracy to resettle missing scientists onto the Moon and Mars in preparation for an imminent environmental cataclysm.

While Alternative 3 is obviously science fiction. Something made clear by the lengthy interview with a fictitious Moon walking Apollo astronaut "Bob Grodin" (played by Shane Rimmer) as well as the list of programme credits run at the end. It is at least interesting that today climatologists are alarmingly forecasting exactly the kind of catastrophic global warming predicted in the mock documentary. A fact which has led to much speculation on the world wide web that the April Fools hoax might have started out as a genuine investigation before having the plug pulled by sinister dark forces ... perhaps the same forces calling for the extradition of Gary McKinnon.

In Jim Marrs' Alien Agenda: Investigating the Extraterrestrial Presence Among Us, the underground bestselling author briefly considered the Alternative 3 controversy. Marrs wrote of respected UFO investigator and television documentary filmmaker Linda Mouton Howe's involvement in investigating the controversial docudrama, reporting: "'I was curious,' Howe said, 'and I had a discussion with a BBC producer about it. I was told that the program began as a BBC documentary on the so-called British 'brain drain' of the 1970s. You might remember that a large number of British scientists were leaving, reportedly for better-paying jobs in America. I was told that the program never came off because the BBC could not locate any of the scientists once they left Britain. It was all very odd. It was like they disappeared.'"

Further, Marrs also writes in Alien Agenda that "Howe said writers Ambrose and Miles wrote a script for Alternative 3 based on real interviews conducted by the BBC."

Journalist and author of Science Fiction Secrets: From Government Files and the Paranormal Nick Redfern wasn't convinced of this, though. When I asked this paranormal investigator about McKinnon's comments in a 2008 interview for the popular esoteric website Binnall of America, Redfern told me "Non-Terrestrial Officers is of course a provocative term that conjures up all sorts of imagery. I think, however, that like much of Ufology, we have a few fragments of a story with what McKinnon found. But what the term might mean is very much down to personal interpretation."

Other researchers, however, have been less sceptical about the possibility of a secret space program. Author of Need to Know: UFOs, the Military and Intelligence and Above Top Secret: The Worldwide UFO Cover-up Timothy Good has gone as far as suggesting an extraterrestrial connection. "In addition to having reverse-engineered some recovered alien vehicles, I believe that we've been given highly advanced technology – including spacecraft – by certain allied extraterrestrials. As Ben Rich stated at the University of California School of Engineering in 1993: 'We already have the means to travel among the stars, but these technologies are locked up in black projects ... and it would take an Act of God to ever get them out to benefit humanity.'"

And Good is not alone. Acclaimed UFO Historian and author of the definitive multi-volume UFOs and the National Security State, Richard Dolan, has also spoken out about the possibility of such a covert program indeed existing. Initially sceptical, the Oxford educated historian writing in a special guest article for my website RichardThomas.eu said that "Slowly, by degrees, I have come to the opinion that there is a secret space program."

According to Dolan he was told by an individual with "impressive scientific and intelligence credentials" that he "should not dismiss" the supposed anomalies located in the Cydonia region of Mars, such as the famous "Face" and "City" photographed by NASA's Viking 1

Orbitor in 1976. And that "there were in fact many people within the classified world who took them seriously."

Dolan wrote, "That's when I realized, very concretely, that the notion of space anomalies was indeed a serious topic. I began to consider: if there is covert interest in the anomalies on Mars, would there be a covert space program to investigate? To this day, I don't know the answer with certainty, but over the years I have encountered no shortage of quiet, serious-minded people who tell me of their knowledge that there is such a covert program. One component of this, it appears, has to do with the Moon. Are there bases on the far side of the Moon? Again, I do not know for sure, but I cannot rule it out. More than once, people I consider to be informed insiders have steered me in this direction."

However, it isn't just the opinions of credentialed but anonymous insiders about the possibilities of alien architecture on Mars and perhaps even the Moon that interests Dolan.

"There is another reason to suppose the existence of an advanced, clandestine space program. An enormous amount of video of space missions has been downloaded and is available for anyone to see. These include missions of NASA, the European Space Agency, Russia, and China. Much of this was downloaded and made available by a gentleman named Jeff Challender, who unfortunately died in 2007. Jeff spent an enormous part of his life downloading and reviewing – very carefully – video recordings of those missions. There can be no denying that there has been a great deal of activity in Earth's orbit. Much of what was recorded undoubtedly has conventional explanations. But, frankly, many events do not offer easy explanations. I firmly believe there is something unusual going on in Earth's orbit. Fortunately, after Jeff's death, I was able to upload his entire site and attach it to my own. His site, known as Project Prove, now has a permanent home at keyholepublishing.com."

This cocktail of tempting space anomalies on the one hand, which if indeed artificial or extraterrestrial would offer whichever nation studied them first tremendous leaps in technology, and video evidence of covert activity in space on the other. Not to mention the US Government's determination to extradite McKinnon after he had gained access into NASA computers, does seem to add up to good grounds for suspecting a covert space program as Dolan suggests. There is only one problem with all this speculation, though, how would the US Government (or anyone else for that matter) fund such a vast and deeply clandestine project – possibly for decades if any of the information presented in Alternative 3 is to be taken seriously – without anyone even noticing? Any space programme along the lines of Alternative 3 or as envisioned by Dolan with bases on the Moon would cost trillions of dollars, surely there would be evidence of such incredible spending?

The short answer is yes, there would be ... and YES there is. In 2001, at the National Press Club, US Secretary of Defence Donald Rumsfeld admitted to the media that amazingly "According to some estimates, we cannot track $2.3 trillion in transactions." What's more, this took place somewhat suspiciously on September 10, the eve of the 9/11 attacks on New York and the Pentagon, guaranteeing the story would get buried by the mainstream media and forgotten about the next day.

This is where things get more complicated. Up to now we've assumed that the US authorities wanted McKinnon because of what he might have stumbled upon in relation to UFOs or a secret space program. However, it's worth considering that McKinnon was active during and in the immediate aftermath of 9/11. While the date of Rumsfeld's $2.3 trillion admission is suspicious it is circumstantial evidence of prior knowledge at best, however, we must ask is it possible Gary stumbled upon something relating to the 9/11 instead? If so, McKinnon is remaining quiet. And with the extradition efforts of the US authorities dragging on, it might be some time before we find out more.

The UK UFO Debate

I live in South Wales, so I was particularly excited by the incident which kicked off an enormous increase in interest in UFOs in Britain, and many more sightings subsequently being reported to the now defunct UFO desk at the Ministry of Defence (MoD).

On June 8, 2008, a police helicopter was apparently forced to swerve sharply to avoid being hit by what the experienced crew termed an "unusual aircraft" near RAF St Athan, a military base near Cardiff. A few weeks later, another dramatic sighting was reported, this time by a member of the military. A soldier, along with three other witnesses, saw several "craft" spinning in the skies above his barracks near Market Drayton, Shropshire, just two hours before the South

Wales UFO-helicopter incident – begging the question, could these two sightings be related?

It would be hard to overstate the excitement generated, not just in UFO-circles, but in the general public and press, by these incidents. The UFO phenomenon was the hot topic of the day and even the official statements about Chinese lanterns failed to stem a tide of new sightings reported by the British public to the press and the MoD. This wave lasted throughout 2008, with The Sun newspaper creating its own online UFO page to cope with the correspondence, and it only began to wane during the latter half of 2009.

Despite this renewed interest and calls for official inquiries from the likes of Nick Pope, who ran its UFO desk for three years (1991-1994), the MoD has decided to take no more calls from the public – which might confirm in some people's mind that there really is a cover-up going on.

So, in order to get a handle of what's going on here, I tracked down the "three lions" of British ufology: the aforementioned former MoD investigator Nick Pope; prolific author and contributor to Paranormal Magazine; Nick Redfern; and the master of UFO cover-up research and author of the "UFO Bible" Above Top Secret; and finally Timothy Good.

What follows are the interviews that I conducted with these three men. The interviews have been labelled "Room 101 Interviews" in reference to the horrific Room 101 found in the great futuristic novel 1984 written by George Orwell. The original Room 101 was a torture chamber in which a prisoner of the state was forced to confront his or her own worst fears. My own interviews were not that bad, but the novel's overtones of an all powerful state misleading its citizens seemed too good to ignore.

A Room 101 Interview with Nick Redfern

Esoteric superstar Nick Redfern is, of course, a big name but I have a special reason for admiring him. Back in 2006, I sent Tim Binnall an email that asked if he could possibly ask a future BoA:Audio guest about the 1974 Berwyn Mountain incident or "Welsh Roswell", in which I have a special interest. A few months later, he asked British Ufologist and author Nick Redfern about the Berwyn case while attending the UFO Crash Retrieval Conference IV. Then, about a year later, Tim had another chance to interview

Nick and this time, on my behalf, he asked him about the Alien Big Cats phenomenon in the UK and related an ABC sighting my younger sister actually had here in Wales. The episode also saw me being brought further into the BoA fold, with Tim coining me the "BoA UK Correspondent." So, I was delighted to have the chance to interview Nick Redfern in the Room 101 format.

Nick, of course, is a highly successful author from the UK who has written several books on UFOs and other esoteric subjects. In such a US-centric field, his decorated writing career has been a huge source of inspiration to someone, from the same side of "the pond," who hopes to become an esoteric author himself someday. At last a chance to interview the man myself ...

Richard Thomas: First things first. Thank you very much for taking the time to answer these questions. One of the first UFO books I ever read was Cosmic Crashes, a book you wrote detailing cases of alleged UFO crashes in the UK. One of the most interesting crash stories investigated in the book is that of a supposed UFO crash somewhere in the UK during WWII. The possible link to the JFK assassination was interesting. What do you think the truth of the matter could be?

Nick Redfern: There have been rumours for many years of an alleged UFO crash – or Foo Fighter crash – in Britain at some point during the Second World War. Unfortunately, the details are very brief and no-one has really been able to pinpoint with any real accuracy what exactly happened, where and when. However, there are stories of elements of the British Government and military supposedly examining such a device – and crew – at some point prior to 1955. The weird thing is that details of this story turn up in a controversial "leaked" document that has ties to the JFK assassination. And as bizarre as it may sound, there are many threads that link UFOs and the JFK assassination, which leads some people to suspect there is a direct connection. Needless to say, it's a highly controversial area, but it's one on which every so often a new bit of data will surface.

Richard Thomas: Perhaps the most interesting case discussed in the book though is that of the 1974 Berwyn Mountain incident or Welsh Roswell. The bit in the book about the alleged transport of dead alien bodies recovered from the crash site was particularly interesting. What do you think might have happened there? Do you think it was a genuine UFO (whatever they may be), the misinterpretation of natural phenomena, some kind of black project or perhaps something else?

Nick Redfern: The Berwyn Mountains crash-story of 1974 is one of the strangest and most enduring cases I've looked into. It's one of those that never goes away, even when down-to-earth explanations have been offered. Back in the mid-90s, I was of the opinion that a UFO had come down, then I changed my mind after reading the research of Andy Roberts. However, I still get accounts now and again from locals and retired military people (all specifically from RAF Valley, interestingly enough) of knowledge of bodies recovered and taken to Porton Down, Wiltshire. So, I'll be the first to admit that, today, it's one that continues to puzzle me. On the one hand, I am convinced that Andy has solved massive parts of the story. But, on the other hand, it's difficult to dismiss the testimony of the military people who have accounts to relate, and nothing to gain by spreading a false story. I think, though, that we have not heard the last of the case by any means!

Richard Thomas: In Cosmic Crashes, you also hypothesize about the existence of an MJ-12-like group operating in the UK, what you call MJ-UK. Do you still think there could be such a covert group and what about the alleged UFO ties with RAF Rudloe Manor?

Nick Redfern: The whole Rudloe-UFO saga has been a puzzle in itself. There's no doubt that the RAF's Provost & Security Services (who were based at Rudloe for two decades) have played a role in official UFO investigations. There are even a few declassified files available at the National Archive, Kew. But the big question is the particularly Matthew Williams in the mid-to-late 90s – that Rudloe's role went far beyond that officially admitted by the MoD. Others merely see it as a minor aspect of official UFO investigations that got blown up out of proportion by the UFO research community. As with the Berwyn case, I still get accounts now and again from people talking about how, at one point at least, Rudloe was involved at a far deeper level. But I will concede that actually proving this has not happened yet.

Richard Thomas: In Body Snatchers in the Desert, you make a fair case that the famous Roswell incident might be explained by classified military experiments carried out after WWII. In light of this, what do you think about the work of Nick Cook (author of The Hunt for Zero Point) who suggests that many UFOs can probably be explained by US military black projects, perhaps even anti-gravity aircraft?

Nick Redfern: There's absolutely no doubt in my mind that the UFO issue has indeed been utilised – and very successfully too – as a cover for classified military activity, such as the test-flying of prototype aircraft, etc. In "Body Snatchers" I reference a number of cases aside from Roswell that might be classic examples of fabricated UFO stories to hide something more down to earth. I definitely think Cook's work is valid and that he has uncovered some genuine material on very radical aircraft and that gravity manipulation and control is linked to that. Around the time of Roswell, however, I think it was more to do with radical designs, rather than super-advanced technology.

Richard Thomas: The recent helicopter UFO incident in Wales happened near RAF St Athan, a military base outside Cardiff. Do you think there could be some kind of military explanation for this or any of the other recent sightings we've had in the UK?

Nick Redfern: Well, the Welsh one is interesting, but I think on examination many of the others were simply Chinese Lanterns. That's not me being a sceptic. Rather, while I believe there is indeed a genuine unsolved UFO presence among us, the fact is that most cases can be explained. And I put much of the recent UK wave in the second category.

Richard Thomas: Maybe some of the many alleged UFO crashes since WWII can be explained by the Pentagon's billion dollar black budget, but what about pre-war cases, in particular the 1908 Tunguska Event in Russia? Do you have any thoughts on that?

Nick Redfern: Tunguska is definitely back in the news with new books, magazine articles etc. There are some odd aspects to the story, such as reports of the "object" changing direction in flight, etc. I keep an open mind on the event, but I suspect that given its age, we'll probably never really know now.

Richard Thomas: In the 1977 spoof documentary Alternative 3 it is suggested that there is a secret space program. More recently, "UFO hacker" Gary McKinnon has claimed he saw evidence of what might be part of such a program while hacking into NASA and US military computer networks. In particular, McKinnon said he found a list of officers' names under the mysterious heading "Non-Terrestrial Officers," as well as a list of "fleet-to-fleet transfers" and ship names. What do you think of this? Any thoughts on the possibility of a secret space program?

Nick Redfern: "Non-Terrestrial Officers" is of course a provocative term that conjures up all sorts of imagery. I think, however, that like much of Ufology, we have a few fragments of a story with what McKinnon found. But what the term might mean is very much down to personal interpretation.

Richard Thomas: What's the scariest thing that has ever happened to you during your investigations?

Nick Redfern: I wouldn't say I've ever got scared on an investigation. I think on-site investigations can be very intriguing, sometimes adventurous and sometimes adrenalin-pumping. But I view it from a positive angle and one to be intrigued and excited by rather than a fear-driven, scared angle, which is more negative-driven.

Richard Thomas: Have you got any good advice for a young aspiring writer with an interest in UFOs and the paranormal?

Nick Redfern: Be enthusiastic about what you do, whether it's writing books, articles, lecturing, or doing research and investigations. There's nothing worse than seeing someone in the subject who has lost their spark and their zest for what they do. Also, don't worry about people's opinions. Do what you want because you want to do it; and don't be force-fed the opinions of others. And try not to be driven by belief systems. At some point, we're all guilty of that to varying degrees; however, wherever and whenever possible, just go where the facts take you. And if the facts go where you want them to go, that's great. But if they take you down a different path to the one you were expecting, then that's how it goes. And avoiding preconceived belief-systems is the best way to deal with investigations, in my opinion.

Richard Thomas: Thanks again and all the best, I look forward to your future books and articles.

A Room 101 Interview with Timothy Good

After many years of following his work, I'm finally getting the chance to ask best selling author and UFO researcher Timothy Good some questions. From Above Top Secret (which many consider the bible of Ufology) to Unearthly Disclosure and his latest Need To Know, Good has written some excellent books. I'm sure you will all enjoy this interview as much as I did.

Richard Thomas: First things first. Thank you very much for taking the time to answer these questions. I really appreciate it.

Your very first book, co-written with Lou Zinsstag, was George Adamski The Untold Story. What most impressed you about Adamski and have your thoughts on him changed much since writing the book?

Timothy Good: Adamski's photographs (and films) impressed me a great deal. Also, his initial encounter near Desert Center, California, in November 1952, was witnessed by six people who signed affidavits testifying to the fact. I knew two of those people, and they weren't lying. His famous photos, taken with a plate camera attached to a telescope, have been authenticated by a number of qualified people. As for his films, the last and best one – showing a craft similar to the one he photographed in 1952 – was taken at Silver Spring, Maryland, in February 1965, witnessed by my friend Madeleine Rodeffer and three US government employees. The 8mm colour film was authenticated by Bill Sherwood, an optical physicist and a senior project development engineer for the Eastman-Kodak company in Rochester, NY. In May 1998 I was invited to the Defense Airborne Reconnaissance Office in the Pentagon, which at that time handled the unmanned spy planes programme. The director, Major Kenneth Israel, implied to me that the film was genuine. Unfortunately, copies of the film (sometimes shown in documentaries) are unconvincing, being darker and more contrasty than the original film. Individual frames light-enhanced by Sherwood show much more detail.

As for Adamski's claim that the aliens he met were from all the planets in the solar system – Venus and Mars in particular – this has understandably given rise to much ridicule. Most likely, this was a smoke screen to protect their actual origin. However, I don't discount the possibility that alien bases exist on the other planets in our system. Indeed, I think it quite likely that Venus and Mars, and several moons of Saturn and Jupiter, for example, qualify in this respect. Any adverse temperatures and pressures can be dealt with by means of advanced technology. And they most definitely have had bases on Earth for a very long time.

I've always been intrigued by the fact that Adamski held a US Government Ordnance Department card, which gave him access to US military bases and other restricted areas. He liaised with many high-ranking military personnel, including Lord Mountbatten (British admiral and former Viceroy of India) and Lord Dowding (Commander of RAF Fighter Command during the Battle of Britain in 1940) on one occasion, and even – in 1963 – with President Kennedy.

Richard Thomas: I understand that you may have had what might be called a "contactee experience" yourself, what do you think happened?

Timothy Good: Yes, in fact I've had several encounters with beings I believe were from elsewhere. The first occurred at a diner near the Arizona/California border in November 1963 while I was on tour with the Royal Philharmonic Orchestra. It would take me too long to go into all the details, but it involved an unusual young woman who – in the presence of three of my colleagues – responded very positively, but non-verbally, to my telepathic question as to whether she was from elsewhere. Just after we left the diner in our convoy of three coaches, I was astonished to see a road sign for Desert Center – I'd no idea we were anywhere near there. Quite a coincidence!

The second encounter took place in the lobby of a hotel in the middle of New York in February 1967, between a rehearsal and concert with the London Symphony Orchestra. About half-an-hour after I'd transmitted a telepathic request for definitive proof that some aliens were living among us, an immaculately suited man walked into the lobby then sat beside me. Following my telepathic request to indicate by means of a certain sign if he was the person I was looking for, he did so immediately. Neither of us spoke. It was a cathartic experience for me.

Richard Thomas: One of your books is called Alien Base. What do you think of the possibility that Earth could have already been covertly colonised by extraterrestrials or, alternatively, that another intelligent species could have evolved here long before mankind?

Timothy Good: I'm convinced that Earth was colonized by ETs millennia ago, and that we humans are a hybridized species. Apparently, hybridization started at the time of Homo erectus. There are many different species of extraterrestrials. The abductions in more recent times seem to involve the use of humans for hybridization purposes. But for whose benefit? In the 1990's I spent a lot of time investigating cases in Puerto Rico and it's clear to me that the animal mutilations and abductions are related to the abduction phenomenon. For example, I interviewed a family who encountered bug-eyed creatures that had developed some human characteristics – specifically wispy traces of hair on their heads. Are they trying to adapt to our planet, and if so, why?

Richard Thomas: Over 20 years ago now, in Above Top Secret, you were the first researcher to make public the controversial MJ-12 documents. What are your current thoughts on the documents and MJ-12?

Timothy Good: As I have stated repeatedly in my books subsequent to Above Top Secret, the MJ-12 papers are forgeries. The purpose, in my view, was to smoke out some of the real MJ-12 members or those who were knowledgeable about the organization. The ruse worked. Several former military and intelligence personnel – e.g. Dr Eric Walker, a British-born scientist – have confirmed that MJ-12 existed (see Need to Know).

Richard Thomas: It is commonly believed in Ufology that the UFO cover-up began in early July 1947 after the famous Roswell Incident. So, when I read your latest book, Need to Know: UFOs, the Military and Intelligence, I was intrigued to learn of a possible 1933 UFO crash recovery in Milan, Italy. The possible existence of a top-secret group – Gabinetto RS/33 – allegedly set up after the supposed 1933 crash, to deal with "unknown aircraft" was also very interesting. How likely do you think it is that a UFO did crash and that an Italian MJ-12 like group was set up in 1933?

Timothy Good: The UFO cover-up seems to have begun in 1933 with the top-secret RS/33 group. Other governments – that of Sweden in particular – also became concerned about intrusions of strange flying machines that year. Unfortunately we don't have an actual description of the type of unknown aircraft which came down in Italy. I think it possible that a UFO did crash, but I have no definitive information on that particular case. However, the RS/33 documents – which include descriptions of unexplained craft seen by pilots in 1936 – are evidently genuine.

Richard Thomas: What do you think of a possible link between Gabinetto RS/33 and flying saucers allegedly built by the Nazis during WWII? Perhaps you might have some thoughts on the Nazi "Bell" device discussed in Nick Cook's The Hunt for Zero Point.
Timothy Good: Roberto Pinotti, who co-authored a book with Alfredo Lissoni on the case, believes that the alleged retrieval led to some German "reverse-engineering". I don't know if that's true. And as I said, we don't have (or at least, I don't have) an actual description of the craft involved. As for the "Nazi hypothesis", one of the world's leading aviation historians, Bill Gunston, who wrote the foreword to Need to Know, believes there is no serious evidence that the Germans actually produced any highly advanced flying discs, though he concedes that they were beginning to work on conventionally propelled craft with circular aerofoils. Re "the Bell", it definitely existed and a great deal of information can be found in both Nick Cook's book and Igor Witkowski's superb Truth About the Wunderwaffe, but there seems no evidence that its use was related to flying machines of any sort. As Witkowski concludes on the final page: "There is no evidence that the Germans mastered the production of 'flying saucers' with a revolutionary propulsion. One may on the other hand prove that they were attempting to use analogous bell-shaped objects as a weapon."

Richard Thomas: One of my favourite cases is the Berwyn Mountain Incident or "Welsh Roswell." What do you think may have happened in the Berwyn Mountains in 1974? And what do you think of the possibility of an MJ-UK group?
Timothy Good: I never investigated this case personally, so I keep an open mind. As to the possibility of a "MJ-UK", probably an equivalent team was set up, but I have no specifics. The top-secret

"Flying Saucer Working Party" (1950-51) would qualify in many respects. Whatever the case, the UK is subservient to the US regarding these matters.

Richard Thomas: What are your thoughts on the recent UFO activity in the UK, particularly the police helicopter sighting near RAF St Athan, a military base outside Cardiff? Interestingly, when I asked Nick Pope about the sightings he said: "Some sightings have clearly been caused by Chinese lanterns, but the MoD appear to be using this as an excuse not to investigate."

Timothy Good: I've yet to see a detailed official report, so I can't comment. Chinese lanterns (or "UFO balloons") have been responsible for nearly all the UFO sightings reported this year – and to a lesser extent, last year. They are a damned nuisance – particularly for us researchers.

Richard Thomas: Given that your latest book is called Need To Know, how much do you think US Presidents and British Prime Ministers are allowed to know about UFOs? Also how much do you think big corporations might know?

Timothy Good: A number of US presidents have been briefed on aspects of the alien problem. They were told as much as they needed to know. However, Eisenhower and Kennedy, for example (and perhaps a few others) also had direct contact with extraterrestrials. The most knowledgeable president, in my opinion, is George Bush senior. As for President George W. Bush, a friend of mine asked him what he knew about the UFO situation. "Ask Cheney," came the terse reply. I doubt that many British prime ministers have been told much. I think that Margaret Thatcher, thanks to her rapport with Reagan, learned a few things. As far as big corporations are concerned, I'm told that there is indeed a degree of corporate involvement.

Richard Thomas: In Alien Contact you interviewed Bob Lazar about his alleged experiences at S-4, a supposed ultra top-secret facility near Area-51/Groom Lake where, according to Lazar, alien technology is being studied and reverse-engineered. How much of Lazar's story do you think might be true? And do you still think reverse-engineering could be going on at Area-51?

Timothy Good: Lazar claimed to be a nuclear physicist. He isn't. However, he is a talented engineer and launches his own rockets and drives and maintains a jet-powered car (or used to). Definitely something odd seems to have happened to him, but I remain dubious about some of his claims. Perhaps he was exposed to S-4 (which does, or did, exist) in case he came up with some original ideas. Or it could have been an experiment to test public reaction, knowing that he would tell the media. I just don't know. It's important to bear in mind that Lazar was drugged on several occasions by the security personnel at S-4. I have no idea what's going on there now.

Richard Thomas: Ben Rich, the second director of the famous Lockheed's Skunk Works and sometimes called the "father of stealth," once made the incredible comment that: "We now have the technology to take ET home." In light of this, how successful do you think any reverse-engineering efforts may have been? And what are your thoughts on the idea of a secret space program?
Timothy Good: In addition to having reverse-engineered some recovered alien vehicles, I believe that we've been given highly advanced technology – including spacecraft – by certain allied extraterrestrials. As Ben Rich stated at the University of California School of Engineering in 1993: "We already have the means to travel among the stars, but these technologies are locked up in black projects . . . and it would take an Act of God to ever get them out to benefit humanity."

Richard Thomas: One of the most interesting chapters in Alien Contact is called "Cosmic Journey." What was Cosmic Journey and what do you think about it now?
Timothy Good: The 1989 Cosmic Journey Project, supported by the US government, NASA and Rockwell International, was a proposal for an international touring presentation of space-related materials, such as a mock-up of the space shuttle, and even 6,000 square feet of UFO-related material. I was invited to become the official consultant on UFO research. The main portion of the show, I learned, would be the future of space and the technical advances predicted over the next 100 years. To my everlasting regret, I was unable to make the private meeting with the organizers in Florida,

and recommended former NASA engineer Bob Oechsler to fill the position. The rest is history (see Alien Liaison/Alien Contact). Suffice it to say that Bob learned a great deal and claimed to have had some extraordinary experiences while working on the project – which eventually was cancelled.

Richard Thomas: What are your plans for the future? Are you working on anything or have any new cases grabbed your attention recently?

Timothy Good: I'm always working on new cases. I have no plans for a new book, however – I've yet to sort all my files relating to the last one, which took several years of intensive work. There's also the question of money. Unearthly Disclosure (2000), for example, cost me around £35,000 – flights, local transport (including hired planes), hotels, researchers, translators, on-site interpreters, a forensic specialist, and so on. As for (relatively) recent cases that have grabbed my attention, the mile-wide craft of unknown origin seen by multiple witnesses in January this year over Stephenville, Texas, impressed me, as did the radar-confirmed sighting by two airline pilots and passengers of two apparently mile-wide craft over the Channel Islands in April last year.

Richard Thomas: Thanks again, I look forward to your future books, interviews and lectures.

Nick Pope : A "Room 8801" Interview

Here, I'll be interviewing none other than former MoD UFO expert and author Nick Pope. For those left a bit confused by the title, "Room 801" is a legend in British Ufology. Located on the ninth floor of the former Hotel Metropole, London, the top secret room was where all British reports of UFOs were allegedly collected and studied by the Air Ministry in the 1950s. These investigations largely marked the beginning of what would eventually become the MoD UFO project where Nick Pope worked.

Nick Pope seemed like the obvious choice for our next interview. I grew up watching his numerous appearances on the BBC and Sky TV, so it was very exciting when he quickly agreed to do an interview. In a field littered with colourful characters making incredible claims, here was a chance to interview a real government insider.

Richard Thomas: First things first, thank you very much for giving us the time to answer these questions, I truly appreciate it and I'm sure our readers will find whatever you have to say (or not say) very interesting.

Perhaps the most interesting case you have been associated with is that of the 1980 Rendlesham Forest incident in Suffolk, England. Jacques Vallee has suggested that this may have been some kind of psyop, pointing out that the American soldiers who went out to investigate the UFO that night were told to leave their guns behind. What do you think of this theory?

Nick Pope: As much as I respect Jacques Vallee, the psyop theory is extremely unlikely to explain the Rendlesham Forest incident. I worked at the Ministry of Defence for 21 years. One of my jobs involved working closely with the Defence Intelligence Staff, while my final post was in a security-related job. If this had been a psyop, there is absolutely no way that the authorities would have allowed a paper trail to be generated in the way that it was. The affair would have been allowed to play itself out, but the moment people started putting things in writing, those running the psyop would have had a quiet word and stopped anything from being committed to paper. Any documents that had slipped through the net would have been quietly withdrawn.

Richard Thomas: The other major case you are associated with is the 1993 Cosford Incident. Do you think this or any other major cases in the UK (e.g. the 1974 Berwyn Mountain Incident) could be explained by black projects in our skies, British or otherwise?

Nick Pope: For obvious reasons, the issue of black projects isn't something that I can discuss in any great detail. Clearly there are aircraft and Unmanned Aerial Vehicles (both experimental and operational) the existence of which are not yet public knowledge. However, there are ways of eliminating this possibility from any official investigation into a UFO sighting. To give one example, we know where we test fly our own experimental craft (in various special ranges and danger areas), so can take this into account.

Richard Thomas: In other interviews I have heard you say that, during your time on the MoDs UFO project, you never had any indication that there was some secret UFO group – an MJ UK if you will – operating above you. However, what about in other countries. Did you ever get any hint of any secret UFO groups (of whatever scale) active abroad, not just in the US but anywhere?

Nick Pope: It's certainly true that I never got any indication that there was any clandestine UFO group operating in the UK, having access to material that was somehow being withheld from me and my colleagues in the Defence Intelligence Staff. So far as the situation in other countries is concerned, I must answer "no comment."

Richard Thomas: You yourself have compared the MoDs UFO project to the US Air Force's defunct Project Blue Book. It is widely believed in Ufology that Blue Book was, far from a serious attempt to investigate UFOs, simply a PR exercise aimed at debunking UFOs in the eyes of the public. Hypothetically, if a UFO had crashed somewhere in the UK (during your tenure at the MoD UFO desk) do you think you would have been told? Perhaps more interestingly who do you suspect would have been?

Nick Pope: Firstly, I disagree with the view that Project Blue Book was a PR exercise. While it had its faults and was, on occasion, conclusion-led, I think that generally speaking most of those involved did their best to investigate sightings in an open-minded way. While they found no evidence that UFOs were extraterrestrial in origin the fact that they couldn't explain a sizeable percentage of reports shows they weren't debunking the phenomenon. The MoD's investigative efforts mirrored Blue Book in relation to both terms of reference and methodology.

In relation to a UFO crash, I believe that as the SME (Subject Matter Expert) I would have been told. I would then have briefed up the chain of command to Service Chiefs and Defence Ministers. A key priority would have been to bring in MoD scientists, to ensure there was no biological or chemical hazard.

Richard Thomas: We've been having something of a new UFO wave in the UK recently. In an interview with The Sun, you went as far as calling for an official inquiry into the sightings over Shropshire. Is this still your position or has it changed in hindsight? Also, what's your take on the recent Police helicopter UFO sighting near Cardiff, Wales?

Nick Pope: My call for a public inquiry was not the result of a single sighting, but a response to the wave of sightings over the UK this summer, coupled with unprecedented media and public interest. Some sightings have clearly been caused by Chinese lanterns, but the MoD appear to be using this as an excuse not to investigate. It would be simple to ensure that witnesses are interviewed, photos and videos analysed and radar tapes checked, yet these basic things are not happening. This is why we need an inquiry. Whatever one believes about UFOs, cases such as the incident involving the police helicopter show that there are air safety issues involved.

Richard Thomas: Out of all the recently declassified British UFO files, what is the most interesting to you?
Nick Pope: A few cases spring to mind:
   26th April 1984: Members of the public report a UFO in Stanmore. Two police officers attend the scene, witness the craft and sketch it.
   13th October 1984: a saucer-shaped UFO is seen from Waterloo Bridge in London by numerous witnesses.
   11th September 1985: 2 UFOs tracked on a military radar system travelling 10 nautical miles in 12 seconds.
   4th September 1986: a UFO passes an estimated 1.5 nautical miles from the port side of a commercial aircraft.
   The National Archives asked me to review the files prior to their release and pick out cases of potential interest to the media and the public. These are some of the cases I selected.

Richard Thomas: Other than those we've already discussed are there any other UFO cases you are particularly impressed with and if so, why?
Nick Pope: As you'd expect, given my background, I tend to be more interested in cases involving the military and cases where visual sightings are corroborated by radar evidence. Other cases that spring to mind include the sightings over Belgium in 1989 and 1990, where F-16s were scrambled; the RAF Lakenheath/RAF Bentwaters radar/visual cases from August 1956; the 1995 near-miss between a UFO and an aircraft on approach to Manchester Airport; Captain Zaghetti's Sighting from 1991 – another near-miss

between a UFO and a civil aircraft; a case from November 1990 involving RAF pilots sighting a UFO over the North Sea, with other sightings and unusual radar returns across Europe; all the cases featured on the Coalition for Freedom of Information's website; and finally, some cases that I can't discuss until MoD releases the files, over the course of the next 3 years.

Richard Thomas: What do you think the future of the MoD UFO desk will be, in an interview you gave in December you said it would almost certainly be shut down soon?
Nick Pope: I'm reasonably sure that the MoD will formally disengage from the UFO issue. They may well do this once they finish the process of releasing the archive of UFO files in about three year's time, but they may well do so before then. They will probably justify this by reference to the US experience and Project Condign. That said, one does not have to have a formal UFO project to look at the phenomenon: any sightings from civil and military pilots are still likely to be investigated and any unusual radar returns will be examined. But inevitably, a lot of potentially interesting cases (i.e. those involving the public) will no longer be looked at.

Richard Thomas: Abductions: what are your thoughts on them? Do you think something physically real, metaphysical, psychological or a combination of these is happening? Is there any particular case that you find most compelling?
Nick Pope: Just as the UFO phenomenon has no single explanation, I believe there are various different explanations for the alien abduction phenomenon. Some cases will be hoaxes and some may be attributable to some form of hallucination or delusion. To this we can probably add vivid dreams, sleep paralysis, false memory syndrome and various other factors. However, this doesn't explain all the cases and I suspect there's some other factor at work here. Scientific studies of the abductees show no evidence of psychopathology or falsehood and suggest that in recalling their experiences they exhibit physiological reactions (e.g. increased heart rate and perspiration) not seen in control groups of non-abductees. My own case files on this run to about 100 incidents. The most compelling involves a young woman called Brigitte Grant

(a pseudonym), who I worked with for a number of years. There's some information about her on the internet, but she's dropped out of ufology now and witness confidentiality precludes my saying anything not already in the public domain.

Richard Thomas: I know that you've also shown an interest in ghosts, crop circles and the cattle mutilation phenomenon, but what about other esoteric subjects? Do you have any thoughts on the Yeti, Loch Ness Monster or any other mysteries?
Nick Pope: I'm interested in the unexplained and the paranormal as a whole. Inevitably, constraints on my time preclude my investigating everything, but I've looked into and commentated on remote viewing, the Bermuda Triangle and a whole host of other mysteries. Cryptozoology is fascinating, though not my specialist subject. I keep an open mind on all this.

Richard Thomas: I hear that pop star Robbie Williams is a big Nick Pope fan. What do you think of this and has he ever contacted you?
Nick Pope: Robbie and I have exchanged a few emails over the last year or so. I met him at the UFO Congress in Laughlin this year. He's a nice guy and genuinely interested in the UFO phenomenon.

Richard Thomas: I always try and tie in Doctor Who to Richard's Room whenever I can. You've written some excellent sci-fi books and seem to be a bit of a fan, so what's your favourite Doctor Who monster and/or story and why?
Nick Pope: As a successful sci-fi author myself I've been greatly influenced by Doctor Who. The revival of the franchise has been brilliant and stories such as Blink, The Girl in the Fireplace and The Family of Blood have been phenomenal, in terms of script, acting, SFX and direction. TV heaven. However, I'll always look back on Genesis of the Daleks as the all-time classic story. I'd love to see this remade or revisited in some way.

Richard Thomas: Thanks again, I look forward to any future media appearances, books or articles.

A Room 101 Interview with Mark Pilkington: Author of Mirage Men: A Journey in Disinformation, Paranoia and UFOs

Is it possible that instead of perpetrating a UFO cover-up the US intelligence agencies have really been promoting ideas like alien abductions, UFO crashes and recoveries, and secret bases all along. That's what Mark Pilkington alleges in his controversial new book, Mirage Men: A Journey in Disinformation, Paranoia and UFOs. Sceptical but putting nothing past the US military-industrial complex I decided to read the book a lot of UFOlogists will try and ignore. Impressed, if not convinced, I decided to get in touch with Mark Pilkington to ask the author a few questions.

Richard Thomas: First things first. Thank you for giving us the time to answer these questions, I really appreciate it and I'm sure our readers will too.

Reading the book you are obviously a lot more sceptical about UFOs or to be more precise the Extra Terrestrial Hypotheis (ETH) than you were when you first got interested in the subject. How did you first become interested in UFOs and how has your view of the phenomenon evolved since that time, and why?

Mark Pilkington: I've been interested in Fortean phenomena all my life – HG Wells' The War of the Worlds was my favourite book aged about 7 or 8 and I grew up reading 2000AD (the British SF comic) and as much SF, fantasy and horror as I could get my mitts on. I found my first copy of the Fortean Times in the mid 1980s aged about 13 and read Timothy Good's Above Top Secret when I was 14 in 1987. UFOs always appealed to me because they seemed to be the most accessible form of anomalous phenomena – you could look up at the night sky wherever you were and imagine seeing one.

I'm not sceptical about UFOs themselves – people see them every day – nor am I sceptical of the existence of ET life, I believe it's out there, and I can accept that it will come here and perhaps even has done at some point in our past. What I am very sceptical of is the popular notion of ET visitation as presented in the UFO lore that has emerged since the late 1940s. This has developed out of a multi-directional feedback loop between UFO experiencers, UFO book authors, mainstream popular culture and those in the military and intelligence worlds who would exploit and shape these beliefs and ideas.

Each era gets the UFOs and ETs that it desires, they are a culturally constructed phenomenon. In the book I demonstrate, for example, that there's nothing alien about flying saucers, which were synonymous with ET visitation from the 1950s through to the 1970s. Whether or not the Germans, British or Americans ever successfully flew disc-craft at great speed, they certainly tried, as far back as the 1930s. Perhaps they did fly but were less useful than more conventional types of aircraft.

Richard Thomas: You write early in the book about some UFO sightings of your own you had (or thought you had) when you were younger. What did you see and is there any doubt at all in your mind that these weren't anonymous like you originally thought?

Mark Pilkington: I open the book with a sighting of three silver spheres seen by myself and two friends in Yosemite National Park in 1995. I still have no idea what these were, though I'm still confident that they weren't balloons. I actually tried to track down my companions, who I've since lost touch with, to ask them to send me their memories of what we saw, as I thought it would be a fascinating demonstration of the fallibility of memory if they described something entirely mundane or different. If I hear from them I will certainly publish their stories on the Mirage Men blog. As I point out in the book, silver spheres were seen at least as far back as WWII, and are still reported to this day. I have no idea what the things we saw were.

Richard Thomas: I haven't looked into it much but after I read the back of your book I automatically thought of Project Blue Beam, a conspiracy theory on the web that the US Government are planning on staging a fake alien invasion to bring about a global police state. Do you think there might just be a seed of truth to such apparently paranoid thinking?

Mark Pilkington: The earliest version of this story I know of is a speech made by British Foreign Secretary Anthony Eden to the UN in March 1947, in which he posits that an invasion by Martians would be the only thing that might unite the world's nations. Of course the Roswell Incident took place four months later, something that was picked up on by former intelligence agent Bernard Newman in his 1948 novel The Flying Saucer. In which scientists stage a fake invasion to bring about world peace.

Reagan famously alluded to the idea again in 1987, also talking to the UN. It's a common motif in science fiction – I was recently pointed to an Outer Limits episode, "The Architects of Fear," which follows the same premise. There are rumours that Wernher von Braun believed that a false ET invasion was on the cards, and it's something that UFO researcher and Manhattan Project scientist Leon Davidson also talked about in the 1960s referring to the contactees, who he thought were being deceived in elaborate setups by the intelligence agencies. It's a very appealing idea whether true or not.

I think it's a reflection on our times that the Blue Beam story uses the same premise to warn of an impending global police state, rather than world peace!

Richard Thomas: Briefly as possible who exactly are the "Mirage Men" and how did you first become aware of them?
Mark Pilkington: Ultimately everyone who talks or writes about UFOs become Mirage Men as their stories influence the field. In the book I'm specifically referring to those people from military and intelligence organisations who have used the UFO lore as a cover for their operations and, in extreme cases, have seeded new material within the UFO culture to further muddy the waters.

Richard Thomas: Perhaps the best evidence for UFOs are radar reports, but in the book you explain quite convincingly how such evidence might not be as convincing as researchers originally thought. Could you explain why this is to the readers, and what this might mean?
Mark Pilkington: Yes I talk about the Palladium system for spoofing radar returns, which I stumbled upon by accident while reading James Bamford's NSA biography Body of Secrets. By the mid 1960s this had got very sophisticated and was being used by the NSA and CIA. It was used with drones for example, to create the impression of much larger aircraft. I later found out that Leon Davidson had talked about the technology in the late 1950s, with reference to the famous 1952 Washington DC UFO overflights.

CHAPTER 1

The radar ghosting phenomenon was actually first observed in 1945. By the mid-late 1950s the technology to create them was being used to train radar operators in the civilian domain. So the circumstantial evidence that the 1952 UFO wave was a demonstration of somebody's radar spoofing abilities is quite compelling.

Richard Thomas: In Nick Redfern's book, Body Snatchers in the Desert: The Horrible Truth at the Heart of the Roswell Story, Nick speculates that horrific Cold War experiments carried out on Japanese prisoners of war might be the truth behind the saucer crash story. Do you think the US Government are using the UFO lore to cover-up this and similar crimes, or, do the "Mirage Men" have other motives?

Mark Pilkington: I don't know what happened at Roswell, and the story has grown far too convoluted now ever to be satisfactorily resolved. Nick Redfern and I certainly think along similar lines at times and aspects of his Body Snatchers theory are quite convincing. We have to remember that the years following World War II were difficult and often desperate. The threat of Soviet infiltration and/or atomic annihilation was extremely serious, and the US government, like those of every nation, was prepared to do awful things to maintain the status quo.

The point about Roswell is that whatever came down, whether it was a Mogul balloon or something more exotic, the saucer deception worked – nobody took the blindest bit of interest in the Roswell story for at least 30 years, though someone in the military and or intelligence world appears to have been promoting saucer crash stories as early as 1950.

So in that respect Walter Haut and the others who put out first the flying saucer, then the weather balloon press releases are amongst the first Mirage Men that we can identify. As an aside, William Davidson and Frank Brown, the two Air Force Intelligence agents who died while investigating Kenneth Arnold in Tacoma, Washington, should also be added to that roll of honour.

Richard Thomas: The idea that the US intelligence agencies might have encouraged or perhaps even invented much of the UFO cannon, i.e., crashed saucers, recovered ET hardware and bodies, etc, I'm sure will be rejected out of hand by most UFO researchers. Why do you think this is?

Mark Pilkington: Some prominent researchers have invested a huge amount of time, energy and credibility in believing and promoting the ETH and tales of an attendant cover-up. It will probably be harder for some of them to consider the ideas I present in Mirage Men without prejudice, though the positions certainly aren't mutually exclusive.

But, as Leon Festinger showed in his book When Prophecy Fails, there's a strange effect that when someone's deeply-held beliefs are challenged or shown to be delusional, especially when issues of credibility are at stake, rather than accept a new set of beliefs, they will cling more strongly to the old ones, reinforcing them with increasingly warped logic. Festinger studied a 1950s UFO group and his findings are just as relevant today as they ever were.

I'm just putting forward my take on a very complex story. I wrote Mirage Men to be an outward-looking book that would interest people outside of the UFO community, I also wanted to present a reasonable and responsible critique of the mainstream ETH to those who are already well-versed with the UFO lore. Most people who have contacted me seem to agree that I've done a decent job of this, though there's also been some hate mail. Generally I think I've only succeeded if I find myself take flak from both sides of the sceptical divide!

Personally speaking, I have no problem with people believing anything they like, as long as others aren't being exploited, harmed or prejudiced against as a result those beliefs. Taken literally, I think beliefs in ET visitation are actually more logical than those of many of the major religions for example.

Most UFO beliefs are quite harmless, even positive, though I think it's a shame that some people use them as a means to undermine human ability and potential, for example suggesting that advanced technologies or the feats of ancient cultures can only be attributed to aliens rather than human ingenuity.

Richard Thomas: What would your answer be to people who say that too many honest and credible witnesses have reported seeing phenomena that Earthly explanations just can't explain?

Mark Pilkington: I accept that there are always going to be cases that refuse to give up their mysteries under even the most focussed scrutiny, and in those instances it's ultimately going to come down to what people prefer to believe.

I'm fascinated by the 1980 Cash-Landrum incident for example [when witnesses to a UFO sighting later suffered health problems]. If even half of that incident was accurately reported by the witnesses then there are either some remarkably advanced toys in the human arsenal, or we really have been borrowing, or stealing them from someone else.

Some of my friends have had some really spectacular and bizarre UFO sightings, but personally I just don't see the need to invoke the extraterrestrial hypothesis. As military analysts have pointed out since the late 1940s, the patterns of behaviour ascribed to UFOs make no sense as part of a surveillance or invasion plan. Meanwhile if some secret cabal has been negotiating with the aliens, then what have they got to show for it? Where are the technological leaps or anomalies?

I've been reading Paul Hill's Unconventional Flying Objects. Although himself an ET believer, Hill, who worked on successful flying platform designs in the 1950s, points out that there's very little about UFO reports that is truly inexplicable – they obey, rather than defy the laws of physics. My own belief, and it's only a belief, is that some highly advanced experimental craft have been flown over the years, perhaps much further back than we realise.

Richard Thomas: Probably the big UFO story of 2006 was Project Serpo, an alleged exchange of information and technology between the US Government and aliens from the planet Serpo. In the book you meet Bill Ryan who runs the website where the most controversial documents since the MJ-12 papers were first posted. How do you think the story first began and if the "Mirage Men" were behind it what might have their intentions have been?

Mark Pilkington: Yes John Lundberg and I got involved with Bill Ryan within a few weeks of Serpo breaking and followed him to Laughlin for his ufological debut. That's a key section of the book. I don't know whether Serpo was a 'Mirage Men' operation, though in the book I do suggest a few purposes it might have had if it was. What we can say for sure is that the Serpo story, ridiculous as it seems, single-handedly reinvigorated, even resurrected, the UFO field at a time when it was almost entirely moribund.

In 2004 when John and I first began mooting the idea of Mirage Men you couldn't get anybody to take the least bit of interest in the UFO subject other than to say that it was a cultural dead zone. Now UFOs and ETs are once again big business with a flood of books, films and TV series headed our way. While interest in UFOs, like anything else, is always cyclical, I really think that Serpo was the seed for this particular wave of interest.

Richard Thomas: Have you found any evidence that Britain or other countries might have their own "Mirage Men."
Mark Pilkington: My understanding – confirmed by a source who wishes to remain anonymous for now (yes, him again!) – is that the USAF's OSI (Office of Special Investigations) and the RAF's Provost and Security Services often work together, or at least keep each other informed of operations on UK soil. AFOSI have certainly run a few Mirage Men type operations over the last forty years, and I'm aware of at least one UFO-themed disinformation operation conducted on UK soil in the 1990s. I hope to be able to write more about this in the near future.

Richard Thomas: Thanks Mark, where can readers find the book and have you got any other projects or a website you'd like to plug?
Mark Pilkington: Thanks Richard. Mirage Men is currently available in the US and the UK via Amazon, Barnes and Noble, Waterstones and the rest. I've set up a web site for the book, which I'm using to explore some of the book's ideas and themes further. Visit www.miragemen.com.

I also run Strange Attractor Press, publishing books including Welcome to Mars by Ken Hollings, which is about America in the heyday of the flying saucer era, and The Field Guide, by Rob Irving and John Lundberg, which is an insider's history of the crop circle phenomenon, including detailed instructions on how to make your own.

CHAPTER 1

A Room 101 Interview with Keith Chester : Author of Strange Company – Military Encounters with UFOs in WWII

Almost every book I've ever read dealing with UFOs seems to start with either Kenneth Arnold's June 24, 1947 sighting, or the early July 1947 Roswell Incident. Sometimes there's a brief mention of the foo fighters from WWII too, and better researched histories might mention the ghost aircraft of WWI or even the phantom airships that made headlines across the United States in the late 19th century. But Keith Chester's Strange Company – Military Encounters with UFOs in WWII is the first book I've come across that exclusively deals with pre-1947 sightings. What follows is an interview with Keith Chester about his unique book and research.

Richard Thomas: Just wanted to start by saying thanks for doing the interview, I remember your appearance on BoA: Audio back in 2007 and you've been on my list of people I'd like to interview for a while now. I know your book Strange Company mainly focuses on "military encounters with UFOs in WWII" and it's slightly off topic, but with the recent passing of Zecharia Sitchin what's your take on the ancient astronaut hypotheses, that is that aliens have been visiting the earth for thousands perhaps even millions of years and might have even played some kind of major role in mankind's genetic and/or technological evolution?

Keith Chester: Richard, glad we're communicating with one another. I have entertained the ancient astronaut hypothesis since the late 1960s, when I was first introduced to the topic by Erich von Däniken's work, especially after seeing the 1973 documentary, In Search of Ancient Astronauts. That film really got me thinking and I remember being fascinated by the possibility that Earth had been visited by extraterrestrials. I didn't start reading any of Sitchin's works until the late 1980s. It was his scholarly approach that attracted my attention. It seemed he had taken the subject matter to the next level. Whether Sitchin interpreted his research findings accurately, I don't know. But, for me, that really does not matter. The ancient astronaut hypothesis was one of the first subjects I discovered as a kid that excited me about the unknown. It was one of the first times I remember learning of such an idea. It inspired me to think outside the box. More importantly, it was responsible for my interest in the UFO phenomenon, of which I'm still passionately interested in studying. I have a very open mind regarding such concepts. That said, I must point out, however, it is important to keep myself grounded by a dose of healthy scepticism, and not fall prey to unfounded faith and belief systems. So, the ancient astronaut hypothesis can't be ignored.

Richard Thomas: Probably the most famous UFOs reported during WWII were the "foo fighters," what do you think these odd balls of light represented?

Keith Chester: When the foo fighters were reported, it was thought by most all they were some kind of secret German technology. Many reports seem to indicate the objects could be explained by a multitude of conventional explanations, such as rockets, flares, balloons and jets. Though the intelligence memoranda indicated the foo fighters were conventional objects, as the war progressed, and the sighting reports kept coming in, allied intelligence could not confirm what these objects were. Aircraft, some absolutely huge in size, that could hover, travel at phenomenal speeds, and conduct seemingly impossible manoeuvres, are mystifying. In fact, after the war ended in Europe and the sighting continued in the Pacific theater of operations, there were still no answers.

The objects seemed to have come right from the pages of science fiction.

The problem is that these incredible sightings are not available in the official documentation. That means we have to take the word of the veterans. And I am in no position to tell them that they are fools, were drunk, poor observers, or were suffering from war nerves. Some of the veterans I spoke with felt the objects were unconventional, meaning they defied known conventional technology of the day.

At this time, I don't see conventional explanations for some of the more remarkable sightings and am willing to entertain an extraterrestrial hypothesis.

Richard Thomas: Perhaps the most famous UFO sighting during WWII has to be the 1941 Los Angeles Air Raid, what do you think the official files say about the incident also known as the Battle of Los Angeles?

Keith Chester: The official documentation indicates something real was observed. Whatever these objects were, and aside from the civilian accounts, the military witness accounts varied dramatically; some observers witnessed one object, while others witnessed multiple objects. Descriptions of size, shape, speed, and colour also varied. We know the anti-aircraft batteries opened fire. We have a dramatic photograph that appears to reveal an object caught in the crosshairs of several searchlights.

And we know a report was made and passed to President Roosevelt concerning the event. In 1942, due to Pearl Harbor, the United States, especially the east and west coasts, were on edge. Official thoughts about what occurred in those early hours on February 25, 1942, ranged from war nerves to a psychological warfare exercise. But, to my knowledge, there has been no official documents released that reveal what happened.

Richard Thomas: In Timothy Good's latest book, Need To Know, the best selling UFO author writes about an alleged 1933 UFO crash recovery in Milan, Italy, and the subsequent creation of a top-secret UFO group – Gabinetto RS/33 – to study "unknown aircraft." In my interview with Good he also mentioned that "Other governments – that of Sweden in particular – also became concerned about intrusions of strange flying machines that year," have you come across any other stories of pre-Roswell crashes and how significant do you think the RS/33 documents are for UFO studies?

Keith Chester: Starting in 1933, Sweden, Finland, and Norway were being over-flown by unknown objects. This was the first time known official military investigations were initiated relating to aerial phenomena. It was a time in UFO history known as the "Scandinavian Sightings." Known in the press as "ghost aviators" and "phantom fliers," the reports ranged from lights in the sky to craft with propellers. Though the objects seemed conventional, there were several issues that puzzled military authorities. They were unable to establish how such flights could occur over rough mountainous regions in harsh weather, including blinding snow storms, especially since most all aircraft flying in the early 1930s were bi-planes. The authorities were further puzzled over the skill needed to operate in such conditions, since it exceeded that of Europe's best known pilots. Unless Russia or Germany, or both countries, were operating very secret and advanced aircraft, then some of the sightings defied conventional wisdom. And that is the primary reason these objects remained a mystery.

Regarding the Italian documents, if real, they are definitely significant. I have not seen any documentation during my research that indicates any crash and retrieval operations took place during the war. I am, however, open-minded about such a possibility.

Richard Thomas: The newspaper headlines from the late 1940s speak of "flying disks" and "ghost rockets" but the idea that UFOs might be from outer space didn't really gain popularity until Major Donald Keyhoe's 1949 article in Fate magazine, "The Flying Saucers Are Real", which in 1950 Keyhoe expanded into his best selling book. (Although, I know Mussolini made some odd comments – probably just in jest – about the "warlike inhabitants of the planet Mars" in a speech once.) Do any of the pre-1947 UFO files you've looked at indicate the Allies thought UFOs might represent something other than Axis weapons or experimental aircraft or vice versa even?

Keith Chester: During WWII, the first, and foremost, thoughts by allied air intelligence were the sightings represented enemy technology, after satisfactorily ruling out conventional ordnance and other possibilities. If the sightings were not misidentifications of conventional weaponry, meteorological and celestial phenomena, war nerves, or secret axis weaponry, then there is reason to suggest an extraterrestrial explanation was explored.

I feel the most important document uncovered that strengthens the case that unconventional aircraft were observed comes from a document discovered by British researchers, Dr. David Clarke and Andy Roberts, in the National Archives in London. Over Turin, Italy on November 28/29, an "object, 200-300 feet long, travelling up to 500 mph, with "four red lights spaced at equal distance along its body", was reported by Lancaster bomber crew. What gives this report real strength that something very unusual was observed appears in a follow-up report to Royal Air Force (RAF) Bomber Command by No. 5 Group: "Herewith a copy of a report received from a crew of a Lancaster after raid on Turin. The crew refuses to be shaken in their story in the face of the usual banter". No. 5 Group's statement to Bomber Command is very telling in that it reveals the air crew reports were not well received by the air intelligence men debriefing them. The reports were too unbelievable. And this is very important.

The intelligence memoranda I uncovered reveals confusion existed at the highest military levels. When reading some of these reports, of which many excerpts are included in my book, one can clearly see the struggle to find conventional answers for the sightings. It's as if the sightings were lifted from the pages of pulp science fiction; truly "Buck Rogers" and "Flash Gordon" material. When these intelligence reports are combined with the witness testimony, not included in the official reports, and are viewed as a collective whole, then the overall picture changes, thus strengthening the extraterrestrial hypothesis. This gives what I've assembled in my book its power. This is what I'm hoping the reader of my book will appreciate.

Richard Thomas: In his book The Hunt for Zero Point, Jane's Defence Weekly journalist Nick Cook speculates that "anti-gravity" aircraft technology captured from the Nazis by the United States during WWII might be responsible for UFO sightings in the post-war era. What are your thoughts on what Cook calls "the legend" in his book, and how strong in your opinion is the evidence for Nazi flying saucers? Also have you looked into the Nazi "bell" device described in Joseph P. Farrell's The SS Brotherhood of the Bell at all?

Keith Chester: If I understand "the legend," correctly, it is basically the accumulation of documents and testimony that collectively address a subject, such as the Nazi UFO story, but when each piece of information is scrutinized, one finds out that particular piece of information is either false or can't be verified, thus becoming what is considered, in the industry, "the legend."

When I read Nick Cook's book, The Hunt for Zero Point, I was fascinated. I knew little about the anti-gravity subject. The book grabbed my attention and I wanted to learn more about the story. I found Cook's investigation fascinating and I definitely began to question if such a breakthrough in anti-gravity had occurred. Aeronautics and aeronautic applications, such as anti-gravity, is subject matter related to Cook's field of expertise, so for him to become interested in following the alleged "Bell" story, I felt compelled to follow his journey. Farrell's research adds a new layer of information to the "Bell" investigation. I must say, though, both Cook and Farrell, and others, have helped open awareness to a possibility that is pretty interesting.

Richard Thomas: What do you think were the most impressive UFO sightings documented in your book, and are there any cases you learned of after publishing you wish you could go back and include now? The WWII RAF sighting that supposedly resulted in PM Winston Churchill calling for a cover-up perhaps?

Keith Chester: For me, the most impressive sightings are those provided by the witnesses. Again, this is information that has not been verified. The most spectacular sightings, for me, were: A June 25, 1942 when a large circular object with high manoeuvrability was fired upon by a RAF bomber crew; A May 28/29 1943 sighting of a cylindrical object with portholes, hanging motionless and then speeding away at thousands of miles per hour; August 12, 1944 similar type sighting; November 1944 sighting of an circular object that some of the crew felt its heat and followed their bomber for 50 minutes; 1945 sighting of small several circular objects low above the ground, moving silently at low altitude; and, of course, Leonard Stringfield's daytime sighting of three tear-drop shaped objects flying in formation, possibly causing malfunction to his aircraft.

The latest release of documents pertaining to one of Prime Minister Winston Churchill's RAF bodyguards, who claimed he heard a discussion between Churchill and General Eisenhower discuss remarkable UFO encounters is very interesting. Unfortunately, the new documents are only those generated by the RAF bodyguard's grandson, wanting information from the British government.

Since publication of my book, I have not located more documentation, but I'm still actively searching.

Richard Thomas: Thanks for doing the interview Keith, where can readers buy the book, and have you got a website or anything else you would like to plug?

Keith Chester: Richard, thanks for giving me the opportunity to have this interview. I enjoyed it. For those interested in my book, you can get it on-line from Anomalist Books. It can also be ordered from Amazon and at your local books stores, including Barnes and Noble and Borders, along with their on-line sites. You can find my web blog at www.keith-chester.blogspot.com.

Silvery-white over Swansea

I saw my first UFO in Swansea Bay, an inlet of the Bristol Channel, in January 2003. I was about 17 years old at the time and my father was driving me and my younger brother home from town along the Mumbles Road, Swansea. Unfortunately, I cannot remember the exact time of the sighting, but it was probably the early afternoon. It was definitely still very light outside.

While we were stopped at a red light, my eyes turned to the relatively cloudless sky and I saw what at first glance I took to be an aeroplane. I quickly realised, by the strange way the object was moving, that it could not have been. As well as being very curious, I remember getting a bit scared at this point because I really did not know what I was looking at.

The object was moving up and down diagonally from right to left over and over again in the sky. It was a shining white line or rod, almost silver in parts, and appeared to have small round lights spaced out equally in a horizontal line along the centre of its body. I got the impression that the lights were moving around the object.

After registering that what I was looking at was very odd, I pointed the strange moving object out to my father and younger brother. For some reason it took them both a little while to find the object in the sky. After watching and discussing this unusual object among ourselves for a couple of minuets, the traffic light turned green again and we began to move off. As we were moving away, I continued to watch the object for another minute or so until, most strangely of all, the object suddenly disappeared in a silver flash.

A few weeks later, on February 1, 2003 (the same day as the Space Shuttle Columbia disaster), my younger brother and I had a second daylight sighting – very different to the first. This was of a yellow and orange fireball and was probably just a conventional meteor.

Whatever these two sightings were, they definitely had a very real and lasting effect on me and were chiefly responsible for my general interest in UFOs turning supernova. Back then I think I only had two or three books on UFOs but now I have a bookcase full, so these sightings definitely fuelled the flames of my interest in a big way.

UFO Disclosure with a Capital "D"

Recently I had an interesting conversation with Tim Binnall for the new BoA: Audio spin-off series After Hours. We touched on many topics but perhaps the most controversial subject discussed was UFO Disclosure and why I think it will probably never come. After I said this Tim went quiet for a moment. I think that I surprised him with my pessimism. Either he totally disagreed with me or he knew much of the audience would. So I thought it might be a good idea to explain just why when it comes to UFO Disclosure with a capital "D" (Government confirmation of an extraterrestrial presence) I'm still a bit of a doubting Thomas.

First, I should make it clear that I definitely believe that there could be some non-human (at least as we understand human) or 'alien' intelligence in control of what we call "genuine UFOs." Although its difficult to know exactly what form that intelligence might take or its origins, we could be dealing with extraterrestrial aliens just like in the films. That said, I suspect it is probably a lot more complicated than that.

One of the more esoteric theories that has intrigued me is the possibility that most other life in the Multiverse might exist outside of our 'normal' universe in other dimensions. Perhaps popping into our reality from time to time for a quick visit. That would certainly explain a lot of UFO and even ghost accounts where phenomena suddenly just disappear. If true, such a hypothesis could also go a long way to providing us with an answer to the famous Fermi paradox. (The apparent contradiction between high estimates of the probability of the existence of extraterrestrial civilisations and the lack of evidence for, or contact with, such civilisations.) The 'aliens' could be literally sitting in your living room and you would probably be none the wiser.

Back to UFO Disclosure. With the French (and now the British) government finally declassifying their UFO files; Moon walking astronauts admitting aliens are real; and Larry King doing UFO special after UFO special on CNN, I can certainly understand why many people believe Disclosure is imminent. However (far from government confirmation of an extraterrestrial presence) I personally think what we're witnessing is, at best, more along the lines of government confirmation of a legitimate UFO mystery or what might be called disclosure with a small "d."

Although I believe its possible that the US government might have recovered UFO technology and perhaps even 'alien' bodies. I also think that if they have them its extremely unlikely that they'll ever let the world know about it.

Lets say, for the sake of argument, that the US government does indeed possess UFO technology and bodies, that doesn't necessarily mean they know where the 'aliens' come from; who or what they are; what their agenda is; or how their technology works. Put in other words, all the things the public would probably demand to know if the US government ever admitted that they really had 'alien' technology and bodies (or any other "smoking gun" evidence of an 'alien' intelligence behind the UFO mystery.) So, until they figure all that stuff out, I don't think their going to release any hard "smoking gun" evidence of 'aliens.' And, since we're likely dealing with technology at least hundreds to perhaps millions of years in advance of us, I don't think this will happen anytime soon.

These were the reasons I raised for my scepticism in my talk with Tim, however, there is another major reason I wish I'd raised in hindsight. That is basically that you can't just have a little bit of Disclosure when it comes to something as big as UFO technology and dead 'alien' bodies, its all or nothing. Think about it, if the US government ever come out and admit to something as fantastic as they've been hiding the existence of 'aliens' for over sixty years then almost anything becomes feasible. All those topics that the mainstream media and official culture now ignore or worse ridicule (everything from the Kennedy assassinations to 9/11 truth) s uddenly become legitimate in a post-Disclosure world. Put simply, Disclosure would finally allow the public to ask their leaders some very, VERY serious questions without any fear of ridicule. These are questions which I strongly suspect those in power will do anything they can to avoid.

There are two ways though I do think Disclosure could take place within the next few decades. One is that the 'aliens' themselves might decide to finally somehow make their presence known to the whole of mankind. Perhaps flying giant sized craft over major cities like in the film Independence Day. But, given the fact that people seem to have been seeing UFOs since at least Biblical times, this probably won't happen anytime soon.

The other, and perhaps the more likely, is that the US government might try to spin Disclosure to use it for their own political advantage. Much like 9/11 was used as a pretext to clamp down on civil liberties at home and wage wars abroad, similarly a new 'alien' threat could be used to unite the nations of the world behind America and step up the national security state. However, at present a new Cold War with Russia and China seems like a far more likely replacement for the stalling War on Terror. As with so many other things we'll just have to wait and see what happens.

A Room 101 Interview with Karyn Dolan

One 'esoteric' type radio show that I enjoy listening to regularly these days is Karyn Dolan's excellent Through the Keyhole. With her characteristically friendly manner and down to earth approach, Karyn's interviews are both fun and informative. Karyn often asks the questions the ordinary, intelligent listener at home wants to ask but that, all too often, other radio show hosts just don't think of.

So after interviewing her husband Richard Dolan, author of UFOs and the National Security State, I was very pleased when Karyn also agreed to answer a few questions for a Room 101 interview. We'll be discussing UFOs, parapolitics, 9/11, Karyn's evolution as an active media member in the esoteric field, the dynamics of the Dolan family, ET elements in childrens' programming and a whole lot more.

Richard Thomas: Thanks for agreeing to this interview Karyn. I'm sure you and your husband are pretty busy with the recent release of Richard's new book UFOs and the National Security State volume II so it's much appreciated.

How did you first become interested in UFOs and other 'esoteric' type topics and where did the idea to do your own radio show come from? Also, do you think you might have ever seen a UFO, or, perhaps had any other kind of paranormal experience yourself?

Karyn Dolan: Thanks so much for asking me, Richard, and thanks for your kind words about Through the Keyhole! I'm so glad to hear that you enjoy it. I started with a guest spot on Live from Roswell, which is hosted by a friend of ours named Guy Malone. He invited me to come on and talk about what it's like to live with a UFO researcher, for a unique take on the subject when everyone else was interviewing the researchers themselves.

I had a great time, even though I was really nervous at first, and our ratings were quite good. After a couple more guest spots with Guy, I was offered a show of my own on the Paranormal Radio Network. I hesitated, but decided that I'd probably never get an opportunity like this again; and besides, the worst that could happen was that I'd be bad at it, maybe be a little embarrassed, and my time slot would be given to someone else. It was nothing I couldn't survive, so I went for it, and I'm so glad I did. I got to interview people like George Noory of Coast to Coast AM after just a few months at it, I've met all kinds of really fun and interesting people, and I've learned so much about their research.

I never thought about UFOs until Rich told me he was writing his first book; but I'd been interested in other esoteric subjects all my life. Since I was a child, I've read ghost stories, books about vampires and witches and the Loch Ness Monster, and any other unexplained phenomena. I've always been fascinated by anything that couldn't be explained by mainstream science. It proves to me that conventional wisdom, in any subject, is simply not all there is to life – there's so much more, if we just open our minds to it.

Also, when I was about eight, I discovered a book on Wicca. The thing about Wicca is that no one ever "converts" to it – people say they finally learn the name for what they've always believed. That's how I felt. Even though I was brought up in the Roman Catholic Church, I've always felt more Wiccan; and that is a religion that embraces all others as valid paths to the Light. Some of the main tenets of Wicca are to harm none, to respect all life, and to take responsibility for your own actions. It also teaches that everyone has potential psychic ability, which appeals to my belief that there's more to life than what appears in the newspapers.

And yes, I actually did see something in the sky that I still can't explain. In the summer of 2006, years after Rich's book came out, I was in a coffee shop with my son. We were sitting by the window, watching the full moon rise, when we both noticed a diagonal shadowy line across the moon. It was motionless, and we spent several minutes trying to find something in the shop that could be causing a reflection on the window, and changing our position to see if it moved. All the reflections on the window moved as we moved around, but that line didn't. After about five minutes, it slowly moved forward and upward, and once it was no longer in front of the moon, we couldn't see it against the darkening sky.

We live near an airport so we see planes all the time. This looked similar to a plane, but it had no lights at all and it was perfectly straight. A plane has a raised tip on the tail. Also, no plane ever remains motionless that long. I wondered whether it had only appeared motionless because it was coming toward us, but we were clearly viewing it from the side. I still don't know what that was.

Richard Thomas: While preparing for this interview, I was conscious not to overload you with questions about your husband. Do you ever get a little tired of being compared to Richard or having to answer questions about him? I'm sure you've been asked numerous times over the last few years about when his next book would be out and that must get a little annoying sometimes.

Karyn Dolan: It used to be common for people to talk to me only when they wanted to reach Rich. Since I've been hosting the radio show, and have been attending conferences, talking with people, reading the literature, listening to presentations...now I'm finding that people want to talk to me as well. I get people contacting me all the time, asking if they can come on the show, and I love that. Sometimes, people will ask me to sign a conference poster or something, and that's really fun too. I'm also now a member of the Board of Directors for the International UFO Congress, and have contributed a chapter to a book on UFO and alien images in society which we hope will be published soon. So I really feel that I can stand on my own feet in this field.

Rich is a brilliant man, an amazing writer and a very talented speaker. He introduced me to this field, and to a lot of the people in it. There are things that each of us does better than the other. At the end of the day, I know that I can't please everyone, so I do my best at whatever I'm doing, and make sure I can still respect myself. I have my own way of doing things and people seem to enjoy it. I'm not Rich Dolan and I don't pretend to be, but I am Karyn Dolan, and I'm very happy with that.

BTW, I never get annoyed by questions about when the next book is coming out. I'm not the one who has to write it, so it really doesn't bother me. :-)

CHAPTER 1

Richard Thomas: In my interview with Richard (I'll mention him just the once, promise), we focused more on what is sometimes called parapolitics, in particular 9/11 and its aftermath. Your husband seemed to be a big fan of Alex Jones' films, especially his latest addition to the InfoWar The Obama Deception. I know your family is primarily associated with UFO research, but given Richard's outspoken take on 9/11, what are your thoughts on that fateful event?

Also, if you had the chance to ask Obama two questions on Through the Keyhole what would they be? They don't have to be 9/11 or Alex Jones related they could be on UFOs or anything.

Karyn Dolan: I completely believe that 9/11 was an inside job, and I said so to Rich the day it happened. By that I mean that someone in our government either helped plan it, perhaps only knew about it ahead of time and didn't do anything to stop it, or did something that day that allowed the attacks to occur. I believe that the most horrifying thing about that day, and there was plenty of horror in it, was the realization that human life is of no account to those who were supposedly elected to lead us, to look out for us. We are totally expendable, and they will sacrifice us in a heartbeat for their personal gain. That kept me up for a lot of nights after 9/11, and sometimes still does.

Rich didn't agree with me at first, but later, as we both watched the investigation and the evidence that was uncovered, he began to believe it as well. What actually happened that day? Setting aside the loss of human life (which was horrific, but clearly of no account to the perpetrators), the World Trade Center was attacked. The two tallest towers and one smaller building were destroyed. So the two most visible parts of the complex were the first to go; that was a shocking visible reminder of the "Terrorist Threat" that was pounded into our awareness over the following weeks, months, years. Yet, the businesses that had offices there, also had offices elsewhere. It didn't really cripple our nation financially, not in the way the newscasters told us it would. The important thing about that was the fear factor. And I think that's a big reason why the towers still haven't been rebuilt, even this many years later. That scar on the skyline is more important in some ways than building the memorial; otherwise, it would be done by now. It's been eight years, for heavens' sake, and the site was cleared quickly – all the evidence was removed immediately and sold as scrap metal before it could be examined by any forensic specialists.

The destruction of the smaller building, Building 7, has never been satisfactorily explained. The best theory I've heard is that the command center for the events of 9/11 was located in that building, and it was destroyed in order to hide evidence of that fact. I don't know enough to say it's true or not, but it sounds more plausible to me than any of the official explanations that I've heard so far.

Aside from that, the Pentagon building was damaged, but not too badly. There was, again, a shocking loss of innocent lives, but the facility was up and running in a very short time. There is also some indication that some embarrassing financial records were conveniently destroyed. Finally, we were told that the last plane was heading toward the White House, but it never came anywhere near hitting its target. So the public's perception was that our nation's capital, our defense system, and our financial system were all attacked, but truly, no real damage occurred to the systems themselves. A couple of buildings were destroyed, a few more were damaged, some evidence of financial misconduct was disposed of, and it was all covered up by the deaths of thousands of innocent people. We were mostly too stunned and grief-stricken to raise any questions, and anyone who tried to do so was labeled unpatriotic and told to go shopping to stimulate the economy. The real result was fear, which allowed the passage of the Patriot Act and a host of other laws that would never have been tolerated prior to the 9/11 attacks.

There's a huge body of research that's been done on this. I highly recommend David Ray Griffin's book, The New Pearl Harbor, for anyone interested in pursuing this any further. I saw enough to convince me that the official explanation requires more credulity than most of the alternative theories, but I haven't tried to solve the mystery of what actually happened that day. Many others have taken up that task, and I urge everyone reading this at least to consider with an open mind, the evidence these people have amassed before making your decision either way.

As far as asking Obama anything...I don't know that I'd bother. I wouldn't expect to get a straight answer from anyone in his position. He may not even have the answers to my questions. I don't think the person holding the office of President necessarily knows all the secrets; I bet people like Dick Cheney and Bush, Sr. have that information. But if I thought he could or would answer, I'd ask Obama who was really behind 9/11, and what's being kept secret about UFOs.

Richard Thomas: Speaking of parapolitics, what are your thoughts on David Icke? Is he somebody you'd like to interview and have you read any of his books? If so, which ones and what did you think? Personally, I'd love to ask him a few questions myself because, if nothing else, he's lived a fascinating life and I think he has a great approach to life.

Karyn Dolan: A friend told me about David Icke years ago, and on that recommendation I went to Icke's web site. My first impression was very unfavourable, and I didn't look at it again for about a year. The second time I looked at his site, however, some of his predictions had come to pass. So I looked again, and found that a lot of what he said made more sense than I had thought. I'm still trying to come to terms with the whole "shapeshifting, cannibalistic reptilian/humans in the royal family" thing, but my impression is that he feels the same way. I read something he wrote about that in which he said that he knew how crazy it sounded, but people kept coming up to him all over the world and telling him about it. It gave him the impression that there must be something to it, and he put it out there in case someone else could make some sense out of it

I think now that it's entirely possible that someone was feeding him ridiculous-sounding stories in order to discredit him; or maybe, just maybe, they're actually true. I'm sure a lot of people will be groaning at how gullible I sound, but the truth is that I haven't looked into it, I don't have the facts, and what do I know? The one thing I do believe is that almost anything is possible. I don't accept stories without proof; but I try not to dismiss them without proof, either.

I think now that David Icke is a brilliant, perceptive and courageous man. I would be deeply honored to shake his hand one day, and I sincerely hope I get a chance to do that. The bulk of what he writes, and talks about, is our own ability to take charge of our own lives if we just stand up to those who are telling us we have no power. They're lying, and all we have to do is realize it and say no.

Richard Thomas: Back to Through the Keyhole, do you have a favourite topic of discussion and is there a topic you haven't covered yet you really want to?

Karyn Dolan: There are a few things I've been thinking about. I'm interested in ancient and anomalous structures in the United States, like Coral Castle in Florida, America's Stonehenge in New England, and the ancient mounds in the midwest. People write to me all the time and tell me about their work, and often it's something I never heard of before, that sounds really fascinating. That's the best part of the radio show for me, getting to talk with all of these people about their work, getting to ask the questions that I believe my listeners would ask if they were in the room with us. I especially enjoy it when my listeners ask questions through the chat room, when it becomes a conversation that includes more than just two people.

Richard Thomas: You've been doing Through the Keyhole for over two years now, which interviews stand out for you as the most enlightening or surprising and why?

Karyn Dolan: I think I would have to say that my interview with Lloyd Pye about the Starchild Skull really stands out in my mind, because there's this incontrovertible piece of physical evidence that no one can explain away. No one has proven that it's an alien skull, or that of an alien-human hybrid, but no one has been able to prove that it's a fake, either. It's a real skull, and no one can get around that. It has cellular structure that's consistent with, but still different from, normal bone. The most anyone has been able to object to is where the skull has been since it was brought out of a cave in Mexico, saying its "provenance is unproven." Fine, but that doesn't change the fact that it exists, that it's composed of real bone cells, and that no one has yet identified it.

This really appeals to me because I'm fascinated by forensics, by anatomy and physiology and biochemistry. I studied veterinary medicine for a while before we decided to start a family. I may go back to it one day.

Richard Thomas: I've often heard it said by some that the 'Space Brothers' are coming to save us. If that's true great but I can't honestly say I see any real evidence for this interpretation. If anything the UFO occupants (whatever they are or represent) seem ambivalent or worst maybe even hostile towards us. What are your thoughts on this?

Karyn Dolan: I'd love to think that the UFO occupants are benevolent. I just don't feel that I have enough information to justify that belief. I've heard people say that if they wanted to harm us, they would have done so by now. To me, this presupposes that we know their motivations. I don't think I know what they want. They may have very good reasons for waiting a while before they harm us. The fact that they're telling us they don't want to harm us doesn't reassure me, either, since we have absolutely no way to judge whether they're telling the truth.

Of course, they may not be as harmful as we think, either. It's true that they haven't tried to round us all up into their spaceships and eat us, or to simply shoot us all with lasers on the ground. (See how goofy it sounds when you actually say it?) Many people have pointed out that they seem to be studying us in the same way that we study animals. Human researchers shoot an animal with a tranquilizer, abduct it, study it, take tissue samples, and return it to the wild – sometimes in the right place, sometimes not. I like to imagine the animal returning to its family and debating whether to tell them about its abduction experience. Will anyone believe the story? Will they be ridiculed? Will they forever have to fight harder for a place at the watering hole?

Contact with aliens can be a terrifying and traumatic experience for those who live through it. I have a great deal of sympathy for people who've experienced this, and I can't tell you how much I admire the courage of the ones who choose to share their stories. Because that's the only way we learn about what's happening, and that's the only way others who go through the same thing can come to terms with their own experiences. It's incredibly important, and it's incredibly difficult to do. These people are heroes in my eyes, just for living through what they have and not letting it beat them down.

I think there is no single answer to this question of whether they mean us harm or good. I believe there are several groups here, I don't know how many, and I don't think they all have the same motivations. So trying to ask, "what do they want?" is an oversimplification, to say the least. It's simply not possible to answer that question without a lot more information, beginning with "whom do you mean by 'they'?"

Richard Thomas: I understand you're not a big fan of the children's BBC series The Teletubbies. You even did a lecture on it for the Crash Retreival Conference in 2007.

The Teletubbies was an incredibly popular children's series in the UK about a decade ago, when it first started. I remember my mum had to try really hard to get my younger sister a toy Teletubby for Christmas once, they would sell out incredibly quickly and people would queue for hours to try and get one. There were even stories of people snatching them from other people's trolies if I remember rightly.

What do you think The Teletubbies could represent that's so dangerous? Do you think this might be an example of predictive programming?

Karyn Dolan: I don't really think The Teletubbies in themselves are dangerous; but I don't like thinking that small children will see creatures that so strongly resemble alien greys presented in such a positive way. As we discussed earlier, I don't know what the alien beings want, but I don't feel that I have enough information to trust them. Because of that, I don't want kids to start thinking they can be trusted either, not without knowing a lot more about them. I raised the question as to whether their appearance might be a deliberate effort to make the general public more accepting of beings who look something like that, and almost immediately found government documents that supported that conclusion.

I first spoke on this topic at the Roswell UFO Festival in 2007, and immediately afterward so many people contacted me with information and leads that I rewrote the presentation with probably twice as much material, and gave that talk at Roswell in 2008. I also presented this material at the Crash Retrieval Conference and at the UFO Congress in Bordentown, NJ. Not everyone agrees with me, and that's fine. I just wanted to get people thinking about it at first, and now I really do think there's something here that's important for people to know about.

I find it interesting that many people have reacted very positively to my presentation, in particular a police officer who works mainly with child victims of sexual crimes. So a man who spends most of his time defending children from predators is totally in agreement with this concept. In fact, he sought me out at the Roswell UFO Festival last year and told me that he watched my presentation on DVD, then went over it again and again in an attempt to analyze the evidence as he would if he were trying to make a case in criminal court. He said that he hasn't been able to poke a hole in my case, and that's very gratifying to me. Had he found evidence to prove that I was completely wrong, I would have wanted to hear about it; but I was glad to know that my work was checked so thoroughly and apparently passed the acid test.

By contrast, only one or two people have told me they disagree with my conclusions, and they were self-proclaimed contactees. I've found that the people who are most insistent that the aliens mean us no harm are those who believe they have had direct contact with these beings. One could say that they're in a better position to know the truth, since they've had more contact than the rest of us; but they're also in a better position to receive whatever information these beings want to give out about themselves, and we have no way of knowing whether the aliens are telling us the truth. Ultimately, I have to ask myself about the aliens – would they have a reason to lie? Yes, if they are here with the intent to harm us, they would have every reason to lie. Does that mean they are lying? No, it means they might be, and I don't have enough information to prove it either way.

Richard Thomas: Since you first started looking into this, have you noticed any more TV shows with ET elements in them you think could be significant?
Karyn Dolan: I actually haven't, since we don't watch TV. I watch The Office, The Simpsons, Heroes and Lost on DVD, but we never watch live broadcasts of anything anymore because I can't stand the commercials. And yes, our whole family loves the Simpsons. The episode in which Homer sees an alien in the woods and is later visited by the X-Files' Mulder and Scully is priceless! I'm just sorry the Lone Gunmen didn't make it into that episode.

Richard Thomas: Aside from the ET elements in children's programming, what other types of big picture issues in Ufology have caught your interest in recent years?

Karyn Dolan: I've been watching the development of physical trace cases that people like Ted Phillips have been working on. I'm also fascinated by the assortment of anomalies that appear together in some of these cases. The Skinwalker Ranch, that George Knapp and Colm Kelleher wrote about, is a great example of that. Researchers found UFOs and cattle mutilations in conjunction with poltergeist activity and Bigfoot sightings. It proves to me that we can't call ourselves UFO researchers and turn our backs on cryptozoology and other fields; these things are all occurring side by side, and there must be some reason for it, which we'll never discover unless we drop the ego and start focusing on the cases. So many people seem to be adopting an elitist attitude toward this field of study, and it's both silly and self-defeating. Yes, we have to weed out the sad cases of people who don't have real information, but claim to have witnessed UFOs in order to get attention. These people do exist. But we also have to be careful not to dismiss or ignore valuable information.

Richard Thomas: I'm not sure how old your children are but are they showing any signs of becoming interested in either parapolitics or the paranormal at all? Given their para pedigree if I was a betting man I'd put serious money on one or more of them becoming big esoteric stars someday. Would you be happy to see this or is a Dolan dynasty of paranormal and/or parapolitical researchers something your trying to actively discourage?

Karyn Dolan: I love the term para pedigree; I'm going to have to remember that one! Our son and daughter are both are very comfortable with the fact that there's a lot more to the world than what you can see and touch. They accept the reality of UFOs as a given; if anything, they wonder why anyone would doubt their existence. They've already moved on to the next question, which is where they come from and who's flying them. Both are also very much interested in the spiritual world, with a strong belief in the existence of ghosts, spirits, and psychism. We've experimented occasionally with Zener cards and they both did quite well.

Mike is very much involved with parapolitics, as is noted on our website, keyholepublishing.com. Although he's only thirteen, he belongs to a local environmental group and is also a member of Students for a Democratic Society, and recently attended the G-20 protests in Pittsburgh with them as well as a protest against the war in Afghanistan that was held here in Rochester recently. He's already had experience with tear gas. I have mixed feelings about that; mostly I'm just glad he's home safe, but we're also tremendously proud of him for standing up for what he believes in.

Our daughter, Elaine, is eleven. She's a very talented musician and filmmaker, and makes a lot of funny animated videos which actually got kudos from someone at the Discovery Channel last year. Both the kids are very talented writers, as well, so I wouldn't be at all surprised to see more books being written in this family.

Every once in a while, I joke about buying an RV, painting it purple and green like the Mystery Machine on Scooby Doo, and driving it around the country to investigate mysteries. We have a big dog now, and there are four of us, so I guess we could do it. But I guess my cats probably wouldn't enjoy it as much. :-)

I never try to push the kids into anything. I'll nudge them to try something new and broaden their horizons, but they choose their own interests. I'm pleased to see them pursuing UFO research if this is what grabs them, but I'd be just as pleased to see them in a different field. What matters is that they find the thing that makes them want to jump out of bed in the morning and get back to it, and that's different for everyone. We've homeschooled them both for years, and I think it really helped them learn to think for themselves and make a lot of their own decisions in a way that public schools simply aren't able to do. I have the greatest respect for public school teachers, I just think they're overwhelmed with the amount of work they have to do, and the number of students they have to teach, with limited resources. It's so much easier for me, with only my two, whom I've known since before they were born. We can allow more freedom since we have so much more flexibility. Both of the kids have tried public school, by the way, and excelled at it, though both chose to return to homeschooling.

Richard Thomas: Thanks again Karyn, please tell our readers where they can listen to Through the Keyhole and find any websites or blogs you might have.

Karyn Dolan: Thanks so much for asking me, Richard. It's been a pleasure. Your readers can find out more about me and about my work at keyholepublishing.com/karyndolan . All the information about Through the Keyhole and my guests can be found there, as well as links to listen live or to access the archives. The show airs on the Paranormal Radio Network at paranormalradionetwork.org. Archives can also be found at blackvaultradio.com and on iTunes, by searching for Paranormal Radio Network and selecting Through the Keyhole.

As I mentioned earlier, I'm now the Media Relations Director for the International UFO Congress. Information on that organization and their yearly conference in Laughlin, NV, can be found at www.ufocongress.com.

I also write occasionally for Women of Esoterica, at womenesoterica.blogspot.com. Other contributors to this blog include Regan Lee, Lesley Gunter, and Farah Yurdozu. I'm very pleased to be able to work with such excellent writers.

And for fun, check out this website, which relates to my day job: I'm an assistant to world-class balloon artist Larry Moss. He calls his work "the fine art of folding air," and you can see his work at www.airigami.com. (I'm trying to get Larry to come to Roswell and fly a balloon UFO over the city.)

A Room 101 Interview With Regan Lee

Regan Lee is a columnist for UFO Magazine and has also written and self published a book on the Oregon Bigfoot legend. Bigfoot and UFOs might sound like an unlikely combination, researchers in both fields sometimes dismiss each other, but there are some parallels.

One of the many categories of alleged alien beings associated with close encounters is known as the "Animal" type. These are large furry humanoid creatures which closely resemble the famous ape-man. More generally, though, like UFOs far from there just being one definitive answer to the Bigfoot mystery there are probably many explanations.

Some Bigfoot sightings might be explained by the traditional hypothesis that there may still be a species of undisclosed primate roaming the forests and mountains of the world, but other sightings might have more exotic explanations, including extraterrestrial visitors and even beings from other dimensions. In my interview with Regan we discussed all of these possibilities.

Richard Thomas: Thanks for taking the time to answer my questions Regan, I want to focus on your Bigfoot research in this interview. I think I first became interested in Bigfoot because of my interest in Doctor Who, the Yeti or Tibetan Bigfoot are in two classic stories from the series, The Abominable Snowmen and the Web of Fear. How did your own interest in Bigfoot begin?

Regan Lee: I've always been interested in anything Fortean or unusual, in mysteries "of the weird..." I don't remember a time when I wasn't curious about all these things. But probably my interest with Bigfoot really took off when I moved to Oregon, and I came across Bigfoot encounters connected with UFO sightings. Stan Johnson's story, an Oregon LTW (long term witness), and other similar tales in Oregon, had me go from "this is ridiculous! – Bigfoot and UFOs all in one tale – to "this is really juicy Fortean stuff!" I think I'm open to the stranger aspects of Bigfoot encounters because of my own life long experiences with UFOs and the paranormal in general.

Richard Thomas: Have you ever had a Bigfoot sighting yourself, or are there any sightings that particularly impressed you?

Regan Lee: I haven't had a Bigfoot sighting myself. I did have one odd experience while discussing Stan Johnson's experiences with someone who knew him. Now, Johnson's story involves psychic communications with the Sasquatch, travels in UFOs, spiritual and religious epiphanies, healings... a sort of UFO contactee-Bigfoot combo. I met Johnson at a UFO conference; he was very charismatic. I literally felt "buzzy" as he was talking; he exuded an energy, that was for sure. So there I am, talking about Johnson with this person, when a cone of light comes down from the ceiling and completely surrounds us. I was seeing colored lights and everything, feeling very "buzzy" as I call these psychic connections of mine. Sound was muffled, as if cotton balls were stuffed in my ears. I thought I was going to vibrate up towards through the ceiling! When our conversation ended, the cone lifted up, back through the ceiling, and everything was back to normal. I've had a couple of other things like that happen – not directly related to Sasquatch, but connected in a round about way.

I told this story to a woman I met at the first OSS (Oregon Sasquatch Symposium) in Eugene. She told me that it was "spirit" that had manifested, responding to being called, in a sense. Or responding to the energy generated while talking about Sasquatch in that context. Come to think of it, it was a lot like a very intense ghostly apparition – a mist or ectoplasm – I had once experienced in a haunted house.

Richard Thomas: Probably the most famous Bigfoot sighting was captured on the Paterson film. What do you think of the footage?
Regan Lee: I saw that film in the theatre the first time in, I think, the late 60s, maybe early 70s. I think it was the Pickfair theatre in L.A. Well, it's one of those things where I keep going back and forth, but I lean towards it's a real film of a real Sasquatch. I have days when I'm not so sure, but I then I go back the other way and say, "Yeah, it's real." Despite the hundreds of attempts to debunk the film, in my opinion no one has been successful in that. Something about the way the creature moves… not so easy to reject as fake. I also believe Bob Gimlin, who I saw at the OSS and just following him through the years. He's either a very good lair or actor or, he's telling the truth. I think he's telling the truth.

Richard Thomas: My own belief is that like UFOs there is no single explanation for Bigfoot sightings, some might be undiscovered animals and others might have some more esoteric explanations. In Doctor Who the Yeti are robots created by an alien intelligence to conquer the earth. You also write about UFOs, do you think there might be an alien connection or something equally strange with Bigfoot?
Regan Lee: I agree with your take Richard. There is a connection with UFOs, what we call aliens, and all kinds of weirdness and Bigfoot. There are plenty of stories of encounters involving Bigfoot and other strange things that forces us to consider them seriously. When I say "there's a connection" I mean that there are stories out there from witnesses that we have to consider. What that means, is another story. Unfortunately, there are those in Bigfoot research that stick strictly to the flesh and blood angle and ignore or reject there weirder accounts. I have no idea what it all means. Like UFOs, it's tangled, complicated, and no one has the answer. I do think Bigfoot is a lot more than just flesh and blood – it's certainly not a simple "giant ape" – there's a lot more going on here than that.

CHAPTER 1

Richard Thomas: I think Mac Tonnies might have been on to something with his Crypto-terrestrial hypothesis to explain UFO sightings. His idea was that instead of beings from outer space, UFOs were really the work of a parallel civilization right here on the earth, possibly another species of human. Have you seen any evidence that far from being lower on the evolutionary ladder, or, a missing link, Bigfoot might be a parallel species to man and might be a lot more advanced than we think? For instance, do you think stories about Bigfoot being able to go invisible might be proof of them possessing superior technology like a Star Trek cloaking device or something similar?

Regan Lee: It is tragic that Mac died so young. He was really on to something with his theory. I still hang to an ET explanation for some of the UFO stuff – but I have been thinking the past few years that it's much more than that, or, more specifically, not only that. Call them Djinn, or whatever, but entities do exist right alongside of us. I think they are more aware of us all the time than we are of them. Sometimes we get glimpses of them, experience them, much to their amusement. I don't know if they control that or if it's just the way it is. I base this opinion on the research and experiences of others but also, on my own direct experiences with entities.

I don't think Bigfoot posses literal technology – like they have machines underground or off in some hidden forest laboratory. Although, Peter Guttilla, in his book Bigfoot Files, relates some very strange stories of Bigfoot, or Bigfoot type creatures, wearing a sort of tool belt with all kinds of electronic gadgets. Lots of other weird stories like that.

I think that, very possibly, Sasquatch posses abilities that allows them to manipulate energy, that causes us to experience things on some level we interpret as, say, paranormal.

Richard Thomas: In 2010 there were reports that Bigfoot had been shot. What was your reaction to this news and do you think we'll ever have definitive proof of the existence of Bigfoot? (I know a Russian expedition made some claims we'll ever have definitive proof of the existence of Bigfoot?

Regan Lee: I didn't believe the story, and I hoped it wasn't true. I am a NO KILL/NO CAPTURE person: very adamant about that. I've offended some in the Bigfoot community by being so ...

opinionated, I guess, about this, but when it comes to killing another being, I am opinionated. Whatever Bigfoot is, it's clearly highly intelligent, and no doubt as intelligent as us humans. Maybe more so. But the NO KILL stance isn't based solely on intelligence – as if that's the only criteria. It's a living being, clearly wants to be left alone in the sense it hasn't come out and camped out on the local wildlife management steps – who are we to go out and kill it, just because we want to? I know all the arguments about doing it for science, and I say: I don't care. It's not justification enough.

Okay, I went off on a tangent there. Back to topic. Like UFOs, I don't know if we'll ever get definitive proof that will satisfy everyone within all the infrastructures that Bigfoot exists. Both have remained maddeningly elusive for a very long time. That elusiveness is part of the phenomena. It's supposed to be forever elusive. I'm okay with that but it frustrates others, and some refuse to accept that. It's not hopeless; within that elusiveness answers can be found. It's difficult to explain. It's sort of a state of being.

I just don't think definitive proof will ever be produced because Sasquatch isn't "definitive."

Richard Thomas: For readers who want to begin their own research are there any books you would suggest they read, magazines they should subscribe to, or groups they should join?
Regan Lee: I come from a kind of folklore, Fortean perspective, so I'd recommend books that discuss the stranger side of Sasquatch encounters. Researchers like Stan Gordon, Henry Franzoni, Peter Guttilla, Lisa Shiel, Nick Redfern. Lee Harper wrote a book with Ida Kannenberg, My Brother is a Hairy Man. Sali Sheppherd-Wolford's Valley of the Skookum about her experiences with Bigfoot years ago; she's the mother of Bigfoot researcher Autumn Williams. Williams isn't specially about the paranormal or UFOs, she does solid field research, but she's open and sympathetic to the kinds of accounts that some others may reject or scoff at. There's Jack Lapserits and Henry Franzoni. I'd also suggest writers like Patrick Harpur, Colin Bennett, George Hansen, who don't write about Bigfoot necessarily, but their views on the paranormal in general and a sort of Gestalt perspective.

There are a lot of blogs out there that I like but among the Bigfoot blogs that address the stranger side of things: Nick Redfern has something like, four hundred blogs or so; I like Thom Powell's thomsquatch, Lisa Shiel's blogs , Autumn Willams at Oregon Bigfoot.com and Melissa Hovey's The Search for Bigfoot, Lon Strickler's Phantoms and Monsters. there are a lot more I can't think of but there are so many dedicated people out there sharing their experiences about Sasquatch and related subjects, it's just amazing.

See if there's a state or local Bigfoot group in your area and join up, depending on their policies. Some are very vocal in their insistence that no discussion of anything paranormal or weird take place. Even if you're not intending to do field research, or believe in a strictly flesh and blood creature, it's good to take part. I belong to a local Bigfoot research organization that is definitely primary flesh and blood, field research but they're open to other theories; and I joined a few others that aren't local, but good people and again, there's a diversity of members regarding all kinds of experiences. So find the one that fits who you are.

No matter what anyone says about all this; Bigfoot, UFOs, ghosts ... no one knows everything and no one has a magic key to unlock the mystery. You are entitled to follow your own truths in all this and make up your own mind. For myself, I change my ideas about things as I continue to both experience events as well as where my studies take me.

Richard Thomas: Thanks Regan, where can readers find your columns and blogs?
Regan Lee: I contribute on-line to UFO Digest, UFO Mystic, Monster Track, Tim Binnall's Binnall of America, Skylaire Alfvegren's League of Western Fortean Intermediates and I run several blogs of my own; Frame 352 is my Bigfoot blog, Mothman Flutterings, Animal Forteana are others. And of course there's The Orange Orb, Vintage U.F.O. and Saucer Sightings, which deals with UFOs. I've written articles for some of Tim Beckley's books and I write a column for UFO Magazine.

Thank you Richard! You do great work and it's an honor.

A Room 101 Interview With Mack Maloney – Author of UFOs In Wartime

From the foo fighters of WWII to the ghost rockets of the early Cold War, UFO sightings have always seemed to be more frequent during times of conflict. In his book UFOs In Wartime author Mack Maloney takes a look at sightings not just from 20th century conflicts but as far back as the time of Alexander the Great too.

Richard Thomas: How did you first become interested in the UFO subject as a writer?

Mack Maloney: I've always been interested in UFOs. Even as a kid, I read anything I could get my hands on having to do with UFOs. I think everyone likes to believe there's more to life than just life, and for me the thought that these things were flying around, appearing to people, things from some other place, I just found it fascinating and still do. So when I had the opportunity to write a book about them, I jumped at the chance.

Richard Thomas: Why did you decide to focus on UFO reports during times of conflict in your new book UFOs In Wartime?

Mack Maloney: I was having lunch with my editor and I mentioned to him that from what I'd read in the past, it seemed that lots of people see UFOs during times of war or just before a war starts. I had just read something about the foo fighters, and I'd known about the UFO incursions over U.S. ICBM bases in the 60s and 70s, and I just had the thought that whatever UFOs are, they might be particularly interested in us when we are either at war or preparing for war. My editor thought that it might be a good idea for a non-fiction book, even though I'm primarily a fiction writer. We went through the process and the book is the result.

Richard Thomas: The sub heading of your book is What They Didn't Want You To Know. What do you think the authorities don't want us to know?

Mack Maloney: They don't want us to know what they know about UFOs. It's as simple as that. But the question is, what do they know? Do they know what UFOs are, and are keeping this news from us? Or do they not know what they are and they're keeping that news from us? It's a 50-50 question it could go either way. But they know a lot more than they are letting on. I'm absolutely convinced of that.

Richard Thomas: One of the earliest UFO reports you discuss in the book is Christopher Columbus' sighting. What do you think Columbus saw that night and would you agree that too much attention has been given to the Kenneth Arnold sighting and Roswell Incident from 1947 as the start of the modern UFO era?

Mack Maloney: What did Columbus see? It seems like he saw what would be normally described as a UFO a bright light, acting strangely in the sky, something that is not a star or the moon, or a meteor falling to earth. Whatever those things are, that's what Columbus saw. As for Kenneth Arnold's sighting being given too much attention, I agree that it has, at least in the context that these unidentified flying objects have been around for centuries. They didn't suddenly appear that day Kenneth Arnold saw them. What happened that day was the American press finally woke up to the story and branded them in this case, as flying saucers. Once that happened then everyone became aware that unknown things were flying through our skies. But up to that point, no one in the media and apparently not in the military either, had ever thought that the foo fighters of World War Two and the Ghost Rockets of 1946, and the Ghost Fliers of 1933 and all these things that were seen by Alexander the Great and by people in the Bible and in medieval times were all connected that they were UFOs too. We just hadn't given them a name yet. So, yes, the popular involvement started with Kenneth Arnold's sighting, but UFOs had been around a long time before that. And as for Roswell – I don't think anything extraordinary happened there. No crashed saucer, no recovered bodies. Nothing.

Richard Thomas: The Los Angeles Air Raid is perhaps the best-known UFO case from WWII in the United States. What do you think of the speculation that the US Army was able to shoot down and recover whatever was in the air on that day?

Mack Maloney: I did not come across anything to indicate the Army or the Navy shot down anything that night. The only thing that came out of the sky were spent anti-aircraft shells falling back to earth after being shot at whatever was flying overhead and missing their target. What is apparent is that both the Army and Navy were completely baffled and confused about what happened and they were at each other's throats the next day.

Richard Thomas: The most famous UFOs from the Second World War are the "foo fighters" spotted by both Allied and Axis pilots during that war. What are your thoughts on Nick Cook's book The Hunt for Zero Point in which he speculates that the Nazis could have been working on anti-gravity saucer shaped aircraft?
Mack Maloney: I haven't read Nick Cook's book, so I can't comment on it directly. However, I will say that as far as the speculation that the foo fighters were actually Nazi super weapons, we reject that notion in the book. Simply put, the Nazis didn't have the resources from 1943 onward to even maintain their armies in the field, never mind create some futuristic flying machines that were seen doing fantastic things. By 1944, the Nazis were building the cockpits of their Me-262 jet fighters out of wood because they didn't have enough metal and steel to do the job. Second, if the foo fighters were Nazi weapons, why isn't there a single instance of a foo fighter firing on any Allied warplanes? If they were Nazi super weapons, why were they seen the Pacific theatre as well? Why was no vast super weapons manufacturing facility ever found in Germany after hostilities had ceased? And finally, if the Germans had these fantastic weapons, why did they lose the war?

Richard Thomas: The Rendlesham Forest Incident is often called the "British Roswell" but Jacques Vallee has suggested that it was a psy-op. How likely or unlikely do you think that explanations is?
Mack Maloney: I respect Jacques Vallee for all the tremendous work he has done in this field. And I've read only very little about his theory that the whole Rendlesham Affair was a psy-ops. But my first reaction would be to question whether the U.S. military or some U.S. intelligence service would actually run a psy-ops over the Christmas holidays. Why then? Government spooks have lives too. They go on vacation. They need time off. It seems like an unlikely time to conduct a psy-ops. Plus how was it done? Did the spooks construct a fake device that was able to float above the forest floor and then take off at a high rate of speed? Where they able to

construct the half dozen large glowing lights that people saw in the sky one of those nights? Were they able to somehow stage the "crash" of some object into the woods and have it shine brightly with three vivid colors? Were they able to manipulate the radiation detection devices on aircraft flying over the forest to make it seem like the area was saturated with radiation? That's a lot of trouble to go through to psychologically test a bunch of Air Force types who, for whatever reason, couldn't get a holiday leave to go home for Christmas.

Richard Thomas: What do you think are some of the other best UFO cases from the Cold War era, not just the 1980s but the Korean and Vietnam Wars too?
Mack Maloney: The Korean War was pivotal in the U.S. government's investigation of UFOs. They'd closed up Project Grudge about six months before war broke out, basically saying UFOs didn't exist and that they were either misidentified aerial phenomena, the work of crackpots or people with delusions. But then, once the war broke out, a lot of U.S. pilots started seeing UFOs over Korea and the U.S. military realized they couldn't say all their pilots were crazy or hoaxers or delusional. So, they were stuck. Some UFO researchers believe that was one big reason the Air Force started Project Blue Book. So many of their pilots were seeing UFOs over Korea, they just couldn't ignore it. And there were some spectacular sightings. About two months into the war, three Navy fighter-bombers were about to bomb a North Korean convoy when they encountered two enormous flying discs. And I mean these things were gigantic. Then there were a couple cases of UFOs orbiting high above U.S. ships out at sea and playing hide and seek with carrier aircraft sent up to intercept them. There's an incredible story told by Dr Richard Haines in his book, Advanced Aerial Devices Reported During the Korean War, about a UFO appearing in the midst of a battle between U.S. infantry and North Korean soldiers. The object took fire from both sides, but then it bathed the American soldiers with some kind of ray, and two days later, nearly all of them were very sick. Really frightening stuff. I highly recommend the Haines book to anyone who wants to learn what happened in Korea when it came to UFOs. We just scratch the surface in our book.

For Vietnam, we came across a number of episodes. All of the sightings from Vietnam are strange because, I believe, the war itself was very strange. The most well-known is probably the Hobart Case, where US fighter planes fired at UFOs off the coast of the DMZ and wound up hitting this Australian warship, the HMAS Hobart, and killing four Australian sailors and wounding dozens of others. A very tragic story that got very little play here in the States at the time.

Richard Thomas: Are there any cases from the recent civil war in Libya or other recent conflicts you would like to include if you ever did a second edition?
Mack Maloney: If we did a second edition, we'd have to start just before 9/11, and cover all the conflicts in the Middle East. That might take up the entire book: Iraq, Afghanistan, Pakistan, Libya, Syria maybe. That whole part of the world is turning upside down and when things like that happen, especially militarily, UFOs are usually on hand. Who knows what stories are out there, just waiting to be documented?

Richard Thomas: Where can readers buy UFOs In Wartime and have you got any plans for another UFO book?
Mack Maloney: UFOs in Wartime is published by Penguin-Berkley Books, so it's on sale at most bookstores. It can also be bought on-line at Amazon.

Whether there will be another UFO book in the near future, time will tell. I would like to do another one, but in a strange way our friends in the UFOs will have to cooperate and provide us some good stories. And so far, they're not returning my calls.

Nineteen Eighty-Six

The 1980s were a boom period for UFOs with bestselling books like The Roswell Incident by Charles Berlitz and William L. Moore (and input from Stanton T. Friedman), Timothy Good's Above Top Secret and Whitley Strieber's Communion. There were also movies and TV series like Steven Spielberg's ET: The Extraterrestrial, Predator starring Arnold Schwarzenegger, James Cameron's Aliens, Star Trek: The Next Generation, and documentaries such as Unsolved Mysteries.

CHAPTER 1

And if all that wasn't enough in 1987 US President Ronald Regan even spoke about "an alien threat from outside this world" in a speech to the United Nations, and that same year the major US soap opera The Colbys featured a storyline in which the character Fallon reported being the victim of an alien abduction!

In a guest article for my Para-News.info website UFO author and historian Rupert Matthews wrote: "The Colbys TV series and Whitley (Strieber) book launched the abduction phenomenon into the mass media. Suddenly the television, magazine and newspaper world could not get enough abduction stories. Many researchers took to hypnotic regression of witnesses in an effort to get more details and more coherent versions of events. Sadly some researchers had little or no training in hypnotic treatments and made some key errors of technique that would later discredit their findings. Nevertheless UFOlogy in the later 1980s became dominated by abduction stories obtained largely by hypnotic regression. It seemed that the answer to the entire UFO riddle might finally be within grasp of researchers."

The decade also ended with Bob Lazar's famous allegations that he had worked at the secret Nevada Area 51 or Groom Lake base back in the late 1980's on a back-engineering program involving captured alien saucers.

There's no doubting then that the 1980s marked a turnaround in the popularity of the UFO subject after years of declining interest in UFOs following the US Air Force's decision to closedown their UFO investigation Project Bluebook in 1969.

One year that seems to stand out is 1986. What with it being the 25th anniversary of the UFO events of that year I asked Nick Redfern, who blogs for UFO Mystic, if there were any good 1986 cases I should include.

Nick replied: "Probably the only 2 good ones I can think of for that year, is one which was (I think) a Jumbo Jet sighting of a UFO over Alaska. I'm pretty sure a Google search will find it. And I know there was a very good Brazilian military UFO chase/sighting in that year, and that the US Defense Intelligence Agency released its files on the case a few years ago, so they may be at the DIA website, as they have their FOIA-UFO files posted there."

A Google search found an AP article entitled "FAA Presses Investigation of Lights Seen Over Alaska" about the Jumbo Jet sighting Nick Redfern had told me about.

(http://www.nytimes.com/1987/01/05/us/faa-presses-investigation-of-lights-seen-over-alaska.html) The sighting took place on November 17, 1986 and involved an encounter between a Japan Airlines Boeing 747 freighter aircraft and three UFOs as it flew over Alaska, en route from Iceland to Anchorage.

According to the crew, "two small objects and one huge Saturn-shaped object were in sight and on radar for more than 30 minutes". The unidentified lights were "yellow, amber and green" and the largest one "showed up on the plane's weather radar".

The pilot changed course and altitude multiple times in an attempt to explain the unidentified objects and VHF radio communications were garbled at the time of the sightings.

In 2006 the pilot, Capt. Kenju Terauchi, was interviewed by two Kyodo News journalists about the sightings. The interview was picked up by various UFO websites. Here is an extract from the interview on UFOcasebook.com:

"Suddenly," Terauchi said, "600 meters below, I saw what looked like two belts of light. I checked with the Anchorage control tower. They said nothing was showing on their radar."

But something was emitting those lights, and whatever it was seemed interested in the jumbo, for it adjusted its speed to match the plane's – "like they were toying with us," said Terauchi.

That went on for seven minutes or so. "Then there was a kind of reverse thrust, and the lights became dazzlingly bright. Our cockpit lit up. The thing was flying as if there was no such thing as gravity. It sped up, then stopped, then flew at our speed, in our direction, so that to us it looked like it was standing still. The next instant it changed course. There's no way a jumbo could fly like that. If we tried, it'd break apart in mid-air. In other words, the flying object had overcome gravity."

But the strange events of flight 1628 were not over yet for Capt. Terauchi and his crew. UFO authority Richard H. Hall wrote about the third "gigantic" UFO Terauchi witnessed that night in the second volume of his The UFO Evidence:

About 5:30pm, while in the vicinity of Fairbanks, AK, Capt. Terauchi checked a white light behind the plane and saw a silhouette of a gigantic spaceship. It was walnut-shaped, symmetrical above and below, with a central flange. Capt. Terauchi said, "It was a very big one, two times bigger than an aircraft career." At its closet point, the large object cast such a bright light that it illuminated the cockpit, and Terauchi could feel heat on his face. Radio communications again became garbled during the close approach.

The veteran crew became frightened by the large object and requested permission to change course. After the course change they looked back and saw the object still following them. Increasingly fearful, they requested a descent to get away from the UFO ("We had to get away from the object.") After they descended and turned again, the object disappeared.

The FAA at first confirmed that several of its radar traffic controllers had tracked the B-747 and the large object, and that US Air Force radar had also done so. Later official statements backed away from this and tried to a ascribe the radar targets to weather effects. On December 29, 1986, the FAA issued a report saying, "We are accepting the descriptions of the crew, but are unable to support what they saw".

More recently the Japan Air Lines flight 1628 sighting was featured on the History Channel's UFO Files series in an episode entitled "Black Box Secrets" and the case has gained a reputation as being perhaps the "best UFO sighting ever" on the internet forums.

Another good pilot aircraft sighting in 1986 happened on May 11, in Sedona, Arizona. A pilot, Robert H. Henderson, and his wife travelling in a Cessna 172 saw a dome-shaped object make a head-on pass at them and fly beneath their plane at an estimated 1,200 mph.

There were a concentration of sightings in Brazil in 1986, including many physiological effects cases between March 19 and June 15. The best of which was the UFO chase case Nick Redfern had mentioned.

The Telegraph ranked this case, known as São Paulo sighting after the airport where the UFOs were tracked from, number eight in a 2009 "list of 10 of the most famous UFO incidents in history". Telegraph contributor Sasjkia Otto wrote in the newspaper that on the night of May 19, 1986 "around 20 UFOs were seen and detected by radar in various parts of Brazil. They reportedly disappeared as five military aircraft were sent to intercept them."

The São Paulo case was discussed openly by high ranking Brazilian officials. It was first reported by Colonel (Ret.) Ozires Silva, president of the state-owned oil company Petrobrás, who was flying on an executive Xingu turbo-prop, when he and the pilot saw and pursued the mysterious lights for about 25 minutes. The incident was covered widely in the Brazilian media at the time, leading to a press conference at the Ministry of Aeronautics in Brasilia on May 23, with air traffic controllers and air force pilots involved in the scramble mission.

At the press conference the Minister of Aeronautics, Brigadier General Otávio Moreira Lima, said: "Between 20:00 hrs (5/19) and 01:00 hrs (5/20) at least 20 objects were detected by Brazilian radars. They saturated the radars and interrupted traffic in the area. Each time that radar detected unidentified objects, fighters took off for intercept. Radar detects only solid metallic bodies and heavy (mass) clouds. There were no clouds nor conventional aircraft in the region. The sky was clear. Radar doesn't have optical illusions. We can only give technical explanations and we don't have them. It would be very difficult for us to talk about the hypothesis of an electronic war. It's very remote and it's not the case here in Brazil. It's fantastic. The signals on the radar were quite clear."

The Minister also announced that a commission would study the incident. Air Force Major Ney Cerqueira, in charge of the Air Defense Operations Center (CODA), added: "We don't have technical operational conditions to explain it. The appearance and disappearance of these objects on the radar screens are unexplained. They are Unidentified Aerial Movements ... The technical instruments used for the identification of the lights had problems in registering them. CODA activated two F-5E and three Mirages to identify the objects. One F-5E and one Mirage remained grounded on alert. A similar case occurred four years ago (1982 Commander Brito VASP airliner radar-visual incident). The lights were moving at a speed ranging between 250 and 1,500 km/hr. [150 to 1,000 mph] The Air Force has not closed the case."

Today São Paulo continues to be a UFO hotspot. In March 2011 a video shown on Brazilian TV of a disc-shaped object hovering in the clouds for a minute or so – before disappearing in a bright flash was widely circulated. The Telegraph writing that: "The television station explained the clip originated from two motorists who saw the object as they were driving near the town of Agudos in Sao Paulo state. They hopped out of the car to shoot the video with their hand-held camera. According to the TV station, the cameramen reported the earth shaking at the same time the unidentified flying object vanished in a blast of light."

Conspiracy Research

H. G. Wells and the New World Order

"Countless people will hate the New World Order
and will die protesting against it."
-- H. G. Wells
The New World Order (1939)

This genuinely chilling quote is the ominous opening to Alex Jones' Endgame. To the informed, the very words "New World Order" alone should be enough to send a shiver down the spine but what makes this quote – which could so easily be mistaken for coming from the pages of Hitler's Mein Kampf – all the more frightening is the fact that it came from a man still so wildly respected and admired even today as a true visionary like H. G. Wells.

But what is the New World Order anyway and what did Wells mean by the phrase? My own understanding is that the term "New World Order" refers to a proposed future world government or pan-Earth union. The first truly global empire that would include and supplement all the nations of the world and, conspiracy researchers say, be ruled by a tiny oligarchy of enlightened elites who believe that they know what is best for us.

If this nightmare future ever unfolds, at best, it would be as if mankind were reduced to being no more than perpetual children, forever under the governorship of a benevolent parent never truly allowed to grow up and make our own choices in life. However, if human history is anything to go by, it would probably be far worse than that ... benevolent dictators are somewhat of a rarity whereas abuse of power and tyrants are common place. Whatever the case, though, the New World Order would mean the complete end to what we now call freedom and, very sadly, in my opinion this is pretty much exactly what Wells calls for in his book of the same name.

The road to Hell is often paved with good intentions and Wells' The New World Order is perhaps an excellent example of this. Spurred on by the tragedy and horrors of the Great War and the beginning of a new war with a revived Germany, Wells makes a strong argument for ending the reign of the nation-states and creating in their place a new "world state" (the New World Order) to unite and rule all the diverse peoples of the globe. A new "world peace" not all that different to the Roman peace of two millennia ago, ending war once and for all by force. Where national sovereignty is a ghost and any nation or person who disturbs the "World Pax" is dealt with "brutally and completely" by a "world police."

Much of what Wells calls for in The New World Order sounds reasonable and sensible enough: an end to war, discrimination and unemployment. But the ends don't justify the means. It is and will always be immoral to force all the world's nations and people into bowing to the demands of a global empire. No matter how elegantly disguised Wells may put it.

Even now in the 21st century, there are parts in The New World Order that make for some genuinely troubling and even scary reading. For instance Wells shows nothing but disrespect for the US Constitution, America's most sacred and important founding document: "I do not know how sane men in America are going to set about relaxing the stranglehold of the Constitution ... and pull America into line with the reconstruction of the rest of the world." But this is nothing compared to Wells' dark vision of a world "disarmament police."

Incredibly, Wells makes the astonishing demand that the whole world, not just ordinary citizens but the nations themselves too, should be forcibly disarmed...everyone except the "world peace" enforcers of course:

"The world has a right to insist that not simply some German government but the people generally, recognise unequivocally and repeatedly, the rights of man asserted in the Declaration, and it is disarmed and that any aggressive plant, any war plane, warship, gun or arsenal that is discovered in the country shall be destroyed forthwith, brutally and completely. But that is a thing that should not be confined to Germany. Germany should not be singled out for that. Armament should be an illegality everywhere, and some sort of international force should patrol a treaty-bound world."

A disarmed world totally at the mercy of a single global authority is an obvious formula for abuse and tyranny. Even Wells is forced to admit this danger: "Its chief dangers are the dogmatist and the would-be 'leader' who will try to suppress every collateral line of work which does not minister to his supremacy." But the international force of young, uneducated thugs, totally loyal to the "world state" Wells envisions policing the globe sound especially dangerous:

"A sturdy and assertive variety of the new young will be needed for the police work of the world. They will be more disposed for authority and less teaching or creative activities than their fellows. The old proverb will still hold for the new order that it takes all sorts to make a world, and the alternative to driving this type of temperament into conspiracy and fighting it and, if you can, suppressing it, is to employ it, win it over, trust it, and give it law behind it to respect and enforce. They want a loyalty and this loyalty will find its best use and satisfaction in the service of world order."

Interestingly, ever the futurist, Wells predicted (somewhat accurately) that this "world police" force would be largely air based: "It is not unreasonable to anticipate the development of an ad hoc disarmament police which will have its greatest strength in the air." Perhaps darkly foreshadowing the many examples of "strategic bombing" of so-called rogue states and terrorists we have seen in recent years.

There is so much more in The New World Order we could discuss but the bottom line has to be that any peace brought about by force is no peace at all. War is not peace and a "World Pax" can hardly be considered freedom.

One more thought. When you take on board Wells' New World Order ideas, new and darker interpretations of his writings become possible. Here is the famous beginning to The War of the Worlds:

"No one would have believed in the last years of the nineteenth century that this world was being watched keenly and closely by intelligences greater than man's and yet as mortal as his own; that as men busied themselves about their various concerns, they were scrutinised and studied, perhaps almost as narrowly as a man with a microscope might scrutinise the transient creatures that swarm and multiply in a drop of water... Yet across the gulf of space, minds that are to our minds as ours are to those of the beasts that perish, intellects vast and cool and unsympathetic, regarded this Earth with envious eyes, and slowly and surely drew their plans against us."

Was Wells really using the Martians as an allegory for colonialism as is widely believed or could the Martians represent something else? The architects of the New World Order perhaps? Read The New World Order with The War of the Worlds and decide for yourself.

Manchurian Candidates, Mind Control Experiments and Assassinations

In this chapter I am going discuss one of the strangest conspiracy theories that I have ever heard of, but still think is somewhat credible and at least half believable. The conspiracy theory is that the CIA have used (and are maybe still using) brainwashing techniques to create "Manchurian candidates."

The term "Manchurian candidate" originates from the 1959 novel of the same name by Richard Condon. The best seller was later adapted into two popular films: the 1962 original version starring Frank Sinatra and Laurence Harvey and the 2004 remake starring Denzel Washington and Meryl Streep. The classic novel is about the creation of a programmed assassin by communist Chinese brainwashers in Manchuria during the Korean War. The brainwashed assassin, an American POW, returns to America unknowingly programmed to kill the President of the United States.

In the real world the Chinese did use public confessions extracted from American POWs for propaganda purposes during the Korean War, more than half of American POWs were said to have confessed to war crimes and, strangely, some former POWs continued to stick to their confessions long after they had been returned back home to the United States. This led some Americans to speculate that the Chinese were not only using traditional torture to extract forced confessions, but that they were also using more exotic techniques such as drugs and even hypnosis to brainwash their prisoners.

Such wild speculation in the paranoid atmosphere of the early Cold War would lead to the CIA MK-ULTRA programme, the most infamous of all the American mind control programmes. Experiments were carried out on people without their knowledge or consent, subjects were hypnotised and given dangerous drugs, very sadly some experiments were even fatal.

Many conspiracy theorists allege that the CIA did not only want to develop the ultimate interrogation technique, but that they were also eager to develop the perfect CIA agent, what could be called a "sleeper agent," that, once activated, would carry out their mission and block any memory of what they had done afterwards. After being programmed these "Manchurian candidates" could be activated at any time and could be used for spying or perhaps even assassinations.

MK-ULTRA and similar mind control programmes like Operation ARTICHOKE are documented history, but whether such programmes were ultimately successful in any such quest to create a "Manchurian candidate" or whether such agents were ever used is much less certain. However, there have been a number of very suspicious assassinations of prominent people in America since the 1960s, from JFK to John Lennon. Is it possible that at least some of these deaths could be the work of a "Manchurian candidate"?

Perhaps the strangest was the assassination of Robert F. Kennedy on June 5th, 1968, in Los Angeles, only 63 days after Dr. Martin Luther King Jr. was assassinated in Memphis and less then five years after his older brother, President John F. Kennedy, was killed in Dallas.

I recently watched a new documentary film about the Robert F. Kennedy assassination called "RFK Must Die" by Shane O'Sullivan. I first heard about this documentary on the BBC's high profile Newsnight programme, Newsnight showed a report by O'Sullivan made up of extracts from his film and interviewed him afterwards. In the report O'Sullivan showed new footage that he believed proved that three CIA agents were present on the night RFK was assassinated, suggesting these men were connected with the assassination in some way. In the film O'Sullivan suggests these CIA agents were perhaps handlers for Sirhan Sirhan, the alleged shooter, who may have been hypnotised to kill RFK or just cause a distraction while someone else shoots him.

Certainly if the CIA or anyone else were looking for someone to hypnotize, they could not have picked a better subject. In the documentary, O'Sullivan covers how Sirhan's defence team discovered that Sirhan was extremely hypnotizable. Amazingly, Defence Psychiatrist Dr. Bernhard Diamond hypnotised Sirhan into climbing his cell bars like a monkey. The unusual idea of Sirhan's defence hypnotizing him arose in the first place because Sirhan claimed he could not remember shooting Kennedy. To this day, Sirhan maintains he cannot remember what happened that night and has only been able to recall what happened under hypnosis.

There are also other signs that Sirhan was hypnotized the night of the assassination. Witnesses who saw Sirhan before the assassination that night said that he looked like he was in a trance and later after the assassination when police shined a torch in Sirhan's eyes his pupils were dilated as if Sirhan had been drugged.

As far as I can see there are three main possibilities. One, Sirhan killed RFK exactly the way the mainstream history books said he did and he is lying about not remembering. Two, Sirhan hypnotized himself into killing RFK, or three, Sirhan was hypnotized to kill RFK by someone else, perhaps the CIA. Personally, I find it hard to believe that Sirhan has been lying about not remembering for 40 years. If he had said he remembered and showed some remorse, he could have been out of prison by now. That leaves us with possibilities two and three, of which I slightly favour three because of O'Sullivan's film evidence that three CIA agents or at least three very strangely behaving people were present the night of the assassination.

Anyone interested in the case should watch Shane O'Sullivan's film "RFK Must Die" and decide for themselves what they think happened. However, whatever the truth, I think Sirhan deserves a new trial where all the evidence is brought to the jury and to let them have the last say on this strange and very sad page in history.

What are they Spraying Us with Now !

"In the event that I am reincarnated, I would like to return as a deadly virus, in order to contribute something to solve overpopulation."
- Prince Phillip, Duke of Edinburgh, in the foreword to If I Were an Animal
"A total population of 250-300 million people, a 95% decline from present levels, would be ideal."
- Ted Turner, founder of CNN
"And I actually think the world will be much better when there's only 10 or 20 percent of us left."
- Dr. Eric Pianka, University of Texas biologist
"Climate change is real. Not only is it real, it's here, and its effects are giving rise to a frighteningly new global phenomenon: the man-made natural disaster."
- Barak Obama

Type "environment, eugenics quotes," or words of that effect, into any search engine and these are just some of the environmental extremist/anti-human comments you'll find. With that in mind, perhaps it shouldn't be surprising that one of the fastest growing conspiracy theories in recent years has been the chemtrail conspiracy or the theory that governments are spraying the air with poisonous chemicals in order to combat overpopulation and/or climate change.

While the mainstream media is dismissing such theories as internet "paranoia porn" and attempting to debunk chemtrail sightings as being harmless aeroplane contrails (the chief difference being vapour contrails should disappear almost immediately or within a few minutes, not linger for hours!), the fact is that, around the world, concerned citizens are reporting and photographing the phenomenon.

Sceptical but concerned about some possible chemtrail sightings of my own, I caught up with filmmaker Timucin Leflef to get his take on the chemtrail phenomenon. Below you can read Leflef's answers to my questions:

Richard Thomas: Assuming chemtrails really do exist is there any evidence of what they might be spraying us with?
Timucin Leflef: Numerous air and ground samples of chemtrail fallout have revealed them to contain high levels of aluminium oxide and barium stearate. The levels of aluminium oxide are at least five times higher than the maximum permissible for health safety standards. The amount of barium is far greater at eight times. It has been taken seriously enough for Congressional Bill HR2977 to be created calling for a ban on "exotic weapons" and Section 7 of this bill seeks specifically to prohibit chemtrails.

Richard Thomas: What do you think the purpose of such a covert program might be?
Timucin Leflef: Although many of the hypotheses regarding chemtrails warrant further investigation, I keep veering towards the population control agenda. Henry Kissinger's NSSM-200 states the global elite's plan to reduce world populations by at least 3 billion by the year 2050. This number could be far greater if you believe the Georgia Guide-stones or Ted Turner's pronouncement that 95% of world populations need to be eliminated. NSSM-200 states that artificial food scarcity can be created and used as a weapon to create famines, thus reducing the world population to more

manageable levels.

Now Monsanto recently developed an aluminium resistance gene in their seeds. This makes you wonder, are these poisonous chemicals being sprayed on us deliberately to cause sterility in natural or organic crops, leaving only the more resilient GM crops behind? Also, since the introduction of chemtrails, beekeepers have begun noticing something called Colony Collapse Disorder. The bees are essentially leaving. When this happens, local farm crops may not be pollinated and food production may again be reduced. Are the global elite creating an artificial food scarcity by spraying our land with poisons? Will GM seeds created and controlled by Monsanto be our only source of food in the future? With the reduction of food productivity, food prices will shoot up and thus only those who are rich enough will survive any artificially created famines in the near future.

Richard Thomas: And what effect might these chemtrail chemicals be having on people's health?
Timucin Leflef: If the US Congress have taken it seriously enough to put forward HR2977, Section 7 of which seeks specifically to prohibit chemtrails, which it deems to be an "exotic weapon," then I would take it as a serious indication that chemtrails are detrimental to our health. They contain high levels of aluminium oxide and barium stearate. Aluminium is a metal associated with Alzheimer's disease and barium is a radioactive substance. If they're spraying large populated areas with these substances, one can only imagine what level of harm it will do to people over an extended period of time.

This would not be the first time they've done this either. Bill Cooper states in his book Behold A Pale Horse that back in the 60's malathion was being sprayed on population centers in California. The excuse they gave was that it would kill the Mediterranean fruit fly, but the tip-off was that orchards were not being sprayed, only people. A warning was issued to cover up automobiles and belongings because malathion could destroy paint, some plastics and other property but they said people would not be injured. Since then, if you look at the statistics, the incidence of heart disease has been increasing rapidly.

Let me put it this way, spraying people with heavy metals does not provide them with any short or long-term health benefits. Whether they're doing it to poison our land, our water supply, cause health problems, or create food scarcity, I don't believe there is one significant benefit to it.

And I have taken photos of what appear to be chemtrails. While I'm far from convinced these were really chemtrails, the reason I took the photos in the first place was because I noticed these earlier in the day and hours later they were still there. I suppose a rational explanation might be these were from other aeroplanes..

A Room 101 Interview with Richard Dolan: Author of UFOs and the National Security State

I first discovered Richard Dolan when he was interviewed for BoA: Audio back in 2006. Still studying for my BA at the time, I was impressed by his credentials and quickly got myself a revised edition of his excellent UFOs and the National Security State. Here we're going to focus a little less on UFOs and get Dolan's thoughts and opinions on some other parapolitical topics instead. Most notably: the Kennedy assassinations, 9/11 and the Terror Wars, secret societies and the New World Order.

Richard Thomas: First things first, thank you so much for giving the time to answer these questions. I've read both editions of volume one of your book several times and am currently reading volume two, so it's really appreciated.

I was only 15 when 9/11 happened. Looking back on it now, I think that event and, more importantly, its aftermath (the wars in Iraq and Afghanistan) probably played the biggest part in me becoming interested in conspiracy research or parapolitics. When the War in Iraq first began, I was studying Hitler's rise to power in Germany for A-Level History and the parallels between what had happened in 1930s Germany and what was happening today, globally, just seemed obvious to me. In particular, how Hitler exploited the Reichstag fire (which he probably started, although he blamed the Communists) to make himself dictator and curtail civil liberties.

How do you think you first became interested in parapolitics (I'm guessing the Kennedy assassination probably played a big part) and do you share my concerns about the parallels between the transformation of the Weimar Republic into the Third Reich and what we see in the world today?

Richard Dolan: I think that there are very serious and scary parallels between what is going on today and what happened in Germany during the 1930s. The connection of 9/11 with the Reichstag fire is the obvious example, but there is much more. The existence and promulgation of The Big Lie, for instance. Hitler (and Goebbels[the Nazi head of propaganda]) shamelessly exploited the fears of German people by repeating the most absurd lies over and over again, whether these were about the Jews, or about the Versailles Peace Treaty, or numerous other issues – and it worked. Or, I should say, it worked enough for them to have their way.

Today in the U.S. under Presidents George W. Bush and now Barack Obama, The Big Lie is promoted and peddled to an overstimulated, overworked, and undereducated American public. 9/11 is the linchpin of the entire edifice of deception that has grown around it.

My interest in parapolitics developed by degrees during the 1980s and 1990s, during my twenties and thirties. It didn't happen all at once. Even during my teen years, I was always a bit unconventional in my tastes: I was reading Plato and Shakespeare on my own when I was 14 or so and never stopped reading classical philosophy and literature. During my twenties I did a lot of standard political theory: from Hobbes through Locke and Marx and Weber and everything else. I studied the rise of Hitler to an excruciating degree. All of that was fairly 'conventional,' you might say. By the late 1980s, I was reading the essays of Gore Vidal, which was very influential on my thinking. Vidal wrote some outstanding analyses of the American political scene during the 1970s, 80s, and 90s. One, in fact, later inspired the title of my own book: an article he wrote in the late 80s called "The National Security State." His piece was a critique of the Reagan administration, but I ended up taking that phrase as a concept to describe all of post-WWII America.

But the early 1990s, around the time I turned 30, I had discovered Noam Chomsky. Rather late in the day, when I look back on this all. Still, better late than never. Chomsky, like Vidal, was very influential on me. Still, his writing stops short of what we would call 'parapolitics.' As anyone who has read him knows, Chomsky doesn't really "do" conspiracies. I have always found this a little strange, as his general "big picture" political analyses is otherwise frequently so very good. He understands how powerful nations and economic entities systematically pillage the world for their own good – and call it "democracy." But perhaps it's because he is in the academic world that he has never taken the final, necessary, step. That is, to recognize not only that the elites "manufacture dissent" and control the very parameters of what most people even think, but that through black-ops and intelligence community manipulation of the academic world and media, are able to create entirely fictitious scenarios – the kind imagined by George Orwell – and pass it off as truth. In other words, the reality of our world is well beyond even the mendaciousness that even Chomsky sees. And that's pretty bad, indeed.

By 1994, when I began studying UFOs seriously, I was still very much in the "Chomsky mindset." During much of the period of writing my first book, UFOs and the National Security State: An Unclassified History, 1941-1973 (later republished with the subtitle Chronology of a Cover-Up), I was in that frame of mind. In other words, that – while there were lots of 'little' conspiracies, I was not a believer in grand conspiracies.

It wasn't until I became fascinated by the UFO topic that I became convinced that there was something bigger going on. I continued asking myself why wasn't this topic handled with more seriousness in the mainstream avenues of our society? Why did the universities ignore this topic? Why did the newspapers? After seeing the deep national security connections to the UFO topic, it became clear to me that a real, bona fide conspiracy is going on.

Coming to grips with the fact that there was a substantial conspiracy in that arena, it became easier to recognize the existence of other types of conspiratorial activity operating on a grand scale. But all of this took a number of years.

Richard Thomas: Lets take a step back in time before we go on. For me, the sheer number of high profile assassinations in the 1960s is reason enough to at least suspect conspiracy: JFK, RFK, MLK, Malcolm X, even Marilyn Monroe died under suspicious circumstances in that decade. Do you think that the same force could have been responsible for these deaths and what are your thoughts on the two Kennedy assassinations in particular? For instance, do you think Sirhan Sirhan could have been a "Manchurian Candidate"?

Richard Dolan: Every one of those assassinations is deeply suspicious, although I confess I've done comparatively little research on the assassination of Malcolm X. Regarding JFK, it is plainly obvious that he was killed in a conspiracy of some sort, most probably involving the CIA. Other researchers have done a vast amount of work on this, much more than I will ever read. Still, it is clear that after you tally up the many pieces of evidence, a conspiracy was involved. Some of these are:

• the protestations of Kennedy's secret service officer (captured on film) after he was ordered away from the vehicle moments before Kennedy was shot;

• the testimony of many eyewitnesses of four or more gunshots being fired at Daley Plaza; the testimony of the Parkland Hospital surgeons, all of whom described a massive exit wound in Kennedy's right parietal lobe – that is, the right side of the back of his head – indicating an entry point from the front of the head and exiting through the back;

• the destruction of JFK's autopsy records;

• the strange connections to the world of intelligence by such innocuous people as Abraham Zapruder, who filmed the assassination. Zapruder, for instance, employed as his secretary the wife of a man named Georg von Mohenschildt. Mohenschildt was ex-Abwehr, currently working for the CIA – and the handler of Lee Harvey Oswald. Strange coincidences.

• Then there is the story of the Warren commission, headed by ex-CIA Dir. Allen Dulles, in which included such up-and-coming stars as Gerald R. Ford.

There is so much about the JFK assassination screams conspiracy. 80% of Americans know it was a conspiracy, and 100% of the rest of the world knows it. Yet, the "official" truth is quite otherwise, as we all know.

Regarding Robert Kennedy, yes, this is deeply suspicious. Sirhan Sirhan has never been able credibly to remember the details of the day of the assassination. He kept a diary in the period leading up to the assassination, and I seem to recall that the contents of the diary were very suspicious to investigators, and suggestive of mind control.

The technology of mind control is more substantial and goes back much farther than many people realize. There were substantial efforts by the CIA and other agencies from the 1940s onward to find ways of harnessing the human mind. We all know about how the CIA pioneered the use of LSD during the 1950s, but many people forget it was in order to find the ultimate mind control chemical. Advances in hypnosis were also far more profound than is generally believed.

When we are dealing with the national security and intelligence community – which steadfastly refuses to open its records for public viewing – we will always be at a disadvantage. Yet, to paraphrase an old comedy routine: it looks like it, smells like it, feels like it, and tastes like it.

Richard Thomas: Moving back to present times, do you still believe that 9/11 was an "inside job" and what, for you, is the best smoking gun evidence? In hindsight, aside from the extremely suspicious way the buildings collapsed, the paper passport, supposedly found in the ruins of the WTC, what was the first thing that really raised my suspicions.

Richard Dolan: Certainly, finding Mohammad Atta's passport on the street of New York City following the collapse of the towers – in perfect condition –is eerily reminiscent of the so-called magic bullet being found on JFK's stretcher at Parkland Hospital in Dallas, Texas. As everybody in the world knows, the wreckage following the collapse of the World Trade Center towers was almost beyond comprehension. My father, who worked at the World Trade Center for its final seven years – and who thankfully had the day off – told me that his colleagues described the remains afterward as absolutely disgusting. Remember, human body parts were liberally distributed throughout the wreckage. I don't mean to be excessively graphic here, but amidst the explosions, fire, dust, rubble, and dead bodies, how did this passport fall all that distance without suffering any damage? Here's another question: how did it get separated from the body of Mohammed Atta? When you travel, you carry your passport with you. Even for an alleged terrorist, he would, after all, need his passport with them in order to have boarded the plane.

But really, the thing that does it for most of us when looking at the evidence of 9/11 is the speed of collapse of the three primary buildings in New York City. All of them dropped at the speed of a brick falling through the air, unimpeded by any resistance. The airliners each struck the North and South towers roughly three quarters of the way up. That means roughly 80 floors of steel below the level of impact. These floors suffered no damage.

Here is a simple question. You can make it multiple-choice, if you like. Would 80 floors of steel offer (A) a lot of resistance, (B) some resistance, or (C) no resistance to the speed of collapse of those buildings? Even if they were to offer as little as, say, one second per floor – which really isn't a lot when you think about it – that would still add roughly 80 seconds to the speed of collapse. And yet the North and South Towers collapsed in about 10 seconds. In other words without any measurable resistance whatsoever. This is simply not credible.

This point is even more significant for the destruction of Building 7 of the World Trade Center complex. This was a 47-story tall steel frame structure which was hit by no aircraft, although it did suffer damage from the North Tower when that tower collapsed. Yet Building 7 came down seven hours later, also at virtual freefall speed, and also in a pile of dust like the other buildings.

It's important to mention these facts because such cases of building collapse are only consistent with those of controlled demolitions. Indeed, fires had never before (nor since) caused steel frame structures to collapse. Never. And there have been fires far worse even than those which ravaged the World Trade Center buildings. The World Trade Center buildings were not made with design flaws, as some people have tried to argue. They were made competently to say the least, and indeed were designed to withstand multiple impacts of commercial airliners.

That's only a beginning, of course. There are so many more questions one can raise, not simply with the New York City aspect of 9/11, but with the Pentagon, Pennsylvania, the fact that NORAD was asleep at the wheel, the connections that existed between members of Al Qaeda, the CIA, and the Pakistani ISI. All of these and more lead us to become very deeply suspicious of what happened on September 11, 2001.

Richard Thomas: Why do you think we're still in Afghanistan?

One of the more alarming things I've heard you talk about in your lectures is that illegal drugs are actually big business, on a par with oil and arms. Do you think this might be the real reason for the continued NATO occupation of Afghanistan?

Richard Dolan: Drug trafficking is unquestionably one of the world's largest businesses. Nobody knows if it's the largest, the second-largest, the third-largest, or even the fourth-largest. You've got weapons, cars, oil, and drugs. Simply because narcotics are illegal doesn't mean that nobody wants all that money. Everybody wants that money, from streetcorner pushers, to police officers on the take, to local public officials, to federal officials, to intelligence agencies, to major banks and financial entities that receive fees for laundering the proceeds. Everybody wants that money. It so happens that the Taliban, for all of their horrible deeds, nevertheless suppressed opium production in Afghanistan during the late 1990s. And it is also true that opium production dramatically rose after the invasion in 2001.

There are other things to note about Afghanistan, however. One is the natural gas pipeline, which had been a dream of leaders of industry and finance for a long time. An enormous amount of natural gas lies to the north of Afghanistan. Getting it to industrial countries like the U.S., is not so easy, however. The idea was to create a pipeline to the sea, compress it into liquid form, and ship it. That's expensive, but in an era of uncertain natural gas availabilities, still an attractive option. If you look at a map of the region, you'll see that a faster, more direct route actually lies to the nation of Iran. But during the late 1990s, Afghanistan seemed to be a more likely route for the pipeline: Afghanistan to Pakistan and then to the sea. Now, that pipeline has had all kinds of problems of construction during these years. Most likely, we can attribute this to the nonstop fighting that has occurred in that country since 2001. Nevertheless, this is a major geopolitical reason for the U.S. presence in that country.

Richard Thomas: I have heard it said that getting control of Iraq's oil was the major reason for the Anglo-American 2003 invasion of Iraq, but what do you think of the idea that capturing ancient astronaut technology left behind in the country could have been another reason?

CHAPTER 2

Richard Dolan: That idea has been put forth by several researchers, most notably Jim Marrs, who has done some outstanding investigation during his lifetime. It's still hard for me to make my own determination on this thesis, so I'm going to pass on that one for now, except to comment on one thing. This was the systematic plundering of the Baghdad Museum. Most people probably remember this. This was a massive and yet surgical-like looting of perhaps the most important ancient museum in the world. All of this was done under the watchful eye of U.S. troops, and the entire world followed the progress, which lasted several days. If there were ancient secrets to be stolen and exploited, we may presume that they existed within that museum, perhaps within the many secret underground layers that have been rumored to exist.

There is no question, however, that international financial groups have wanted to privatize Iraq's oil for many years. Indeed, David Rockefeller himself met with Saddam Hussein during the late 1980s. Also, representatives of Kissinger Associates. Back in the bad old days of Saddam, all that oil was owned and controlled by the Iraqi government. That meant that, yes, Saddam and his family could skim and live like kings, but it also meant that the oil paid for the Iraqi infrastructure: hospitals, schools, roads, and so on.

The problem, however, from the point of view of international finance, was very simple. They did not own that oil, and hence could derive no profit from it. After the Gulf War of 1991, Saddam's government retained control over the Iraqi oil fields. However, after the US invasion of Iraq in 2003, all changed. It's one of the great, unremarked stories of our time how the Iraqi oil has now gone over to multinational – that is private – control.

Well, not unremarked upon in Iraq, of course. Those people know full well what has been going on.

Richard Thomas: 9/11 was eight years ago and Bush as well as Blair are long gone. Do you share my concerns that the general public seem to think President Obama, in and of himself, is some kind of resolution to the last eight years, even though Obama has actually only expanded the War in Afghanistan and neighbouring Pakistan? Also, have you seen Alex Jones' latest film the Obama Deception and, if so, what are your thoughts on it?

Richard Dolan: I think The Obama Deception is a fine piece of journalism. Barak Obama campaigned on a platform of "change you can believe in." But as you suggest, there has been no change. One journalist recently made the apt remark: "want to know what Bush's third term would have looked like? You're living it." And it's true that Obama's major policies are all extensions of what we were seeing under George W. Bush. From the expansion of the war in Afghanistan and Pakistan, to the trillion dollar "stimulus package" for which there is no money to pay, to the ever-increasing power of federal agencies to spy on citizens, and especially to the increasing speed of the creation of a kind of global hegemony by financial elites. One fact pointed out in the Obama Deception was how this current administration is dominated by Wall Street finance to a greater degree than any previous U.S. presidency. All of Barack Obama's top advisors come from Wall Street. Barack Obama attended, along with Hillary Clinton by the way, the 2008 Bilderberg Group meeting. This is now an open secret.

Richard Thomas: Speaking of Alex Jones, in his film Endgame, he documents the dark history of Eugenics and argues that the whole point of the New World Order super-state being constructed is to carry out Eugenics on an unprecedented global scale. The elimination of at least 80% of the world population and the transformation of the global elite into super beings via the merger with advanced technology.

I know you have at least some interest in Transhumanism and what is called the Technological Singularity (as do I) so what do you think of Jones' Endgame scenario and assertion that Transhumanists are crypto Eugenicists?

Also, do you think we need some kind of international law or agreement to insure the technology involved in creating a Trans or Post-human is not abused?

Richard Dolan: I think all of these points are valid and there needs to be a greater public discussion about it. Our technology is evolving so rapidly, and I'm afraid our ability to grasp the implications of what we are doing is continually lagging far behind. We have now deciphered the human genome. We are very close to having advanced nanotechnology. The combination of those two sciences can mean all kinds of things. It could mean a virtual utopia for all human beings, provided that such technology were used for the benefit of humanity at large.

And yet, we must assume that those individuals who have hitherto been "Masters of the Universe" would have no desire to for this outcome. It isn't hard for them – or for most of us, for that matter – to see that we are in the midst of a dangerous population explosion. We are sucking down global resources at a rate that is probably not sustainable. A mere century ago there were about 2 billion people in this world. We are now approaching 7 billion people, with each person using vastly more natural resources than did our ancestors. It's almost certainly not sustainable in the long term.

The global elites who are creating this new world system presumably see this and more. They also see the opportunity of creating their own form of Utopia. Most of us, unfortunately, are standing in their way.

Richard Thomas: While on the topics of Eugenics and population reduction, like me, will you be refusing any compulsory Swine Flu vaccination or are you unconcerned? Also, do you give any credence to the idea that Swine Flu could be some kind of manmade bio weapon?

Richard Dolan: There is no way that I will allow anyone to poke me or members of my family with a swine flu vaccination. There are too many risks associated with the vaccination that have already come to light. We don't do many medications in my house, anyway. I'll stick to my carrot juice, thank you very much.

As to whether or not the current swine flu is a bio weapon, I'll wait until I encounter tangible evidence before I make a strong statement about. But this is the kind of thing has been done before. We know for sure that U.S. military and intelligence groups have played games with diseases in the past. This goes back to the 1940s and 50s at the least. Indeed, the anthrax scare of 2001 has now been traced to Fort Detrick Maryland. I assume most people can readily understand what that means.

Richard Thomas: Somewhat disturbingly, of course, the idea of using advanced technology to create a new super species isn't too far removed from David Jacobs' hybrid theories as outlined in The Threat. Also, we can't really talk about human-alien hybridisation and the New World Order without at least mentioning David Icke's extremely controversial reptilian ideas.

I suppose my question is do you think the alien agenda and the New World Order endgame could in fact be one and the same, or, to put it another way, could the aliens be the secret rulers of the world? If so, how old do you think this conspiracy could be: for instance, do you think its possible mankind could be their creation?
Richard Dolan: With questions like these, we naturally enter a realm of speculation. Jacobs' theory does have a certain compatibility with what you're talking about. The real question is, if there has been a long-standing alien presence on our world in some form or another, have they been manipulating us? Although definitive proof eludes us, there are suggestive reasons for thinking this is the case.

One of my friends, Colleen Clements, who has a PhD and formerly taught at the Rochester Institute of Technology, has written a number of books that suggest this scenario. If so, if we have been "developed" in some way, it's not much of a stretch to assume that these other beings would consider us something of an investment. Would they want to control, at least in broad terms, our social and political and intellectual development? Might they be doing so now? These are the themes that people like David Icke discuss, and as crazy as they sound to the uninitiated, responsible investigators are obligated to inquire. We may not have answers easily forthcoming. But when you are doing an investigation, you have to do it honestly and courageously. You can't rule things out because they seem absurd to you at first glance. You have to look at the facts and decide what scenarios fit within those facts.

Richard Thomas: We've discussed some deeply dark and scary topics in this interview do you have any solutions to the problems the world faces that our readers can put into practice?
Richard Dolan: We all need to keep in mind that human history is filled with crisis and suffering. There has been no period, ever, in our history in which people did not face serious difficulties and even questions concerning their very survival. It's nothing new.

For all people, at all times, facing difficulties requires a kind of calm courage. You have to stay calm in order to learn the facts that you need to know. And you have to be brave. I've come to see our life as something akin to flying a glider plane through a hurricane. It's a hell of a wild ride, and at the end of it we all crash and burn. There is no way out of that. So what we have to do is first accept the hurricane, and secondly experience all that we can from it – learn from it, and enjoy whatever we can along the way. Because that's our life.

We have been handed this precious gift. We could just as easily not exist at all. And yet here we are. What do we choose to do with this existence of ours? Sadly, most people basically throw it away. But for every person there is the opportunity to begin the long journey of expanding their awareness and consciousness. It is only through heightened awareness of ourselves and our world that we can find meaning in what we do, and organize with each other to the extent that we can actually effect positive change.

To put it another way, most of us sleepwalk our way through life. Now it is time to wake up.

Richard Thomas: Thanks again Richard, please tell our readers how they can get signed copies of both volumes I and II of UFOs and the National Security State and when they may expect to see Volume III ?

Richard Dolan: My books are available at my website: keyholepublishing.com. I sign all copies of books that are sold directly from my website. Of course the books are also available at Amazon.com.

I do not expect the third volume of my history to take nearly as long as it took for the second one to appear. Nearly all of the research for volume 3 is already completed. I think two to three years is reasonable to expect. At that point I will have completed a three-volume, 1,600 page history of UFOs. Even now, it surprises me when I think about it. I've enjoyed this journey of mine, of delving into this topic and having the opportunity to learn the things I've learned, and to communicate what I've learned to other people. There is still a long way to go, and there is still a great deal for me to learn. I want to live long enough to make some real progress on this issue.

Mac Tonnies : A Room 101 Interview with a Transhumanist

Mac Tonnies is the author of After The Martian Apocalypse, an excellent book on Mars anomalies. He is perhaps better known in UFO circles, though, for his controversial cryptoterrestrial hypothesis. In this interview we're going to focus more on his views and beliefs as a Transhumanist. In particular, we'll be getting his take on many of the problems people have with the whole idea of Transhmanism. So is Mac Tonnies a real life Davros-like mad scientist or the next Arthur C. Clarke? Maybe a bit a both, you decide ...

Richard Thomas: First things first, thank you so much for agreeing to do this interview.

In this interview, I want to mainly get your take on the Transhumanist movement and some concerns many (myself included) have about the whole idea of upgrading humanity. But first there is something else I've been wanting to ask you about that kind of relates to transhumanism a little bit.

I'm a huge fan of Nigel Kneale's Quatermass serials and films, particularly Quatermass and the Pit. What do you think of the central premise of the story: "That we owe our human condition here to the intervention of insects"?

Mac Tonnies: Cultures all over the world seem to have a special affinity with insect intelligence, a theme we seem to see reiterated in Western pop culture's eponymous image of the "Gray" alien. "Trippers" who ingest DMT sometimes describe similar insect-like entities. The question that naturally arises is whether we're indeed making contact with an intelligence external to our own minds or else tapping into some neural legacy.

Colony collapse disorder is at least as disturbing, albeit for different reasons. The global die-off of bees reminds us how intricately connected we are with the planet. Ultimately, there are no dispassionate, clinical observers; we're embedded in the experiment with no clear sight of its purpose – assuming, of course, that it has one.

Richard Thomas: For people who don't know, what is "transhumanism" and why do you support the idea?

Mac Tonnies: Transhumanism is a simple blanket term for people who view technology as a means by which to augment and expand human prowess – physically, cognitively and perhaps even spiritually. We're already knee-deep in an era of smart-drugs, genetic therapies and molecular manufacturing, so it's not exactly rash to attempt to anticipate future breakthroughs. For instance, there's reason to suspect that aging itself will eventually come to be viewed as a degenerative disease, much how we currently view diseases like polio or cancer. Given the ability to avert disease, relatively few among us will refuse to take advantage of new cures. So I suspect most of us are "closet transhumanists," whether we're explicitly familiar with the philosophical arguments or not.

Richard Thomas: Sci-fi is littered with examples of what might be called transhumans or post-humans: from the Daleks and Cybermen of Doctor Who to the Borg and Augments of Star Trek. But how do you imagine these future creations? For example, do you think some might have a group consciousness like the Borg or maybe removed their emotions like the Cybermen?

Mac Tonnies: The Borg is a wonderful cautionary metaphor: the transhumanist equivalent to the Party in Orwell's "1984." Could transhumanist technologies be used unwisely? Certainly. But the same could be said for any technology, old or new. As with any endeavor with the potential to fundamentally alter our relationship with ourselves, we need to apply caution and forethought, which is what much of contemporary science fiction represents.

Richard Thomas: I'm all for giving sight to the blind, replacing missing limbs and that kind of thing. Restoring or making up for lost ability seems fine, since we're already doing it with things like false teeth and eye glasses, but I have to draw the line at trying to make "improvements" or "upgrading" people. Trying to create better or even "perfect" beings suggests there is something wrong, or worse, inferior about people now. Historically, this is a very, VERY dangerous idea. What are your thoughts on this?

Mac Tonnies: I would argue that we're all "inferior" in the sense that we're ill-adapted to essentially any lifestyle other than the one in which we happened to evolve. (Ask an astronaut.) I don't think any transhumanist thinkers want to create a "perfect" being; the operative goal is to empower the human species on an individual level. In a foreseeable future scenario, instead of being saddled with the genome one blindly inherits, one can choose to become an active participant – and I find that possibility incredibly liberating and exciting. Transhumanism is not eugenics.

Richard Thomas: The whole idea of the post-human seems dangerously close to Friedrich Nietzsche's concept of the Übermensch or Superman. How do we prevent transhumanism from being hijacked and turned into something evil the way Nietzsche's ideas were by Hitler and the Nazis?
Mac Tonnies: That's a legitimate risk. As with the "digital divide," it's likely that, at first, only the relatively wealthy will have access to modification technology – whether a brain-computer interface, anti-senescence treatment or access to intelligence-expanding pharmaceuticals. But one of the appealing outgrowths of digital manufacturing is the ability to build on the atomic level: the sort of technology that could mature into a nanotech "assembler" that can produce desired goods from scratch. Machines like this could do an immeasurable amount of good for the developing world; one hopes they're inevitable, like the now-ubiquitous cellphone.

Richard Thomas: Human beings seem to find it hard enough to get on with other humans, never mind post-humans. What sort of relationship do you think will exist between us and post-humans? Will they be our slaves or will we be their pets?
Mac Tonnies: Neither. A posthuman civilization will probably have enough to think about without harassing its neighbors -- especially if they pose no threat. When I see the Amish, I'm tempted to speculate along similar lines. Almost invariably, some of us will eschew transhumanism for various philosophical or metaphysical reasons, but that doesn't necessarily entail antagonism or hostility.

Richard Thomas: Closely paralleling transhumanism, of course, is the whole idea of the "Technological Singularity." A point in our future history when computers advance beyond the limits of human intelligence and become the new leading source of great invention and breakthroughs in the world. How likely do you think Ray Kurzweil's predictions are that it will occur in the next few decades?
Mac Tonnies: I think Kurzweil's overly optimistic – and naive in a sort of endearingly infectious way. Specifically, I don't think the

post-biological future will arrive as abruptly as Kurzweil suspects. While I think many of his forecasts will indeed happen more or less as advertised, I foresee a more gradual – and markedly less utopian – transition. On the other hand, we might direly need the technologies Kurzweil describes in order to survive the excesses and hazards of the next century, and necessity is often the mother of invention.

Richard Thomas: Do you think the Singularity is something we should be preparing for in case it really does take place? For instance, do you think we need any new laws or other safeguards to prevent any possible dangers? (e.g. Robot rebellion.)
Mac Tonnies: Absolutely. We can continue to engage in a healthy dialogue about when and how the Singularity might arrive – if ever – but there's enough momentum to suggest some very real challenges in coming decades. Possible dangers include "designer" viruses and weaponized nanotech: inventions that could conceivably render us extinct. I don't think that's a risk we can afford to underestimate, regardless of one's intellectual biases.

Richard Thomas: Some speculate that super intelligent machines might develop their own goals that could be inconsistent with continued human survival and prosperity. What do you think of AI (Artificial Intelligence) researcher Hugo de Garis warning that such entities may simply choose to exterminate the human race?
Mac Tonnies: Roboticist Hans Moravec thinks the opposite is more likely: our mechanical offspring will think of us as parents and allow us to join them or perish of our own accord. Perhaps it seems cold, but that's evolution. If Homo sapiens in ultimately usurped by something wiser and more capable, that's quite OK with me.

Richard Thomas: What are your plans for the future? I understand you've been working on a book on your cryptoterrestrial hypothesis, when do you think we might expect that?
Mac Tonnies: I'm fascinated by accounts of apparent UFO occupants and have been rethinking who or what we might be dealing with. I'm of the opinion that the extraterrestrial interpretation is incomplete. Could we be interacting with

indigenous humanoids? That's the question I'm posing in the book I'm writing. Time will tell if it helps resolve the UFO enigma; I'll be satisfied if it makes readers a little less complacent.

Richard Thomas: Thanks again, I look forward to your future projects.

Note: Very sadly Mac Tonnies passed away October 24th, 2009 about a year after doing this interview.

A Room 101 Interview with Dean Haglund: Star of The X-Files and The Lone Gunmen

Did the US Government have foreknowledge of the 9/11 attacks and filter it out to the writers of The X-Files spin-off series The Lone Gunmen? It might sound unlikely to some but that's exactly what Dean Haglund – who played the recurring character Langly in both series – seemed to be hinting at when The X-Files star appeared on a memorable December 15 edition of The Alex Jones Show back in 2005.

To summarise: The Lone Gunmen pilot (broadcast before 9/11) involved a government conspiracy to "hijack" a commercial airliner via remote control and fly the aircraft into the World Trade Centre. 'Why?' you ask. According to dialogue in the script the plan was to blame the terrorist atrocity on rogue third world nations and launch a new global conflict against terrorism to replace the much missed Cold War that had given America so much direction and purpose in the world ... not to mention keep the arms trade afloat following the collapse of communism in the early 1990s.

"The Cold War is over, John. But with no clear enemy to stockpile against, the arms market's flat. But, bring down a fully-loaded 727 into the middle of New York City and you'll find a dozen tin-pot dictators all over the world just clambering to take responsibility and begging to be smart-bombed."

Intrigued by his more recent appearance on the AJ Show earlier this year and the news that Mr Haglund is in the midst of making a new feature documentary about believers in conspiracies and their search for "the truth," I thought the Lone Gunman might make an interesting interview.

Richard Thomas: First I just want to say thank you for agreeing to answer my questions, I've been a huge fan of The X-Files since it first aired on the BBC back in 1993, so you doing this interview is much appreciated.

Your first line in The X-Files was, "Check it out, Mulder: I had breakfast with the guy who shot John F. Kennedy." That still makes me chuckle, but I'm a lot more open to that kind of thing now. What did you think of that line when you first read it in the script and have your own perceptions of the character you played changed at all since then?

Dean Haglund: I didn't know what the writers were really talking about then. My brother was more up on that stuff than I was, so I started talking to him. The other part of that line was... "old dude now, but said he was dressed as a cop on the grassy knoll". And that was funny, because a year later I was down in Dallas and went to the book depository which is now a museum and went to that grassy knoll. From then on, it was fun tracking down these theories and ideas and experiencing first hand so many of the things that The X-Files talked about. That naturally changed my perceptions and they continue to change to this day.

Richard Thomas: Did you do much research for the character, i.e. did you read any conspiracy related books or magazines, or start listening to paranormal talk radio shows or anything like that?

Dean Haglund: Yes. I got to be on the paranormal talk radio programs as a guest. Then I was introduced to many of the researchers in the various fields and really got to know them well. Everything branched off from there. Many of them appear in my documentary that we are doing called The Truth is Out There.

Richard Thomas: There are other characters in the first series of The X-Files that we never saw again, why do you think The Lone Gunmen kept returning and were ultimately even given their own spin-off series?

Dean Haglund: One word: Internet. The early newsgroup alt.tv.x-files was one of the first online gathering spots for the fans of a TV show. There they would talk about the episodes, and the writers would lurk in there and get honest feedback of the show. Thus, the Gunmen sort of reflected this culture and even some of our lines came from this news group. And they would bring us back to boost chatter on the newsgroup, and use that traffic as a proof of our popularity. It was a fun symbiotic relationship.

Richard Thomas: Do you have a favourite episode or moment from either The X-Files or The Lone Gunmen? And is there a particular type of episode you prefer to watch yourself as a fan?
Dean Haglund: In our origin episode, called Unusual Suspects, my playing Dungeons and Dragon for money, was a really fun moment. And got me invited to a lot of games. I liked the monster of the week shows that they did, but the story was compelling when you had the time to invest in it all.

Richard Thomas: The subtitle of the new X-Files film was "I Want To Believe," do you think people really simply "want to believe" or do you think something more meaningful might explain the growth of the 'alternative media' in recent years? Guess I'm really asking do you think people believe in conspiracy theories because they're true or because they need to believe in something and religion etc doesn't make the cut?
Dean Haglund: Belief and Truth! Two great ideas that are often jammed into one. For the last year, as a camera followed me around the world and we interviewed many people, like Alex Jones, Jordan Maxwell, etc, I asked them the question what is the truth and why do they believe they know it and not the other guy with a completely alternative viewpoint. Some said because they felt it or that history beard them out. But the thing that all of them had in common was the need to follow this path regardless or the personal toll it took. That the truth, however subjective it may seem, was ultimately an objective quantity that they were getting to.

Richard Thomas: What was your reaction after 9/11 and what's your current opinion on The Lone Gunmen pilot? In your interview with Alex Jones you said the writers would sometimes be approached by people from the CIA, FBI and NASA, was this the case with the pilot?
Dean Haglund: I asked Vince Gilligan (Breaking Bad) this very question when he was on my podcast and he said that this was a case of an artist tapping into some bizarre collective un-conscience

item, and he said that he read about the idea in a Tom Clancy novel, so there was no direct involvement in this case. My current opinion is that the pilot now stands as a chilling time capsule when we were just a little less scarred by real life events.

Richard Thomas: If the pilot was indeed based on insider knowledge of some kind, why do you think they would feed it to the writers of The X-Files of all people? Do you think the purpose might have been to discredit the "government did it" theories in advance?

Dean Haglund: Separate from the pilot, I have heard that the popular culture is used as a tool by whatever elite (business, govt, Illuminati, etc.) to both gauge and control the populace. That is, the conspiracy is the conspiracy theory itself, making its way into the mainstream culture, thereby usurping the power of the populace to alter it, because one can diminish some researcher or whistleblower as someone who "just watches too much X-files."

Richard Thomas: What's your take on the theory that sci-fi shows like The X-Files and Star Trek are intended to be a form of 'predictive programming' aimed at slowly acclimatising the public to ideas they would otherwise be hostile towards, i.e. world government?

Dean Haglund: This seems to give more power to an elite ruling body and removes the power of the artist to create shows that are tapping into the zeitgeist of the moment. It involves the idea that we all already know the future and we just connect to shows or artwork that reflect what we are thinking in a pre-cognitive level. To say that a small group dictate those idea memes into our minds and then have Hollywood or the BBC then make entertainment that matches what they preloaded I don't think can work. I think that they would like that to happen, but ultimately, creating art is not a simple cut and dry business exercise, it has to include some 'other' things to make it a "hit"

Richard Thomas: The final X-Files episode "The Truth" left us with a very ominous prediction about 2012, is it possible that this might have been based on some kind of insider information? Perhaps even preparation for something very nasty coming down in

2012?

Dean Haglund: Here is an excellent example of a collective fear manifesting itself into popular culture. Since this airing, 2012 has become the hot topic at all the conventions, however, as Paul Dean said in our documentary, when he was talking to a Mayan priest about all of this, he said that "western society has it all wrong" and that since we cannot hold a duality in our minds, a quantum "Schrodinger's Cat" scenario if you will, then we can only picture the end of something as a finite disaster and not both that and the re-awakening into the light.

Richard Thomas: It took the best part of thirty years before Oliver Stone's 1991 film JFK broke the taboo and featured a pro-conspiracy plot about the assassination. How long do you think it'll take before Hollywood or even TV do the same thing with 9/11? Also do you think if The X-Files had not ended in 2002 Chris Carter might have tackled the issue?

Dean Haglund: I think that The X-Files would have been painted into a corner because it would have had to address it in some way, and yet to come out on the conspiracy side would have sat very harshly for some. Because the implication on the 9/11 truth movement is very sinister and somewhat hopeless even, in that, if it was all an inside job and all the people that had to be involved to make that happen, means that the cynicism that runs through whatever entity was behind that and whatever motive that was the compelling force to achieve that, is a lot of negative energy. Whether greed of Halliburton, or terrorist zeal of Al-Queda, either case makes for some heavy karmic weight some are carrying regarding that day. And to put that on TV even now would require either fancy footwork or a counterbalance. I think that the only work thus far that was able to embrace that would be Art Speigleman's comic book about the day called "In the Shadow of No Towers". His fun drawing style works to balance out that story nicely.

Richard Thomas: I noticed on your website, that you've done a comic book called "Why The Lone Gunmen Was Cancelled," so why do you think The Lone Gunmen and ultimately even The X-Files were cancelled? Jack Bauer was quite a departure from the kind of American hero the Gunmen and Spooky Mulder represented, do you think there was an agenda to replace pro-conspiracy type programming with pro-government shows like 24?

Dean Haglund: To answer the first part, you have to get my comic book because it is a long story. Here again, popular culture reflects the times we live in. The X-Files would never get off the ground today because we don't have room in our brains to contemplate an "evil syndicate that is working with Aliens to create a human hybrid." When you think back to the time the show started in '93, there was so much optimism – the wall had just come down, there was the Oslo accord, the atomic clock was set BACK, etc. – so that we could be entertained by a "Trust No One" anti-hero, who rarely even used a gun. Now Jack Bauer is more comforting in our times because as all elements seem to spin out of control, this guy can work non-stop (within 24 hours) to stop and solve global crisis. That is cathartic at the same time as it is soothing.

Richard Thomas: I understand since the end of The X-Files you've been working on a documentary film about people who believe in conspiracy theories, what exactly is the film about and why did you decide to do it after doing The X-Files for so long?

Dean Haglund: As I alluded to earlier, The Truth is Out There, is a documentary about why conspiracies exist in the first place and what function do they serve, and ultimately, about what is "truth" and how do you know in our present 'information blizzard' when you have found it. I decided to do it after my co-host on my podcast, Phil Leirness, came to a couple conventions and saw that my life was interesting in that I dealt with these concepts daily, and because of the people that I knew from researching my role as one of The Lone Gunmen I had unique access to many people in the field that probably would not talk on camera to anyone else. So what I thought would be a few interviews has become a year long travelling document about what is really TRUE and how that affects all those who seek and live it.

Richard Thomas: I know Alex Jones is one person you've interviewed but who are some of the other personalities you've encountered, and does anyone stick out in particular?

Dean Haglund: Jordan Maxwell, Dr. Roger Leir, David Sereda, Dr. Miller who started the Institute of Noetic Sciences with Edgar

Mitchell, and many more. Alex Jones was illuminating because for the number of times I had been on his show I didn't really know that much about him. So for me to ask him questions and to see his passion behind why he slaved away on the radio and fighting against the machine was really cool. This documentary should be ready in November and then we head off to the film festivals for some screenings.

Richard Thomas: Other than 9/11, what other conspiracy theories have you investigated or looked into? For instance what's your opinion on the 1960s assassinations of JFK, RFK and MLK; the New World Order conspiracy theories surrounding the Bilderburg Group and other secret societies; and, of course, Roswell and UFOs?

Dean Haglund: Let's see, we look into the GMO food alteration of our diet. Our food has been the same for 50,000 years except for the last 30 where we have completely changed how and what we eat. This may or may not be a specific plan to reduce the human population back down to workable levels using nothing other than our own gluttony. We saw labs where experiments are going on in a level of science that is beyond the orthodox three dimensional sciences that would require this answer to be about 25 pages long. My theories on all of these are now, after hearing all of these people in a state of flux, since all of it, even though it contradicts each other, seems to be true is some way. Hopefully, we'll find an answer in the editing.

Richard Thomas: What other projects are you working on and where can people contact you and find out about the documentary?

Dean Haglund: I am reconfiguring everything as we speak. So go to Deanhaglund.com for links to everything, and you can contact me there for more info.

Richard Thomas: Thanks again Dean, hope we can do this again sometime.

Room 101 Interview with Steve Watson: Webmaster for Infowars.net

Steve Watson is the webmaster for independent journalist, political activist and documentary filmmaker Alex Jones at Infowars.net. He is also a regular contributor to and editor of Jones' Prisonplanet.com. Holding a BA Degree in Literature and a Masters Degree in International Relations, Steve and his brother Paul Watson first became aware of Alex Jones after watching Jon Ronson's Channel Four documentary series: The Secret Rulers of the World. In 2005 both brothers appeared in Alex Jones' documentary film Terrorstorm.

Richard Thomas: Thanks for taking the time to answer these questions mate, I'm sure your constantly busy so it's really appreciated. Have you always been interested in what the mainstream media like to dismiss as "conspiracy theories" or was there a particular book, documentary etc that first caught your attention and things developed from there?

Steve Watson: I was always interested in alternative theories and questioning the accepted version of the truth regarding major historical and political events. I remember when I was in school, about 13 years old, my history teacher (who was also my brother's history teacher) would show video of the JFK assassination and would raise questions over the government's explanation of what happened. That stuff wasn't even part of our curriculum – we were supposed to be learning about the Second World War – but before the lessons began, as we filtered into the classroom, he would be playing these videos and telling us about the facts and discrepancies of the lone gunman explanation – I'm certain that prompted me into exploring things more and looking for alternative explanations and I thank him for that.

Richard Thomas: How was it that you and your brother, two "red coats," started writing for Alex Jones' website infowars.com?

Steve Watson: We both saw Alex on a British documentary called Secret Rulers of The World made by Jon Ronson, who went on to write The Men Who Stare At Goats. It was 2000, when Alex infiltrated The Bohemian Grove. We began listening to his radio show on the internet, Paul started up his website and his own radio show, as Alex always encourages his listeners to do. I began helping him with the website and eventually it got popular enough for Alex to notice it. He liked what he saw and asked Paul to write for him and create the websites that became Prisonplanet.com and Prisonplanet.tv. I was studying at university during this time, but I kept contributing and helping out and in 2005 when I finished studying, Alex brought me in full time.

Richard Thomas: What do you think the biggest misconception is towards people interested in the kind of topics you cover at infowars.com?

Steve Watson: That we are pushing a one sided political viewpoint like the mainstream media does. Left and right is part of the same control system, anyone who looks at what we do for long enough will see that.

Richard Thomas: I noticed your brother goes by "Number 6" and I've heard the classic 1960s Doctor Who theme more than a few time on the Alex Jones Show. Are you, your brother and Alex Jones big science-fiction fans, and if so what are some of your favourite shows/films/novels etc?

Steve Watson: I am not particularly a science fiction fan (sorry!). In terms of entertainment culture I am a fan of anything stimulating and thought provoking, no matter what genre of entertainment it belongs to. In relation to science fiction, Patrick McGoohan's The Prisoner fits into that category for me, as does the writing of Philip K. Dick and some of John Carpenter's films. I can't say I like Dr Who at all, especially in its modern incarnation. I think Alex just uses the theme tune because it sounds good!

Richard Thomas: About 90% of what Alex Jones talks about seems to be based directly on what governments have already openly admitted to. In light of this what do you think the most disturbing document you've ever come across is?

Steve Watson: The ones that relate to biowarfare and eugenics. There are countless examples of the US government having illegally tested and used bio-weapons on its own citizens. The Tuskegee Syphilis Study, The Program F fluoride study, Project SHAD which used live toxins and chemical poisons on American servicemen on American soil, spraying clouds of bacteria over San Francisco, releasing toxic gases into the New York subway, holding open-air biological and chemical weapons tests in at least four states in the 1960s, the list goes on. These are only a few examples of what has become public knowledge. Then there are documents like the 1974 declassified document of the National Security Council, entitled "The Implications of World-wide Population Growth on the Security and External Interests of the United States" in which Henry Kissinger calls for programs of sterilization and depopulation in the third world in return for increased aid. John P. Holdren's Eco-Science is another eugenicist's masterpiece. The most disturbing material is covered in Alex Jones' film Endgame.

Richard Thomas: Did you vote in the recent General Election? And what, if anything, do you think the result showed?
Steve Watson: Yes I did, though I didn't expect anything to change because all three candidates are establishment career politicians with broadly the same agendas. The result showed that people are utterly sick of the political system in the UK. The relatively high turn out also showed that people are desperate for some meaningful political change. Some people say everyone should stop voting in protest – I don't think that would achieve a great deal other than devaluing our right to vote. You have to effect change from the bottom up, that means ensuring the right candidates win locally. Though there is a great deal of optimism in our movement, there is also a great deal of defeatism – I mean people declaring that it doesn't matter whether they vote or not because everything is controlled and manipulated by the powers that be. Power is as much a state of mind as it is an actuality.

Richard Thomas: What role, if any, do you think the British Royal family plays in the New World Order?
Steve Watson: They represent an elite bloodline that has for centuries declared itself as God's appointed rulers over half of the planet, killing, torturing and maiming anyone who crosses it in order to hold on to that mantle. Are we supposed to believe they've had a sudden change of heart? Today many people in Britain suggest that these facts are no long relevant because the royal family has very little power. This is a huge myth. The Queen is the head of state and as such she can simply replace the British government at

any time she chooses, should she wish to do so. The royal family still owns vast swathes of land throughout Britain and the rest of the world, and the Queen still presides as head of state in Canada and Australia. They also exert influence on the global stage through groups, bodies and corporations they charter and provide patronage to.

Richard Thomas: Why do you think Russia Today is the only mainstream media channel to take subjects like the recent Bilderberg meeting in Spain seriously?
Steve Watson: I understand why you ask this question, but I don't believe it is. This year there was much more mainstream media coverage of the meeting this year, though it takes someone like Charlie Skelton to approach it from out of leftfield for it to get into mainstream sources such as the London Guardian. Russia Today has become a prominent news provider because it has embraced the internet, while much of the mainstream resides in dinosaur land.

Richard Thomas: How long, if ever, do you think it'll be before the BBC are forced to let serious 9/11 researchers and climate sceptics on shows like Question Time?
Steve Watson: Never. The BBC is a state controlled propaganda machine. If you buy a TV or any form of television receiving equipment in the UK you have to pay for the BBC by law. If you gave the British people a choice of whether to pay for the BBC or not, as part of a subscription deal for example – which should happen because it has violated it's charter over and over again – the majority would opt out and the BBC would cease to exist – simple as that.

Richard Thomas: I know Alex Jones doesn't discuss them much on his show, but what's your take on UFOs?
Steve Watson: It's a very broad subject, and I'm no expert. Some of the research into the topic is interesting, some of it is useless and ridiculous from what I've seen. I've never personally seen a UFO, but my gut feeling is that some are advanced military technology and the others are natural phenomena. That doesn't mean I don't believe there isn't life on other planets though – of course there is.

CHAPTER 2

Richard Thomas: Thanks again mate, where can people contact you and read your articles? (Please feel free to plug anything you like here mate)

Steve Watson: prisonplanet.com, my Myspace page, and Infowars.com – because there's a war on for your mind!

The Top Ten Weirdest Paranormal and Conspiracy Theories

In 2008 I begin writing a regular column for the website binnallofamerica.com. Called 'Richard's Room 101' this bi-weekly column mostly focused on the paranormal and what most people know as conspiracy theories.

Topics like 9/11 and how much the US Government and its alphabet agencies really knew ahead of the attacks, as well as secret societies, the JFK assassination, UFOs and other government cover-ups. The column also gave me the chance to interview some of the best known researchers on these topics. Men like Jim Marrs author of Crossfire: The Plot That Killed Kennedy, UFO authors Timothy Good, Richard Dolan, Nick Pope and Nick Redfern, as well as Zoological Director for the Centre for Fortean Zoology (CFZ) Richard Freeman and writer for Alex Jones' alternative news website Infowars.com, Steve Watson, and many others. I even interviewed Dean Haglund, better known as Langley in the popular 90s TV series The X-Files, who had his own opinions on why some people believe in the paranormal and conspiracy theories:

"Belief and Truth! Two great ideas that are often jammed into one. For the last year, as a camera followed me around the world and we interviewed many people, like Alex Jones, Jordan Maxwell, etc, I asked them the question what is the truth and why do they believe they know it and not the other guy with a completely alternative viewpoint. Some said because they felt it or that history bears them out. But the thing that all of them had in common was the need to follow this path regardless or the personal toll it took. That the truth, however subjective it may seem, was ultimately an objective quantity that they were getting to."

What follows are ten of the weirdest sounding paranormal and conspiracy theories I researched while writing my column. It's worth remembering, though, just because something might sound a bit weird doesn't mean it's not true, decide for yourself.

TEN: British Big Cats

Pumas and other big cats are not supposed to be roaming wild in the remote hills and countryside of Britain, but in 2010 newly released documents obtained under the Freedom of Information Act revealed that a government agency tasked with investigating more than 100 big cat sightings across England since 2005, concluded that 38 were genuine.

But if these creatures are in fact real, and not just the stuff of myth and human imagination, where could they have come from?

According to Cryptozoologist, people who study unknown species of animal, these beasts are the descendents of escapees.

Richard Freedman of the CFZ told me, 'Until the Dangerous Wild Animals Act in 1976 anyone could keep anything they wanted as a pet and up until the early 1980s any old duffer could start a zoo in their backyard! The nucleus of the current big cat population in the UK was from these irresponsible people.'

Another theory is that these British big cats are a form of 'Zooform'. In the words of author of Monster! – The A-Z of Zooform Phenomena Neil Arnold, 'a term coined by Fortean researcher Jonathan Downes who runs the CFZ to describe 'a void of creatures' which clearly aren't flesh and blood, yet which cryptozoology and the paranormal realm attempts to file, and yet such 'monsters' fit into neither.'

NINE: UFO Crash Retrievals

Everyone has heard about the famous Roswell incident, the alleged crash and recovery of a UFO by the US Government in the New Mexico desert in the summer of 1947. Few realise that there have been rumours of other UFO crashes, however, including some British cases.

Nick Redfern author of The Real Men in Black and other UFO books told me, 'There have been rumours for many years of an alleged UFO crash – or Foo Fighter crash – in Britain at some point during the Second World War. Unfortunately, the details are very brief and no-one has really been able to pinpoint with any real accuracy what exactly happened … However, there are stories of elements of the British Government and military supposedly examining such a device – and crew – at some point prior to 1955.'

Some British ufologists even speculate that there might be a link between this UFO crash and the JFK assassination in 1963.

According to Nick, 'details of this story turn up in a controversial 'leaked' document that has ties to the JFK assassination. And as bizarre as it may sound, there are many threads that link UFOs and the JFK assassination, which leads some people to suspect there is a direct connection.'

The best known alleged British UFO crash, however, is the Berwyn Mountains crash-story of 1974. Nick Redfern said of this case, 'Back in the mid-90s, I was of the opinion that a UFO had come down, then I changed my mind after reading the research of Andy Roberts. However, I still get accounts now and again from locals and retired military people (all specifically from RAF Valley, interestingly enough) of knowledge of bodies recovered and taken to Porton Down, Wiltshire. So, I'll be the first to admit that, today, it's one that continues to puzzle me.'

Another famous British crash case is the 1980 Rendlesham Forest incident, which involved American airmen from RAF Woodbridge who reported seeing mysterious lights and a landed craft.

French-born American scientist Jacques Vallee has suggested that the Rendlesham Forest incident may have been some kind of psy-op, pointing out that the American soldiers who went out to investigate the UFO that night were told to leave their guns behind. Former MoD UFO investigator Nick Pope is sceptical about this theory, however:

'As much as I respect Jacques Vallee, the psy-op theory is extremely unlikely to explain the Rendlesham Forest incident. I worked at the Ministry of Defence for 21 years. One of my jobs involved working closely with the Defence Intelligence Staff, while my final post was in a security-related job. If this had been a psy-op, there is absolutely no way that the authorities would have allowed a paper trail to be generated in the way that it was. The affair would have been allowed to play itself out, but the moment people started putting things in writing, those running the psy-op would have had a quiet word and stopped anything from being committed to paper. Any documents had had slipped through the net would have been quietly withdrawn.'

EIGHT: RAF Rudloe Manor

If crashed UFOs have been retrieved by the British then where do they take them? Many in the British UFO research community believe that alien saucers in the possession of the British Government may have been kept at Rudloe Manor, a Royal Air Force station located south-east of Bath, between the towns of Box and Corsham.

In a guest article for my website Para-News.info historian Rupert Matthews wrote about the rumours linking the base with UFOs:

'By the later 1990s the rumours had begun to take a more definite form ... According to these reports, there was a vast underground complex beneath the apparently innocuous barracks and office buildings scattered in the grounds of the old manor house. This much could be checked out and was accurate. The manor had been taken over by the RAF at the start of World War II precisely because these huge underground caverns existed. They were the abandoned workings from which the much prized Bath Stone had been quarried out in the 19th century. Being deep underground the tunnels and caves were, of course, proof against German bombing. From 1940 onward a whole range of government and military units and installations were located in the tunnels of Rudloe Manor where they would be safe from the Luftwaffe. Much of what went on there at the time is now well known and while it was all vital to the war effort is hardly controversial.'

Nick Redfern has also investigated Rudloe Manor-UFO connection, telling me:

'The whole Rudloe-UFO saga has been a puzzle in itself. There's no doubt that the RAF's Provost & Security Services – who were based at Rudloe for two decades – have played a role in official UFO investigations. There are even a few declassified files available at the National Archive, Kew. But the big question is the extent, or otherwise, of those investigations. Some researchers have suggested – and particularly Matthew Williams in the mid-to-late 90s – that Rudloe's role went far beyond that officially admitted by the MoD. Others merely see it as a minor aspect of official UFO investigations that got blown up out of proportion by the UFO research community. As with the Berwyn case, I still get accounts now and again from people talking about how, at one point at least, Rudloe was involved at a far deeper level. But I will concede that actually proving this has not happened yet.'

SEVEN: The Illuminati and Secret Society Symbolism

Fans of Dan Brown's novel Angels & Demons will be familiar with the Illuminati and the conspiracy theory that this secret society behind world events hides its secret symbols and messages in art and architecture. One film riddled with examples of alleged 'Illuminati

Symbolism' is Ridley Scott's Blade Runner, a film based on a novel by sci-fi author Philip K. Dick.

In that film, there are numerous examples of symbols and ideas often associated with the Illuminati and other popular secret society conspiracy theories on the web. 'The Owl of Bohemia,' the 'all-seeing eye,' even David Icke's Reptilians (an extra-dimensional race of reptiles, of which, Queen Elizabeth II is supposedly a member) are given a nod to in the form of a replicant snake! And all this in 1982 … which was more than a decade before the internet gave conspiracy theorists the power to reach millions around the world with their exciting mix of in-depth research and New Age paranoia.

Author of the popular Secret Sub blog Christopher Knowles has his own thoughts on Dick and Blade Runner:

'Well, we know that Dick was all over anything weird or mystical, but I don't think he had much involvement in the movie itself. Blade Runner kind of presents us with this kind of technocratic dystopia that some of these elite cult types would see as the paradise of their apotheosis. The cognitive elite in their penthouses and the poor, teeming masses huddled in the streets and the middle class a distant memory. The constant rain is kind of like the piss of the new gods in that regard. Maybe Scott incorporated some of those symbols as part of the overall social critique of this world that runs throughout the film. Maybe it was the screenwriter David Peoples, who also did similar films like Twelve Monkeys and Soldier.'

SIX: Mind Control and Assassinations

About 80% of Americans say in polls that they believe there was a conspiracy to kill President Kennedy in Dallas, Texas, in 1963. But many believe that there was also a conspiracy to kill his brother Robert Kennedy. The gunman Sirhan Sirhan has never been able to consciously remember the details of the shooting and has only been able to recall what happened under hypnosis. In the pages of a diary Sirhan kept leading up the assassination he wrote over and over again phrases like 'RFK must die' and 'RFK must be assassinated', leading some to believe he was being mind controlled.

There are also other signs that Sirhan was hypnotized the night of the assassination. Witnesses who saw Sirhan before the assassination that night said that he looked like he was in a trance and later after the assassination when police shone a torch in Sirhan's eyes his pupils were dilated as if Sirhan had been drugged. Richard Dolan, author of

UFOs and the National Security State, thinks that Sirhan may have been the victim of a CIA programme called 'MK-Ultra'.

'The technology of mind control is more substantial and goes back much farther than many people realize. There were substantial efforts by the CIA and other agencies from the 1940s onward to find ways of harnessing the human mind. We all know about how the CIA pioneered the use of LSD during the 1950s, but many people forget it was in order to find the ultimate mind control chemical. Advances in hypnosis were also far more profound than is generally believed.'

FIVE: The Cryptoterrestrials

The initials UFO stand for Unidentified Flying Object. The extraterrestrial hypothesis is simply the most popular explanation for the UFO phenomenon. But if these mysterious objects don't come from outer space where else could they come from? The only other alternative is that they originate from this world, either built by a parallel human civilization we know nothing about, or perhaps even stranger another species native to this planet existing in the remotest parts of planet Earth. Perhaps deep underground or beneath the seas.

Before his untimely death in 2009, Mac Tonnies wrote a book entitled The Cryptoterrestrials exploring this theory.

'Cultures all over the world seem to have a special affinity with insect intelligence, a theme we seem to see reiterated in Western pop culture's eponymous image of the 'Gray' alien. 'Trippers' who ingest DMT sometimes describe similar insect-like entities. The question that naturally arises is whether we're indeed making contact with an intelligence external to our own minds or else tapping into some neural legacy.'

FOUR: Alien Abductions

Just as the UFO phenomenon has no single explanation there are various different explanations for the alien abduction phenomenon. Some cases will be hoaxes and some may be attributable to some form of hallucination or delusion. To this we can probably add vivid dreams, sleep paralysis, false memory syndrome and various other factors. However, these explanations can't explain all cases.

Scientific studies of the abductees show no evidence of psychopathology or falsehood and suggest that in recalling their experiences they exhibit physiological reactions (e.g. increased heart rate and perspiration) not seen in control groups of non-abductees.

Nick Pope told me, 'My own case files on this run to about 100 incidents. The most compelling involves a young woman called Brigitte Grant (a pseudonym), who I worked with for a number of years. There's some information about her on the internet, but she's dropped out of ufology now and witness confidentiality precludes my saying anything not already in the public domain.'

When I interviewed best selling UFO author Timothy Good he told me about two encounters with extraterrestial beings he thought he had had.

'Yes, in fact I've had several encounters with beings I believe were from elsewhere. The first occurred at a diner near the Arizona/California border in November 1963 while I was on tour with the Royal Philharmonic Orchestra. It would take me too long to go into all the details, but it involved an unusual young woman who – in the presence of three of my colleagues – responded very positively, but non-verbally, to my telepathic question as to whether she was from elsewhere. Just after we left the diner in our convoy of three coaches, I was astonished to see a road sign for Desert Center – I'd no idea we were anywhere near there. Quite a coincidence!

'The second encounter took place in the lobby of a hotel in the middle of New York in February 1967, between a rehearsal and concert with the London Symphony Orchestra. About half-an-hour after I'd transmitted a telepathic request for definitive proof that some aliens were living among us, an immaculately suited man walked into the lobby then sat beside me. Following my telepathic request to indicate by means of a certain sign if he was the person I was looking for, he did so immediately. Neither of us spoke. It was a cathartic experience for me.'

THREE: The Secret Space Programme

Back in 2005 Garry McKinnon made international headlines after he was charged with various counts of hacking into Pentagon and NASA computers, in search of what the computer hacker described as 'free energy technology,' which McKinnon believed the US Government had reversed engineered from recovered UFOs.

While the mainstream media largely concentrated on the US Government's dubious claim that McKinnon caused some $700,000 worth of damages to its computers, some truly out this world comments the supposed 'cyber terrorist' made to the author of The Men Who Stare At Goats, Jon Ronson, in an interview printed in the July 9, 2005 edition of The Guardian were all but ignored. In particular, McKinnon's assertions that while hacking into the US space command he discovered 'lists of officers names' under the tantalising heading 'Non-Terrestrial Officers' as well as records of what McKinnon called 'fleet-to-fleet transfers' and a 'list of ship names.'

Rather than extraterrestrials, though, the computer hacker told The Guardian columnist that he thought he had found evidence of a secret space program of some kind. When Ronson asked McKinnon 'The Americans have a secret spaceship?' McKinnon answering, 'That's what this trickle of evidence has led me to believe.'

Author of UFOs and the National Security State Richard Dolan has speculated that advanced technology obtained via UFO crash retrievals in the 1940s and 50s could of lead to the creation of a 'parallel human civilisation' separate from any government with its own secret space program:

'That's when I realized, very concretely, that the notion of space anomalies was indeed a serious topic. I began to consider: if there is covert interest in the anomalies on Mars, would there be a covert space program to investigate? To this day, I don't know the answer with certainty, but over the years I have encountered no shortage of quiet, serious-minded people who tell me of their knowledge that there is such a covert program. One component of this, it appears, has to do with the Moon. Are there bases on the far side of the Moon? Again, I do not know for sure, but I cannot rule it out. More than once, people I consider to be informed insiders have steered me in this direction.'

TWO: Chemtrails and Population Reduction

Chemtrails, not to be confused with airplane contrails, are a new phenomena which has struck all over the world. Chemtrails differ from conventional airplane vapour contrails in that they usually extend continuously and expand to transform into a cirrus type cloud layer.

Texas author Jim Marrs wrote about the chemtrail phenomenon in a guest article for my blog Para-News.info:

'High levels of Barium, along with aluminum oxide, already had been identified among the contents of chemtrails by tests. During a three month period in 2002, three separate rainwater and snow samples from Chapel Hill, North Carolina, were collected and submitted for formal double-blind laboratory analysis. Therese

Aigner, an accredited environmental engineer, found significant amounts of barium, aluminum, calcium, magnesium and titanium in the samples, all of which had a verified chain of custody. Ms Aigner concluded that that the consistency of the findings indicated "a very controlled delivery (dispersion) of chemtrails by aircraft in your area." She added that whoever was responsible for the chemtrails was violating more than a half dozen federal laws and regulations.'

But if the governments of the world are conspiring together to covertly spray the global population with dangerous chemicals, why are they doing this?

The Bilderberg conference is an annual secret meeting of approximately 140 of the world's most influential politicians and business leaders. In the documentary film The New World Order chemtrail researcher Timucin Leflef is seen protesting the Bilderberg Group meeting in Turkey in 2008. Lefef and other researchers believe the covert spraying is part of a long term plan to reduce overpopulation:

'Although many of the hypotheses regarding chemtrails warrant further investigation, I keep veering towards the population control agenda. Henry Kissinger's NSSM-200 states the global elite's plan to reduce world populations by at least 3 billion by the year 2050. This number could be far greater if you believe the Georgia Guide-stones or Ted Turner's pronouncement that 95% of world populations need to be eliminated. NSSM-200 states that artificial food scarcity can be created and used as a weapon to create famines, thus reducing the world population to more manageable levels.'

ONE: NASA's Project Blue Beam

Project Blue Beam is an alleged NASA plan to stage a fake alien invasion using holograms and use this staged crisis to create an authoritarian world government. The basic premise of Project Blue Beam that the US alphabet agencies like the CIA encouraging the belief that UFOs = aliens was explored by Mark Pilkington in his book Mirage Men.

'The earliest version of this story I know of is a speech made by British Foreign Secretary Anthony Eden to the UN in March 1947, in which he posits that an invasion by Martians would be the only thing that might unite the world's nations. Of course the Roswell incident took place four months later, something that was picked up on by former intelligence agent Bernard Newman in his 1948 novel The Flying Saucer. In which scientists stage a fake invasion to bring about world peace.

'Reagan famously alluded to the idea again in 1987, also talking to the UN. It's a common motif in science fiction – I was recently pointed to an Outer Limits episode, "The Architects of Fear," which follows the same premise. There are rumours that Wernher von Braun believed that a false ET invasions was on the cards, and it's something that UFO researcher and Manhattan Project scientist Leon Davidson also talked about in the 1960s referring to the contactees, who he thought were being deceived in elaborate setups by the intelligence agencies. It's a very appealing idea whether true or not.'

As a screenwriter and filmmaker himself conspiracy researcher Timucin Leflef sees evidence that we are all being programmed via TV and films to fear an alien invasion:

'The alien invasion hoax is also another reason why so many Hollywood science fiction movies involve aliens arriving in vast armadas to destroy us and take over our planet. They were quite prevalent in the 50s and you can find modern-day examples like Independence Day, War of the Worlds and even Mars Attacks. Very few movies about extra-terrestrials actually involve aliens with peaceful intentions. E.T. certainly comes to mind, but even movies where they arrive as our benevolent 'saviours' like The Day The Earth Stood Still, is still another permutation of the New World Order hoax, in which case it's about giving up our sovereignty, our 'petty little differences' as Reagan put it, and joining a fascist global regime in order to achieve an alleged 'world peace'. It will be world peace but with a seriously heavy price on our freedoms.'

A Room 101 Interview with Jim Marrs

One of my favourite films is Oliver Stone's 1991 film JFK. Although Stone took a lot of creative licence in the film, for instance merging different historical characters into a single character like the "MR X" character, the film was largely based on two non-fiction assassination books. The first was On the Trail of the JFK Assassins, written by former New Orleans district attorney Jim Garrison, the only prosecutor to bring a trial for the assassination of John F. Kennedy, and who is played by Kevin Costner in the Oliver Stone film.

The second book which informed the film was Crossfire by Jim

Marrs. I remember listening to Jim being interviewed about assassination on The Alex Jones Show and that interview really captivated me and I began reading more and more books about the assassinations of the 1960s. What follows is my own interview with Jim Marrs about the JFK assassination and some of the parallels with 9/11.

Richard Thomas: I've always had an interest in the paranormal and unexplained, but Oliver Stone's film JFK and your book Crossfire played a large part in me becoming interested in the JFK assassination and other conspiracy topics. How did you first begin researching the JFK assassination and what exactly do you think happened in Dallas, Texas, on November 22, 1963?
Jim Marrs: On Nov. 22, 1963, I was a journalism major at the University of North Texas and I began looking into the JFK assassination on the day it happened. I still have the Dallas and Fort Worth newspapers from that day to include the UNT campus special edition. I knew something was funny right from the start because witnesses were on TV stating that two shots came one on top of the other – Bang! Bang! At the time I was a deer hunter and had bolt-action rifles of my own and I knew that the bolt on a bolt-action rifle had to be cycled before firing again. Therefore, one could not get two shots close together. But at that time, although I was puzzled, I had no alternative but to believe the official version.
  As to what happened in Dallas, President Kennedy was killed in a military-style ambush involving organized crime with the active assistance of elements within the federal government of the United States to include the CIA, FBI and military. Pressure from the top thwarted any truthful investigation. The Kennedy assassination was a true coup d'etat—a sudden and violent shift of power to the right in this country. And that power remains with us today.

Richard Thomas: The final documentary in Nigel Turner's 9-part series The Men Who Killed Kennedy, "The Guilty Men," which speculated about Lyndon Johnson's involvement in the assassination was banned after its initial broadcast on the History Channel back in 2003. How significant do you think LBJ's involvement was in the assassination, and are there any parallels to be made with 9/11 and George Bush's War on Terror continuing under President Obama?

Jim Marrs: Common sense would dictate that one does not kill the president of the United States without being assured that his successor would not track and prosecute the culprits. I do not personally believe that LBJ had any foreknowledge of the details of the plan as he would have wanted "plausible deniability." However, I think he generally knew what was up and was in agreement as it was his lifelong dream to become president and he would stop at nothing to achieve his goals.

The parallels between the JFK assassination and 9/11 are numerous. In many ways, the aftermath of the 9/11 attacks fit the same template as the assassination of President Kennedy in 1963:

• Within hours, despite a lack of real evidence, one man was blamed for the event along with hints that he was connected to foreign enemies.

• Official pronouncements were widely publicized only to be quietly admitted as errors later on.

• Although within the jurisdiction of the local authorities, the entire case was usurped by the FBI and CIA, both agencies under the control of a president who benefited from the tragedy. In 2001, FEMA, also controlled by the president, was added to this list.

• A group of specialists (medical in the JFK's case and engineers in that of the WTC) was convened but limited in what they could view and study, blocked from conducting an objective probe by federal officials.

• Evidence in the case was hastily removed and destroyed, forever lost to an impartial and meaningful investigation.

• More evidence was locked away in government files under the excuse of "national security."

• Federal malfeasance was excused by claiming lack of manpower and resources and no one was disciplined or fired. Federal agency budgets were increased.

• Any alternative to the official version of events was decried as "conspiracy theory" and "unpatriotic."

• The federal government used the event to increase its own centralized power.

• A foreign war (Vietnam in JFK's case and Iraq and Afghanistan today), which otherwise would have been opposed, was supported by a grieving population.

• A top government leader (then LBJ and now Bush), formerly under suspicion for election fraud and corrupt business dealings, was suddenly propelled to new heights of popularity.

• Many citizens knew or suspected that the official version of events was incorrect but were afraid to speak out.

• A compliant and sycophantic mass media was content to parrot merely the official version of events and studiously avoided asking the hard questions that might have revealed the truth.

• In yet another strange parallel to the Kennedy assassination, in the months and years following 9/11, an increasing number of potentially crucial witnesses began suffering untimely deaths.

Richard Thomas: Your second most recent book is called The Rise of the Fourth Reich. The Third Reich was born out of Hitler's Enabling Act and the end of the democratic Weimar Republic, would you agree that in the wake of the JFK assassination and 9/11 America has undergone a similar metamorphosis to 1930s Germany or the Roman Republic in the wake of Julius Caesars' assassination in 44 BC?

Jim Marrs: The American Republic has been lost to a National Security State Empire with many parallels to Rome and Hitler's Third Reich – 9/11 = Reichstag fire; the PATRIOT Act = the Enabling Act; Homeland Security = Secret State Police; secret detention centers = concentration camps; Nazi National ID cards = National ID Act of 2005, etc.

Richard Thomas: In Alex Jones' 2000 film Dark Secrets Inside Bohemian Grove, the popular alternative radio show host exposed the bizarre annual "cremation of care" event, in which, as strange as it sounds, many of America's biggest names apparently meet up to conduct a mock child sacrifice to a forty foot stone owl deity, allegedly called Moloch. Have you seen any evidence of similar occult overtones in the JFK assassination or 9/11, or, even anywhere else?

Jim Marrs: There are many odd and puzzling aspects to both the JFK assassination and 9/11, for example, the strange similarities in names and places between the death of Kennedy and Abraham Lincoln, of which many people are aware. Dealey Plaza sits on the 33 degree parallel which has significant Masonic meaning. There are many other such oddities but we must not let this fascinating aspect distract us from the hard factual evidence of conspiracy in both cases.

A Room 101 Interview with Len Osanic : Host of Black Op Radio

When Room 101 first made its Binnall of America debut back in April 2008 I wrote about how it was the JFK Assassination, and its modern day counterpart 9/11, that first really got me seriously interested in events and ideas that way too many intelligent people sadly debunk as "conspiracy theory." Looking back on it now, I used to be one of these "intelligent people" until I started listening to shows like Len Osanic's comprehensive Black Op Radio (easily the best podcast dealing in the realms of parapolitics) so I was very excited when Len agreed to do an interview with us. What is more, it will allow us to cover the JFK conspiracy, and cover-up, with some depth.

Richard Thomas: First things first, thank you so much for giving the Room 101 readers the time to answer these questions. I'm a big fan of the show and I'm sure many of the RR readers are too, so it's really appreciated. I believe you hail from outside the US, like me. Some might think it a little unusual that you host a show dedicated to researching the death of a US President. How did you first become interested in the JFK Assassination and what's the origin of Black Op Radio?

Len Osanic: Years ago, I wrote to Col. Fletcher Prouty [Chief of Special Operations for the Joint Chiefs of Staff under President John F. Kennedy and later a prominent critic of the CIA - ed.]. We became friends and I produced a CD-ROM for him. I started doing radio show interviews with him. When he became ill, I continued on my own. After that, I thought I could do a better job asking the questions, since I knew the topic quite well. That was back in 2000 some 430 shows ago.

Richard Thomas: Growing up with the Zapruder film footage regularly played on various documentaries about the assassination, I'd always just assumed Kennedy got shot from the front. So it was a bit of a shock to discover that according to the Warren Commission, Lee Harvey Oswald supposedly shot the President from behind. What, for you, is the best smoking gun evidence pointing towards a conspiracy?

Len Osanic: The photo of CIA General Edward Lansdale in Dealey Plaza on November 22nd, the day of the assassination.

Richard Thomas: If you had to point out another two or more reasons for dismissing the so-called Lone Gunman Theory what would they be?

Len Osanic: The fraud of CE399 (The bullet) and almost all of the Warren Commission. I mean, all the evidence exonerates Lee Oswald. Of course, The Sixth Floor Museum is the biggest fraud of all, trying to obscure the fact that Dallas was the city that allowed the murder to happen. ˙

Richard Thomas: Other than the ridiculous lone nut Oswald theory, there seems to basically be three main schools of thought among researchers on who was responsible for the assassination. Roughly they can be broken down as: the Communist (the Soviet Union and/or Cuba), the Mob and CIA. Personally, I think "the Communists" is exactly what the real conspirator's wanted us to think, but what are your thoughts?

Len Osanic: It appears that the Joint Chiefs wanted to invade Cuba and I suspect Lee Oswald was supposed to have been flown there by Jack Ruby. It may be that Officer Tippit refused to escort Lee to the airport once he learned JFK had been shot and he was killed before he revealed the plot. [according to the Warren Commission version of events Tippit was shot while trying to arrest Oswald - ed.]

Richard Thomas: If you agree the conspirator's wanted us to think that Cuba and/or the Soviets were behind the assassination, why do you think the Warren Commission found no such conspiracy?

Len Osanic: I cannot guess what the members of the Warren Commission really thought or really found. We only have the report and who knows how many people were misrepresented or misquoted. Some members did not agree with the final conclusion, but were kept quiet.

Richard Thomas: Personally I've come to believe that Oswald was probably exactly what he claimed to be: "just a patsy." What is your position on Oswald and how involved do you think he was in any conspiracy: for instance do you think he was really one of the shooters or not?

Len Osanic: I do not think he shot anyone and no evidence has been presented to indicate he did either.

Richard Thomas: My personal favourite documentary about the assassination has to be Nigel Turner's excellent nine part series The Men Who Killed Kennedy. Do you know what the latest on Badge Man is? ['Badge Man' is the name given to a figure wearing a badge and allegedly holding a gun-like object seen in one photo of the assassination scene - ed.]

Len Osanic: I think the gunmen were professional military men on duty. I have no idea who Badge Man really is.

Richard Thomas: We could go on forever about who might have been responsible, but I think the X character (based on Col. Fletcher Prouty) in Oliver Stone's epic film JFK knocks it on the head when he says the more important question is why? Although there were probably many reasons, the big two seem to be the Vietnam War and Kennedy's plans to audit the private run-for-profit Federal Reserve. What do you think was the major reason and why?

Len Osanic: Fletcher Prouty has indicated that pulling out of Vietnam was the final straw. Kennedy was removed by his enemies. In this case, "final straw" meant there were many reasons, and finally (after Vietnam) they made the decision, "He's got to go." It certainly wasn't a lone nut. Who told the Presidential Protection team to "Stand Down, you're not needed in Dallas Nov 22nd" ? That's where the power is, to allow gunmen near, and then to control the autopsy and continue the cover-up. And have a patsy in the wings. I must stress: read the Jim Douglass book JFK and the Unspeakable. I interviewed him six times, once for each chapter.

Richard Thomas: Whatever the truth about the assassination, there's no question, in my book, that many of the people who have investigated the conspiracy over the last four decades are true

heroes. Mark Lane has be my personal favourite, but who do you feel most privileged to have had the chance to interview and why?
Len Osanic: Without question, it is Col L. Fletcher Prouty. There is no other person who wrote about this topic who was there. Prouty worked in the military for 23 years and 9 years in the Pentagon. He was the focal point officer between the CIA and the Air Force. He was there. He worked with these people day in day out for 9 years. Everyone else writes from details and evidence they discover, but not from being there.

Richard Thomas: Inevitably, time will take its toll. It's a pity you'll never get a chance to interview Jim Garrison (whose autobiographical On the Trail of the Assassins was turned into the Oliver Stone film). Who else do you wish you could have had a chance to interview before their passing?
Len Osanic: No one I can think of. I learned so much from Fletcher. But it would've been worth while to spend time with Jim Garrison. Who knows how much more he knew about that was not brought up in the trial. Things that he may have not had the time to investigate.

Richard Thomas: It's been nearly 50 years now since that tragic day in Dallas. Do you think we'll ever know, for certain, what happened and who exactly was involved, and why do you think it's still important to find out today? Also, does it bother you when people just dismiss us as "JFK Buffs" or "Conspiracy Theorists"?
Len Osanic: If you read the Jim Douglass book JFK and the Unspeakable, there is enough there for one to discover who killed JFK. Then if you want to know more details get the Col Prouty CD-ROM.

I consider interest in this as political research. It bothers me that someone like George Bush was president 8 years. It bothers me Rush Limbaugh is still on the air. But, I am Canadian so it's not that big a deal. Really, working with Fletcher taught me more than I ever set out to learn. So if people don't have time to question 9/11 right in front of them, and find it easier to criticize those researching the world in which we live as "theorists," well that's their loss.

Richard Thomas: Some wildcard questions at the end here. One of your semi-regular guests on Black Op Radio has been Jim Marrs, author of Crossfire and The Terror Conspiracy, two books very well regarded among JFK researchers and 9/11 truth activists. What are your thoughts on the topics covered in some of Marrs' other books like secret societies, remote viewing and the UFO cover-up?

Len Osanic: I'll let Marrs speak for himself. I don't believe remote viewing. Americans should have stormed the White House and tried the administration for treason on 9/11. I believe it was an inside job.

Richard Thomas: Another of your guests has been Shane O'Sullivan, author of Who Killed Bobby and director of RFK Must Die. What do you think of the idea that Sirhan Sirhan (the convicted RFK shooter) could have been a "Manchurian Candidate"? Also, what about John Lennon's killer Mark David Chapman, do you think he might have been a victim of CIA brainwashing too?

Len Osanic: I agree there is something troubling about Sirhan. William Pepper is looking into reopening a trial on new audio evidence. Mae Brussell knew more about the Chapman story. I don't know anything really to add.

Richard Thomas: Thanks again Len for answering our questions, perhaps we can do this again sometime. Why not tell the readers where they can listen to Black Op Radio and maybe buy some of your cool gear?

Len Osanic: I host Black Op Radio and run the Col. Fletcher Prouty Reference Site which can be found at www.prouty.org.

NASA's Project Blue Beam – Will the US Government Stage UFO Sightings in 2012?

Not since the Millennium Bug panic in the years running up to the year 2000 has a specific date been the subject of so many apocalyptic theories about the end of the world as December 21, 2012. The date believed to be the end of a 5,125-year-long cycle in the Mayan Long Count calendar.

The Maya civilisation used many calendars to measure time and record history. The main two calendars used by most ordinary Maya would have been the 260-day Tzolkin and the 365-day Haab. Because neither of these calendars numbered years, a combination of both the Tzolkin and Haab dates was used to identify the precise date. This method was sufficient because a particular combination of the two dates would not occur again for about 52 years, which was above the general life expectancy of the time.

To specify dates that occurred more than 52 years ago the Maya used another calendar called the Long Count. This calendar identified a date by counting the number of days from the day when the Maya believed that time began, on August 12, 3114 BCE. The Long Count used a 360-day year called a Tun, in which 20 Tuns made up a Katun (72,000 days) and 20 Katuns made up a Baktun (144,000 Tuns). The 13th Baktun will be completed on December 21, 2012, which is said to be the end of the 5,125-year-long "Great Cycle." However, sceptics say that this is a misinterpretation and that there is no evidence that the Maya believed the world would end on that day.

Whatever the truth about 2012 it would seem that someone wants us to believe something Earth shattering will happen on December 21 in that year. The doomsday theory has been featured in bestselling books, as well as documentaries, films and popular TV shows.

In the last episode of The X-Files (tantalisingly called The Truth) it is discovered by agents Mulder and Scully that aliens plan on colonising the Earth on December 21, 2012.

When I asked Dean Haglund, who played Langly in The X-Files, about the 2012 revelation in the final episode of the sci-fi cult, he told me he was sceptical about 2012 doomsday scenarios.

"Here is an excellent example of a collective fear manifesting itself into popular culture. Since this airing, 2012 has become the hot topic at all the conventions, however, as Paul Dean said in our documentary, when he was talking to a Mayan priest about all of this, he said that 'western society has it all wrong' and that since we cannot hold a duality in our minds, a quantum Schrodinger's Cat scenario if you will, then we can only picture the end of something as a finite disaster and not both that and the re-awakening into the light."

Haglund was less sceptical, however, about the possibility that US government agencies could have been feeding information to The X-Files writers.

"I have heard that the popular culture is used as a tool by whatever elite, business, government, Illuminati, etc., to both gauge and control the populace," The X-Files and Lone Gunmen star told me when I asked him about his comments on The Alex Jones Show back in 2005 about the script writers being approached by members of the CIA, FBI and NASA with ideas for episodes.

But why would US Government insiders want the viewers of The X-Files to associate 2012 with an alien invasion? One popular theory on the internet is NASA's alleged partly declassified Project Blue Beam, a supposed plan by the US Government to create a "New World Order" by staging a fake UFO invasion using holograms and other advanced technology. As Timucin Leflef, who appeared in the documentary film The New World Order and is a screen writer himself, explains.

"The alien invasion hoax is also another reason why so many Hollywood science fiction movies involve aliens arriving in vast armadas to destroy us and take over our planet. They were quite prevalent in the 50s and you can find modern-day examples like Independence Day, War of the Worlds and even Mars Attacks. Very few movies about extra-terrestrials actually involve aliens with peaceful intentions. E.T. certainly comes to mind, but even movies where they arrive as our benevolent 'saviours' like The Day The Earth Stood Still, is still another permutation of the New World Order hoax, in which case it's about giving up our sovereignty, our 'petty little differences' as Reagan put it, and joining a fascist global regime in order to achieve an alleged 'world peace'. It will be world peace but with a seriously heavy price on our freedoms. Mostly, though, these movies are programming us to believe that once we see vast armadas of classified military vehicles hovering in the sky, that they will in fact be UFOs driven by 'extra-terrestrials' who are here to 'kill us and take over our planet.' And then the only solution we'll be presented with will be a heavy reliance on a Militarised 'New World Order' to save us. That's where the real agenda lies."

While many UFO researchers are sceptical about some of the specifics about Project Blue Beam, the basic premise that the US Government might be fostering the belief that UFOs represent aliens from outer space is another matter. The US government definitely has technology a lot more advanced than what they admit to having. In 1993 the "father of stealth" Ben Rich, director of Lockheed's Skunk Works from 1975 to 1991, stated at the University of California School of Engineering in 1993: "We already have the means to travel among the stars, but these technologies are locked up in black projects

... and it would take an Act of God to ever get them out to benefit humanity."

Other government insiders have also made comments implying the US Government were behind UFOs or at least hyping the ETH (extraterrestrial hypothesis). In his book, The Secret Team, Colonial Fletcher Prouty, who was the real life basis for the Mr X character in Oliver Stone's film JFK, speculated that with the fall of communism in the early 1990s UFOs and aliens would take the place of the Soviet Union as the new major threat to the United States.

"This is the fundamental game of the Secret Team. They have this power because they control secrecy and secret intelligence and because they have the ability to take advantage of the most modern communications system in the world, of global transportation systems, of quantities of weapons of all kinds, and when needed, the full support of a world-wide U.S. military supporting base structure. They can use the finest intelligence system in the world, and most importantly, they have been able to operate under the canopy of an assumed, ever-present enemy called 'Communism.' It will be interesting to see what 'enemy' develops in the years ahead. It appears that 'UFO's and Aliens' are being primed to fulfil that role for the future. To top all of this, there is the fact that the CIA, itself, has assumed the right to generate and direct secret operations."

More recently Mark Pilkington in his new book Mirage Men has argued that instead of perpetrating a UFO cover-up the US intelligence agencies have really been promoting ideas like alien abductions, UFO crashes and recoveries, and secret bases all along.

"In the book I'm specifically referring to those people from military and intelligence organisations who have used the UFO lore as a cover for their operations and, in extreme cases, have seeded new material within the UFO culture to further muddy the waters," Mark Pilkington told me when I interviewed him in 2010. Although Mark didn't think all UFOs were explainable.

"I'm not sceptical about UFOs themselves – people see them every day – nor am I sceptical of the existence of ET life, I believe it's out there, and I can accept that it will come here and perhaps even has done at some point in our past. What I am very sceptical of is the popular notion of ET visitation as presented in the UFO lore that has emerged since the late 1940s. This has developed out of a multi-directional feedback loop between UFO experiencers, UFO book authors, mainstream popular culture and those in the military and intelligence worlds who would exploit and shape these beliefs and ideas."

So will the US Government or one of its alphabet agencies really stage a massive UFO sighting on December 21, 2012? We'll have to wait to see. But with the London Olympics, Queen's Diamond Jubilee and the US presidential election all taking place in 2012 perhaps we shouldn't be so focused on December 21 in particular.

A Room 101 Interview With Gerrard Williams – Co-Author of Grey Wolf: The Escape of Adolf Hitler

Last year the web was ablaze with conspiracy theories when the news of Osama Bin Laden's death was announced to the world on the exact same day as Adolf Hitler's death was 66 years earlier, May 1. Most of these conspiracies included the belief that Osama bin Laden hadn't been killed at all, because the Al-Qaeda founder and leader had been dead for years. Similar uncertainty has surrounded the fate of Hitler after WWII, only instead of dying years before the war's end, many believe the Nazi Fuhrer escaped Germany to begin a new life in South America or elsewhere. And like Bin Laden, except for a few skull fragments which could belong to anyone, no body was ever shown to the war weary public, so why shouldn't people question the official story?

In there new book, Grey Wolf: The Escape of Adolf Hitler, Gerrard Williams and his co-author Simon Dunstan investigate claims that Hitler not only escaped to Argentina after the end of the war but that the deposed dictator even fathered children and lived until 1962.

Richard Thomas: Thanks for taking the time to answer my questions Gerrard, I read your new book Grey Wolf over the Christmas holidays and have lots to ask you about, but how did you start your writing career and have you always had an interest in the Second World War?

Gerrard Williams: Thanks for asking me Richard. I trained as a Journalist with the NCTJ in Cardiff, but had always written for school competitions (Eisteddfod in Wales). Most of my life has been spent in international TV News with Reuters, BBC and SKY as well as time in Australia and Kenya. For people of my generation (I'm 52) WW2 always figured heavily in our lives. My Dad was a "Desert Rat" (8th Army N.Africa/Italy) and my mum was in the

Army when they met. That and films, comics and books about the War always kept it at the forefront of our minds.

Richard Thomas: Last year the internet was ablaze with conspiracy theories surrounding the death of Osama Bin Laden being announced on the same day as Hitler's death was made public, May 1. And oddly enough Prince William and Kate Middleton got married on the same day as Eva Braun and Hitler as well, 29 April.

Do you think theories like these are in part due to the failure of historians to sufficiently investigate the fate of Hitler after the war, or, are there other reasons why people are still fascinated by conspiracies linked with the Nazis?

Gerrard Williams: I'm not a great one for conspiracy theories. In 33 years as a journalist any I've come across – and there have been a few – always seemed to fall apart at the first serious investigation. We should remember that the Nazis were the embodiment of Industrialised Evil, and also the biggest criminal gang in history. They cast a long and fascinating shadow, why would a civilized nation like Germany behave so badly?

Richard Thomas: What first persuaded you that the rumour about Hitler's escape from Germany in 1945 was anything more than just another conspiracy theory? Was it the revelation that the fragment of a skull the Russians have couldn't have belonged to Nazi dictator?

Gerrard Williams: I was filming a series of documentaries in Argentina partly on the Malvinas/Falklands War anniversary when I came across the story. I was going to do a silly conspiracy theory film about it – it would have been my first – but so many people I met and talked to were so sure that he had escaped and lived in their country, I decided it needed more investigation. I teamed up with my old-friend and respected historian Simon Dunstan and what we discovered shocked us both. There is far more evidence to his escape than to his death.

Richard Thomas: If Hitler did escape from Germany why do you think this wasn't discovered or maybe even ignored by the Allies and mainstream historians?

Gerrard Williams: The amazing thing is that there were dozens of quite serious stories from news agencies and other sources that detailed his escape. I think elements in the US helped him and thousands of his supporters get away. Some people in Britain were complicit in the cover-up. Why did the head of MI6 hire an obscure medieval historian, Hugh Trevor-Roper to write the "definitive" detective story of the deaths? Why didn't we put in serious investigators, Scotland Yard?

Richard Thomas: What do you think happened in Hitler's bunker in 1945 and how do you explain the account of Hitler's bodyguard that the bodies of Hitler and Eva were burned and buried?
Gerrard Williams: The details are in the book, but simply Hitler and Eva were swapped for two look-alikes. AH fled, and Bormann and "Gestapo" Mueller executed the two stand-ins when they were sure Hitler was clear. These bodies were allegedly burnt – although the Soviets at the time did not find any evidence of the bodies. They did find Josef and Magda Goebbels charred, but recognisable corpses and happily put them on display.

Richard Thomas: How did you begin your research and what led you to Argentina?
Gerrard Williams: I was sitting in a car-park in the Green Zone in Baghdad in 2005 wearing a flak-jacket, helmet in 35 degree heat smoking a cigarrette and a realization came over me. At 46 I was too old for "hard" news. I had always loved making long-form films and decided to see if I could make a living doing documentaries. I had never been to South America and starting with the letter "A" seemed sensible, hence Argentina. Since then I have been back 13 times, each time discovering something new and backing this up with intense research on-line, wading through literally hundreds of books, at Kew, in Berlin and in the US.

Richard Thomas: Where are some of the eerie places you visited in Argentina and was there a witness or other evidence that particularly impressed you?
Gerrard Williams: Hitler's home at Inalco is a strange place, a lovely estate which when built was virtually inaccessible, and the deserted Nazi-Funded Hotel Viena at Mar Chiquita is worth a visit.

CHAPTER 2

Richard Thomas: I've often heard it said Hitler was suffering with Parkinson's disease by the end of the war and wouldn't have lived long even if he hadn't committed suicide. What evidence is there that Hitler lived until 1962? And what do you think happened to the former German Fuhrer's remains after his death?

Gerrard Williams: There is no evidence Hitler had Parkinson's. It's pure supposition based on a couple of home movies which show his right hand "trembling" while he holds it behind his back. Hitler was 56 in May 1945, probably massively stressed and known to have been suffering gastric problems – today they'd probably call it IBS – but still a relatively young man. The evidence is pretty detailed in "Grey Wolf" the FBI taking sightings seriously, numerous eye witnesses to his life in Argentina. Since publication we have had new information which adds to this. As for the body, I don't know. My best guess it was cremated and scattered on Bormann's orders to maintain the fiction that he died in Berlin.

Richard Thomas: One of the strangest revelations in the book is that Hitler and his wife may have had children. If this is true what do you think happened to Eva Braun and where do you think Hitler's children are now?

Gerrard Williams: Eva Braun was 33 in 1945. There is a lot of information about the birth of their daughter "Uschi" in Germany pre-war and also a still-born child in the middle of the war which was attested to by Eva's Mother. She seems to have also been newly pregnant – according to close members of their circle – in May 1945. There were rumours – which we so far have been unable to prove or disprove – that she was still alive in 2000 when she would have been 88. The two daughters would now be in their late 60's and early 70's. We still have leads to follow up. Our last confirmed sighting was from a senior Buenos Aires Human Rights lawyer who says she met "Uschi" in the late 80's.

Richard Thomas: Why do you think it is still important to find out the truth about the events of the final days of WWII over 65 years later?

Gerrard Williams: I'm a journalist – of the old school – I think the truth is something that needs to be told.

Richard Thomas: Thanks Gerrard, where can readers buy the book and have you got a website you would like to plug?

Gerrard Williams: Thanks very much Richard. The book's available on-line at Amazon across the world, Barnes and Noble stores in the US – and on-line from them, Waterstones and all good book shops in the U.K. People who are interested can check out www.greywolfmedia.com. We're currently working on our follow-up.

The Paranormal

The Stone Tape Theory

The "Stone Tape" theory originates from a television play of the same name by the iconic sci-fi writer Nigel Kneale (of Quatermass and the Pit fame). Combining science fiction with the ghost story genre, in the 1972 BBC Christmas special a group of scientists investigate a supposed haunting in the hope of discovering a brand new recording medium. Their theory is that somehow limestone (and perhaps other materials) can retain moments of the past. That perhaps human memories or experiences (particularly ones involving intense emotions like the last moments before death) can be someway psychically recorded in the stonework of buildings. The idea, of course, being that later someone psychic or sensitive enough could act as a kind of psychic video player. Hence the title of the Kneale's original play "The Stone Tape."

As a credit to Nigel Kneale's genius as a writer, despite making its début in a fictional setting, his idea proved very popular with many of the more scientifically inclined paranormal researchers. Finally offering them a real, and perhaps almost equally engaging, alternative to the standard "life after death" explanation of the traditionalists. What's more, if true, the "Stone Tape" theory might also go some way to explaining some of the problems and inconsistencies often associated with paranormal encounters.

For instance, why do people always seem to report "ghosts" from only a few centuries ago? Why so rarely from pre-history?

Perhaps the answer to this peculiarity might be that, much like domestic VHS video tape, "Stone Tape" recordings have a limited lifespan too. Steadily degenerating over the ages until they are completely erased and forgotten forever.

This explanation might also provide the answer to another popular problem in the paranormal. Why is it that some people see full blown solid apparitions where others only see transparent figures, shadows or, worse, nothing at all? Again like a conventional video tape perhaps the older a "Stone Tape" recording gets the more the sound and picture quality suffers.

Alternatively, of course, perhaps a better explanation opened up by the theory might be that some people may simply make better psychic video players than others. Maybe an important point to make here is that according to the theory, the "ghost" or recording is seen (perhaps "played" might be a better term) inside the mind rather than in the outside physical universe. Therefore, depending on the sensitivity of the witnesses, it's quite possible that several people might experience the same encounter very differently.

The idea that "ghosts" might really be some kind of psychic tape recording rather than the spirits of the dead might not be desirable to some die hard researchers who believe "ghosts" offer us proof of life after death. (Though the two ideas are not mutually exclusive, it's possible that there could be more than one type of "ghost" each representing something very different.) However, if ever proven the theory would raise perhaps almost equally important questions about the true nature of consciousness and the human mind.

Think about it. The only way such a recording could be made and replayed would be if there was some kind of direct connection between the human mind and stone. It would have to be some form of telepathy between two "minds" (for lack of a better word) suggesting that inanimate matter might have some form of highly primitive consciousness or awareness. It's an exciting, be it somewhat crazy, idea. However, the "Stone Tape" theory is still a very long way from being proven.

Timeslip: Is Time Travel Possible?

Recently, my old interest in 'ghosts' and what might best be described as the "pure paranormal" has been somewhat reawoken by watching the complete series of Ghost Hunters on DVD. I'm referring to the excellent British scientific documentary series from the mid 1990s, of course. Not the terrible (but undoubtedly far more successful) American reality TV show of the same name.

In hindsight, it was probably over-the-top melodramas like the American Ghost Hunters and its many British counterparts (full of people just screaming in the dark) that put my hitherto strong interest in the grip of a sleeper hold in the first place. Anyway, while my rekindled interest in 'ghosts' and the like lasts, I thought it might be a good idea to write up some paranormal type pieces. So, here we're going to examine probably the strangest, but no doubt also most absorbing of paranormal happenings ... the "timeslip" or time travel experience.

Put simply a "timeslip" is an alleged paranormal phenomenon in which a person, or even group of people, seem to somehow travel through time via apparently supernatural (as opposed to technological) means. Now, admittedly, the whole notion sounds like it was ripped straight from the pages of a Doctor Who script. Time travel, naturally, has been a stable of science fiction and fantasy ever since H G Wells wrote the Time Machine.

Before we dismiss the possibility out of hand, though, perhaps it's worth remembering that a wide range of highly prestigious theoretical physicists and other scientists (both past and present) have gone on record with some very strange ideas about the true nature and behaviour of the fourth dimension. It was no less than Albert Einstein, remember, who first laid down the foundation for the theoretical possibility of time travel with his famous "special theory of relativity." One of the very strange (but now proven) consequences of special relativity being that time slows down as you approach the speed of light, stopping completely for anything able to travel at light speed. Which, of course, logically implies that time might conceivably run backwards if you were somehow able to travel faster than light.

Further, the theory that time could run in reverse might sound ridiculous but that's exactly what Steven Hawking suggests might be the fate of us all in his excellent book A Brief History of Time. In the bestseller, the "smartest man alive" not only speculates that our expanding Universe might eventually begin contracting but, further, that if this "Big Crunch" ever really does take place it's perfectly possible that time might start reversing too. Strange as it sounds, we might all one day be forced to live our lives again. Only this time backwards!

Back to the timeslip phenomenon. There is no question that some of mankind's greatest intellects have taken the theoretical possibility of time travel very seriously. However, as discussed, only in the most extreme circumstances imaginable. Such as travelling at superluminal velocities or the Universe imploding. But what about in our daily lives? Is it possible to go round a strange corner and walk into another time and place?

Amazingly, there are many accounts of sane and credible people who believe this is precisely what has happened to them. One of the most well publicised cases, in Britain at least, is that of the Simpsons and the Gisbys. The 1979 incident featured prominently in a memorable episode of the ITV television series Strange But True? In the programme (now being regularly shown in the UK on the Paranormal Channel) the two English couples described how while traveling through France en route to a holiday in Spain they stayed the night at a strangely antiquated hotel. Bedding in somewhat basic rooms they were a little unnerved to discover no glass in any of the building's windows, only wooden shutters that closed from the outside.

It wasn't just the building though, all the people they met (everyone from police officers to locals) seemed strangely old fashioned too. Dressing almost as if they had just stepped out of the 19th century. In fact, everything even the knives and forks everybody ate with seemed outdated. Not being able to speak much French, the English couples couldn't ask about it.

Putting all the strange anachronisms down to simply being in rural France and impressed by the mere 18 francs their stay had cost them, the four decided to look for the same hotel again on their return journey. However, this time, despite searching for several hours, they were unable to find it again. What's more, when they returned home they were puzzled when all the photos they had taken there turned out blank. As if the hotel and its inhabitants had somehow simply vanished, disappearing even from their film negatives.

If Simpsons and the Gisbys really did, as it seems, travel back in time about a hundred years or so though: why did their hosts accept 1970s style currency? Assuming the foursome didn't just invent their story (though why would they?) it would seem to suggest there could be a lot more to this type of experience than one might first imagine.

Any serious student of the paranormal, of course, could come up with a whole range of incredible suggestions. Perhaps we're dealing with god-like Tricksters playing games with mortal men for their own childish amusement? However, before we begin to speculate perhaps it would be wise to briefly consider another well known case first. There are plenty to choose from but easily the most credible involved no less than the great philosopher and psychiatrist Carl Jung. According to the famous thinker, while traveling through Italy in the 1930s he visited the tomb of a Roman Empress in Ravenna. Impressed with the remarkable beauty of the mosaics depicting maritime scenes in an eerily pale blue light, he discussed them with his companion for about half an hour and, on leaving the mausoleum, even tried to purchase postcards of them. Surprisingly though there weren't any.

Some time later, Jung asked a friend visiting Ravenna if he could obtain pictures for him. It was only after seeing them that he finally learned the truth. The mosaics he had seen and discussed in great detail were totally different to the mosaics now decorating the mausoleum. However, they did exist once but had been destroyed in a fire some 700 years previously.

So what is going on? Jung was personally convinced that his consciousness had somehow traveled back in time to when the mausoleum had been first constructed, 1400 years prior to his visit to Ravenna. As discussed earlier, time travel is thought by scientists to only be possible in the most extreme of circumstances. However, what if the laws that govern nature are different to the laws that govern the mind? If so, then maybe it would be possible for consciousness (free of the limitations of the laws of physics) to travel through time much more easily.

Further, many timeslip witnesses report strange bouts of depression or unease just prior to or at the start of their experience. Perhaps this indicates that the mind is indeed involved in some key way. The theory would definitely explain why the Simpsons and the Gisbys weren't able to get any photographs. Which brings us back to the question of why their French hosts didn't make a fuss about their modern money? Maybe they simply saw money from their own era. Unless scientists someday break the light barrier or maybe even develop a "science of the mind" though, it's impossible to ever know.

Swansea Museum

Originally set up by the Royal Institution of South Wales (a local group who wanted to investigate all aspects of history, the arts and science at the beginning of the 19th century) Swansea Museum was completed in 1841 in the grand neo-classical style, and is the oldest museum in Wales.

The main museum on Oystermouth Road contains all kinds of unusual objects from Swansea's past as well as the wider world. The building's six galleries house everything from an ancient Egyptian mummy to a traditional Welsh kitchen.

In addition to this treasure trove of both ordinary and extraordinary exhibits the museum also has three floating exhibits in its collections which are kept at the marina: the lightship "Helwick," a tug boat called "Canning" and the "Olga," a Bristol Channel Pilot Cutter built in 1909. Other popular items kept at the museum's collection centre in Landore include old vehicles like a travellers' van, lorries, a fire engine and two lifeboats, the "Naomi Beatty" and the "William Gammon."

On March 27th, I attended an evening investigation at Swansea Museum. With so much history surrounding not only the main building itself but more significantly the items within it, I was hopeful for some activity. And although most of the night was admittedly very quiet, I did experience what might be interpreted as paranormal activity.

Most significantly, while I was downstairs with three others, we could hear clear and distinct footsteps and knocks coming from the library room above us when nobody should have been in that location at the time. Also, later in the evening one member of the investigation team I was with felt someone pinch his backside. I was standing directly behind this person at the time and can say definitively it wasn't me!

However, if anyone was to have experienced anything out of the ordinary at the museum – just as with any allegedly haunted location – surely it would be the staff that work there day in day out. During the investigation, I spoke with one of the staff, Catherine Perrie, who told me she and two colleagues (Paul Giuffrida and Trish Nicholls) had seen a "dark-cloaked figure" walking up and down the stairs. Intrigued, I arranged to return to the museum in the daylight hours to see if I could find out more. I wasn't disappointed.

When I interviewed Catherine further she told me that she saw the strange figure on top of the stairs twice, on two different evenings. While reading, she saw the outline of a figure on the top of the stairs. When she turned to see who (or what) it was, though, the apparition quickly turned and ran up the next flight of stairs leading to the "Cabinet of Curiosities" gallery room, where, according to Catherine, the strange activity in the building "seems to be mainly focused."

When I talked with another staff member who saw this "cloaked figure" on the stairs, Paul Giuffrida shared with me two other strange experiences he had had at the museum. The first of these took place in the "Cabinet of Curiosities" gallery. While putting a window in for one of the exhibits, "The Victorian Room" (where Catherine told me visitors had reported cold spots and a "presence"), Paul said he heard "a lot of noise ... tapping and banging" coming from the corner opposite the lift. Naturally, he assumed someone must have come upstairs but, on investigation, he discovered nobody had.

On another occasion, this time at the museum's collection centre at Landore, Paul told me that while he was working in the storage area he heard "loud whistling" in his ear.

In addition to these two accounts, Paul also related to me that when a medium had been brought in to investigate the strange activity at the museum, they were told the ghost of someone who committed suicide on the lightship "Helwick" now haunted the museum; this might even be the cloaked figure who had been seen on the stairs.

Roger Gale, Swansea Museum's Exhibition and Events Officer, wasn't convinced about this, though, since he doesn't believe in the abilities of mediums and other sensitives. Despite this, however, Roger did admit after some coaxing to seeing and experiencing things at the museum. Although a little embarrassed, Roger went into some detail about a full-bodied apparition he saw. It had "come out of the wall" and walked along a corridor before vanishing. Roger said the apparition was in view for at least 15 to 20 seconds and that it looked so lifelike that for a moment he thought it was one of his colleagues.

"It was as real as you are now," he said.

When people think of haunted locations, they tend to think of ancient castles, theatres or pubs. But with so much history surrounding them, museums should not be overlooked when considering haunted hot-spots, as the experiences of the staff at Swansea show.

Quirky History – Mumbles

The gateway to the Gower Peninsula, an area of immense unspoilt natural beauty unparalleled in South Wales, Mumbles in Swansea is best known for its historic pier, castle, lighthouse and other popular seaside attractions.

What is less well known, however, is that holidaymakers risk getting more than they bargained for at 'The Mumbles', as the old fishing village is slowly gaining a spooky reputation for haunted locations. But maybe this isn't surprising as Mumbles has always been considered a place apart, as this old poem has it:

Mumbles is a funny place,
A church without a steeple,
Houses made of old ships wrecked
And most peculiar people.

The seaside town began its status as a popular tourist haunt when Mumbles Pier, designed by W. Sutcliffe Marsh and promoted by John Jones Jenkins of the Rhondda and Swansea Bay Railway, first opened on May 10, 1898.

Stretching 225 meters out into Mumbles Bay, the Victorian built pier was once the only way to visit Swansea in style. The White Funnel paddle steamers of the Bristol-based P & A Campbell Ltd company would dock on the end of the pier unloading tourists who would then make their journey via the Swansea and Mumbles Railway, which was the world's first passenger railway. And although in recent years the pier has fallen into a state of disrepair with a large section fenced off to visitors and other areas patched up to maintain safety; the bustling holiday magnet still welcomes thousands of visitors each year from across Wales and the world, all of them attracted to the beautiful beaches, pubs, restaurants and famed scenery of the Mumbles coast.

With such a happy history Mumbles Pier isn't automatically the first place ghost hunters might think to look for proof of the paranormal. Nevertheless, there is at least one ghost story linked with the popular Victorian walkway. The figure of a young woman wearing a long dress and what looks like a scarf or shawl wrapped around her face has been seen walking on the pier late at night, long after closing at 8.00pm. The apparition allegedly disappearing before anyone can ask her who she is? Or why she is haunting the pier?

And Mumbles Pier isn't alone. Oystermouth Castle (aka Mumbles Castle) built sometime around 1100 by William de Londres, and later rebuilt in the thirteenth century by the infamous de Breos family, after being burnt down by the native Welsh twice, also has a resident spectre. Known as the 'White Lady of Oystermouth Castle'. This apparition of a woman dressed all in white has been experienced many times by visitors to the battlement.

The 'White Lady' is usually seen weeping, with the back of her dress ripped away and a series of brutal welts on her back. The woman then abruptly vanishes as if she had never existed before witnesses can offer her any help. Reports of the 'Woman in White' allegedly go back centuries, leading some paranormal investigators to believe she might have died after being tied to the medieval whipping post – which still stands in the castle's dungeon, and tortured.

A Room 101 Interview With Richard Holland : Author of Haunted Wales

I've been lucky enough to get a special interview with Richard Holland, editor of Paranormal magazine and author of Haunted Wales. We're going to be discussing poltergeist phenomena and what might be the cause of such activity.

Richard Thomas: First things first. Thank you very much for agreeing to do this, I'm sure you're always busy with the magazine so I really appreciate you taking the time to do this interview. I'm sure our readers will enjoy it too. From reading Paranormal magazine, I understand you had a childhood encounter with a poltergeist yourself. What sort of things happened and how did you deal with it?

Richard Holland: As poltergeists go, I guess it was fairly tame in that it almost entirely limited itself to audio effects, most particularly a tapping on the wall above my bed which I found very unnerving, even threatening. I think the worst thing about it was this atmosphere that would build up at night before it manifested. One night it groaned at me out of a darker patch in the dark above my brother's bed. That was horrible. But it would also do things like mimic people walking around upstairs when there was no one there – this on sunny afternoons. On one occasion it mimicked the sounds of my brother's footsteps running towards where I was kneeling down by a bed where I had a board game laid out, and it kind of knocked me over. That is to say, I found myself lying on my back, but I was placed gently on the floor and felt no hands touching me. That was the most dramatic thing. You ask me how I dealt with it, but I didn't really. It came in two waves and then just went away for good.

Richard Thomas: Do you think this sparked your interest in the paranormal or do the origins of your interest lie elsewhere? I know that, like me, you're a big Doctor Who and Hammer Horror fan, do you think that might have played a large part too?

Richard Holland: It obviously helped spark my interest in the paranormal, although it's also left me with a nervousness of the subject, too! I was never tempted to carry out vigils in 'haunted houses', partly because I knew my imagination might run away with me and partly because I believe that I might be asking for trouble – inviting something unwanted, if you know what I mean.

But I suspect I'd have been interested in the supernatural anyway, because I've always loved monsters and weirdness – ours was very much a Dr Who family back in the 60s/70s and I already loved dinosaurs at a time when it wasn't as obvious a thing for small boys to be into as it is now. When I was 5 my dentist asked me: 'And what do you want to be when you grow up?' Expecting 'fireman' or something. 'A paleontologist', I promptly told him.

Richard Thomas: Looking back on it now, I think my own interest in these subjects lie in three things really: my interest in Sci-Fi, my own personal little brushes with the paranormal, and, last but not least, my father's interest in Graham Hancock's theories and other esoteric type subjects. Were any of your parents or other family interested in the paranormal at all when you were growing up?
Richard Holland: No, my parents weren't interested in the supernatural at all. My father read a lot of good quality sci-fi but he was one of those blokes who, instead of learning from it that all things are possible, used it as a prop to his untrained wannabe scientific outlook. He was a member of the Humanist Association and a big fan of Carl Sagan et al. He'd hate what I'm doing now for a living. My mum is much more open-minded about such things and recalls seeing a white lady glowing a vivid white sitting on the end of her bed when she was a child in the Blitz. She doesn't think of it as an 'angel' either – it terrified her!

Richard Thomas: Back to the subject of poltergeists, there seems to be two main schools of thought on what might be responsible for such phenomena. The first, of course, is that we are really dealing with the spirits of the dead, and the second (and probably far more interesting) is that we could be dealing with the psychic abilities of the living. Personally, I think it could very well be both, but what are your thoughts on the subject?

Richard Holland: I'm not sure – well, who is? But the feeling of a presence has stayed with me, that there was something trying to get at me in some unidentifiable way. I'm not sold on the 'wild talents' concept entirely for that reason. Nor does a lot of poltergeist behaviour tally with a conscious, reasoning spirit – why spread marmalade down the banisters or lay flowerpots out in a line on the kitchen floor like the Pontefract polt did? When I was at university I read about bacteriophages, viruses so primitive that they can barely be called life at all. They attach themselves to bacteria and pump in their RNA. The rest of it, a protein shell, drifts away. The RNA recodes the bacterial DNA and – lo! – two viruses where once there was one bacterium.

It made me wonder about a primitive consciousness, scarcely a mind at all, just a mass of electrical discharges that floats about and like the phage can only exist in any real form by latching onto a human mind. Perhaps puberty makes our brains susceptible to such encroaches. Perhaps similar twilight entities answer our subconscious needs according to our current superstitious beliefs – become fairies when we believe in fairies, then aliens when we believe in aliens. Perhaps they created some crop circles, too. More recently, I've been getting interested in the Islamic concept of the Jinn, incorporeal spirits created out of 'smokeless fire' at the same time as Man, and living alongside us. That comes quite close to what I've been groping at.

Richard Thomas: Anyone interested in "ghosts" and the like should have heard of the famous Enfield Poltergeist. What are your thoughts on that case and as a writer/researcher from Wales do you think there is a Welsh equivalent? If not maybe you could share some of the more compelling Welsh ghost stories you've heard of or researched.

Richard Holland: I don't think I really have anything to add to the Enfield story. It seems like a genuine one to me. I remember the story appearing as it happened in the Daily Mirror about the time I had my polt. The 'dirty old man' who spoke through one of the girls might have been an example of the Jinn-type thing I was chuntering about above. Part It, part Her. I'm sure in another culture, priests/wise women/ village elders or whoever would have got rid of the bugger with a couple of rituals. In ours, though, that family had to suffer months of indignities and fear. There isn't really a Welsh equivalent but I was pleased to find a first-hand account of a poltergeist outbreak preserved in a letter dated 1812 in the Flintshire Records Office. The St Asaph farmer who was suffering from it wrote to his landlord about it. 'That night it was so terrible that the women left the house and went to a neighbour's house and it threw stones, bricks and the like that they had no quiet to milk by throwing dung up on them' etc etc. Great stuff.

Richard Thomas: It was probably nothing, but I've seen objects fly through the air seemingly without explanation. Also, recently my dad told me that a woman from where he works thinks she has a poltergeist. How common do you think poltergeist type phenomena might really be?
Richard Holland: Much more common than people realise. After all, I didn't tell my family about what was happening to me, although one or two people, like my younger brother who shared a room with me, experienced it, too. But it took me a long time to tell my parents. I wonder how many other frightened kids there are who just don't talk about it. Also, I'm sure a lot of the 'just one of those things' experiences people have regularly are related phenomena. Putting something down then being unable to find it moments later, only for it to turn up exactly where you thought it was and had checked and checked and checked… That sort of thing. The Missing Biro Phenomenon. 'Eerie Indiana' had an episode about it, I seem to remember.

Richard Thomas: Whatever people might believe, there is no doubting the very real fear this type of phenomena can cause. What is your advice to people who think they are living in a house with a poltergeist?
Richard Holland: Talk about it! Let it become part of family life and try not to be scared of it. Laugh at it good-humouredly. Shout at it if it does something really irritating or frightening. That seems to help defuse them. There's certainly no point getting in a priest/exorcist and most mediums should probably be avoided. You never know, a nice quiet person from your local Spiritualist Church might be some good, but it's a risk – things often get worse. Alas, there are no experts.

Richard Thomas: I have already written about the timeslip phenomenon and on what is called the "stone tape" theory. Do you have any opinions or thoughts about these two genres of esoterica?

Richard Holland: 'Time slip' is a very loaded phrase, isn't it? I suspect a lot of time slips might be ghosts of what people have previously seen and otherwise experienced rather than someone falling through the 'timey-wimey things' of Stephen Moffat's Dr Who. It might fairly be suggested that many apparitions are ghosts not of the person himself per se, but the ghost of what someone else has seen. This might explain the dramatic appearances of some ghosts – they are not that former person playing out an emotive incident or the moment of their death, it's the witness to it who has created the ghost through their shock at seeing the incident. This wouldn't perhaps explain the detailed ladies of Versailles walking about for ages type experience – although they might just have got caught in a groove of someone else's previous existence for a while.

As for the 'Stone Tape': it's a very engaging idea but with no science as yet to back it up (not that anyone's really tried, of course). But we don't necessarily need stone – whatever happened to Ether? I can accept Ether as an abstract concept – some form of energy/interdimensional glue we have no knowledge of as yet (like electricity, magnetism, radioactivity and radio waves in their day – all around us but unperceived till science caught up). Perhaps it's dark matter? A psychic material on which impressions of personalities and/or emotions can be imprinted or fossilised in, and which our brains can connect to for reasons we simply don't understand – if reasons there are. Much of it might be totally random, like so many ghosts – an old horse and cart manifesting briefly, or somebody pottering about an old ruin with their legs disappearing into the ground – innocuous and meaningless.

Richard Thomas: Tell people about your books and how to get the excellent Paranormal magazine.

Richard Holland: Well, I've written five books on Welsh folklore/ghostlore. These are mainly 'stocking fillers', not great scholarship to be honest, just a collection of yarns culled from various sources, including correspondence through various newspaper columns I've written over the years. I did work very hard on 'Haunted Wales' (Landmark, ISBN 978-1843061779), though, and I'm not showing off when I say it's the best book on Welsh ghost-lore in print. I delved into lots and lots of old and obscure sources to write that, finding trends and then putting the whole lot into a gazetteer so that people could read the ghostly folk stories from their region, many of which hadn't seen print for up to 200 years. I also researched Welsh fairy-lore and witchcraft in depth but decided the work to put that into book form wasn't worth the reward. Maybe when I'm retired.

In the meantime, I have my blogsite and Paranormal Magazine to keep me busy. Paranormal is devoted to the whole gamut of the supernatural, mainly ghosts but including UFOs, cryptozoology, magic, ESP and the rest. It's all about phenomena – no mediums or New Age stuff. Regular writers include Nick Redfern, Karl Shuker, Janet Bord, Nigel Watson and the guys from the CFZ, and this month I added Brad Steiger and Colin Wilson to the roster.

I'm very proud to be involved with such excellent people and also to chat to new writers (new to me, that is) like Jimmy Lee Shreeve and Mark Greener. Visit us on www.paranormalmagazine.co.uk – if you want to buy one online to try it out, you'll be glad to know postage is free in the UK, so it costs no more than buying it in the shops.

Richard Thomas: Thanks mate. Hope we can do this again sometime, maybe a Sci-Fi Worlds interview where we could talk about Hammer Horror, Doctor Who and other cult Sci-Fi.

Paranormal Dichotomy

The sheer mountain of eyewitness testimony, photographs, audio recordings, not to mention film and video evidence should be ample enough to show that the pantheon of phenomena popularly described as "ghosts" or "apparitions" exist. That's NOT to say any of this accumulating evidence approaches anything near scientific proof or verification of the paranormal. The fact that, by definition, paranormal activity falls outside the normal realm of scientific understanding and can't be repeated within a laboratory setting has left many researchers believing we'll probably never have irrefutable proof.

However, few investigators would argue that the phenomena continues, nonetheless, and is all too real for a wide spectrum of witnesses that come from all walks of life. Which raises two important questions: if paranormal activity really does exist, what does it represent and how might the answer, or answers, effect our collective understanding of the universe and ourselves?

Other than hallucinations caused by ultrasound, sleep paralysis and similarly mundane explanations, parapsychologists and other paranormal investigators basically subscribe to three main schools of thought on the matter. The first, and most obvious, of course, being that "ghosts" are exactly what psychic mediums and other sensitives have always claimed they are: the spirits of the deceased or whatever it is that survives of the human consciousness after bodily death.

It is the second and third alternatives that seem to be the preferences of most contemporary parapsychologists. That is that paranormal phenomena such as "ghosts" are either some kind of 3D psychic recording / temporal replay, or alternatively, the manifestation of the latent telekinetic powers of the human mind. When I interviewed Richard Holland editor of Paranormal Magazine the author/investigator, himself a witness to poltergeist activity, he speculated about a possible fourth alternative.

"When I was at university I read about bacteriophages, viruses so primitive that they can barely be called life at all. They attach themselves to bacteria and pump in their RNA. The rest of it, a protein shell, drifts away. The RNA recodes the bacterial DNA and – lo! – two viruses where once there was one bacterium. It made me wonder about a primitive consciousness, scarcely a mind at all, just a mass of electrical discharges that floats about and like the phage can only exist in any real form by latching onto a human mind ... Perhaps similar twilight entities answer our subconscious needs according to our current superstitious beliefs – become fairies when we believe in fairies, then aliens when we believe in aliens. Perhaps they created some crop circles, too. More recently, I've been getting interested in the Islamic concept of the Jinn, incorporeal spirits created out of 'smokeless fire' at the same time as Man, and living alongside us. That comes quite close to what I've been groping at."

The danger, of course, when discussing "ghosts," just as with UFOs and pretty much any Fortean type mystery, is that people want a single definitive answer. The classic example being that UFOs are either "nuts and bolts" spacecraft from Zeta Reticuli or they're extra dimensional vehicles. And, as alluded to, a similar dichotomy seems to be entrenched in the paranormal field. It might be a bit of a overgeneralization, but generally speaking "ghosts" are either seen as evidence of survival after death, or else, they're interpreted as being some form of alternative psychic phenomena we currently don't understand as the parapsychologists would suggest. The problem being, why does it have to be one or the other: why can't it be both or as conspiracy author Jim Marrs likes to say: "all of the above" or even something else entirely?

Traditional style hauntings, poltergeist activity, stories of possession and timeslips: there is certainly no shortage of paranormal phenomena to choose from, however, perhaps none defy this paranormal dichotomy better than the "crisis ghost phenomenon."

Crisis ghosts are different from most other apparitions in that they appear to be person-based rather than location-based. They typically involve close friends or family members of witnesses appearing at a time of crisis, usually just before or after the person appearing dies. So common is the phenomenon that there is actually a case within my own family we can discuss.

I won't bore readers with all of the details but basically, years ago, while on holiday in Tenerife, my father had a strange dream involving several deceased relatives "all dressed in white" and a close childhood friend he hadn't seen in about "two and a half years." According to my father, the white figures in the dream told him that "they were all alright and not to worry." After waking up, my dad assumed it was just a strange dream and got on with enjoying his holiday. On returning to the UK, though, he discovered, to his shock, that the friend in the dream had, unbeknownst to him, been ill for some time and had died while he was away.

Had the spirits of the departed somehow invaded my father's subconscious that night in Tenerife, or alternately, had my father somehow psychically picked up on his friends passing or imminent passing and this is how his subconscious mind dealt with it. Either explanation can be made to fit.

Stranger still, though, are the crisis ghost cases that take place while the witness (or witnesses) are wide awake. For instance, there are many cases from the two world wars of soldiers returning home only to suddenly vanish or walk through a wall. News of their death arriving not long afterwards.

A classic example of this was featured in a memorable episode of

CHAPTER 3

Ghosthunters (the UK 1990s documentary series) focusing on the alleged ghostly happenings at Ireland's Castle Leslie. In the documentary we're told that "Uncle Norman" Leslie was seen by the old game keeper and others "walking the gardens" when last they heard he was in France fighting in the 1914 war. Thinking the army captain must have gotten unexpected leave, the servants rushed to get a meal prepared for the returning war hero. Strangely, though, he never turned up. Not long later, however, (within a week) the family learned the truth. "Uncle Norman" had died attacking a German machine gun post.

When you consider the wide spectrum of crisis experiences (some awake, some asleep, some alone, some with others etc) is it really likely that every case has the same explanation, or, is it more reasonable to think that some might be traditional "spirits" and some might be evidence for something else. Ultimately, though, as is the case with all Fortean or esoteric type topics, it comes down to a matter of personal belief.

Cryptozoology

Quirky History – Alien Big Cats in Pembrokeshire

Pembrokeshire is best known for its rugged natural beauty and tourism magnets, including Oackwood Theme Park and Folly Farm. In recent years, however, the idyllic maritime county has made national headlines for quite a different reason. Mystery "big cats" have been sighted wandering the county, and leaving paw prints and the gory remains of mutilated livestock in their path.

As late as last January 2011, it was reported that a former police officer, Michael Disney, had had an encounter with an animal described as being similar to a "puma or panther". In a statement passed to the police, Mr Disney said he was travelling around 10 to 15mph on a single-track lane when the animal crossed just five meters in front of his car.

"I immediately stopped my vehicle and stared at this animal. It had a large cat-like head, muscular build and was approximately three feet tall ... I am 100% certain that this was a puma or panther-like animal and was definitely not a dog, cat or any other domestic animal. It was not something I had seen before other than in a zoo."

Mr Disney's close encounter with an ABC or "alien big cat", which took place near the village of Treffgarne, six miles north of the market town of Haverfordwest, was touted by the Pembrokeshire council as being the "most definitive yet." However, big cat sightings in the region and throughout England and Wales are nothing new.

Members of this writer's own family have on occasion heard "growls" and once even saw what they thought was a puma or panther, "carrying a dead sheep in its mouth." And during the last decade there have been hundreds of similar reports of large big black cats roaming the remote hillsides and valleys of Wales – many of these sightings taking place in the Pembrokeshire region.

Between April 2004 and July 2005, 123 sightings in Wales were reported to the research group Big Cats in Britain. And in March of last year newly released documents obtained under the Freedom of

Information Act revealed that a government agency tasked with investigating more than 100 sightings across England since 2005, concluded that 38 were genuine.

But if these creatures are in fact real, and not just the stuff of myth and human imagination, where could have they come from?

The Centre for Fortean Zoology is the only fulltime scientific organisation in the world dedicated to the study of unknown animals. In 2009 I subscribed to their journal Animals & Men and had an opportunity to interview their Zoological Director, Richard Freeman, about the evidence for a breeding population of big cats roaming wild in the British countryside.

"There is no doubt big cats are alive and well in the UK", Richard Freeman, told me. The former Zookeeper from Leeds added: "A female puma was captured in Inverness in 1980. These are descendants of escapees and deliberate releases", he explained.

"Until the Dangerous Wild Animals Act in 1976 anyone could keep anything they wanted as a pet and up until the early 1980s any old duffer could start a zoo in their backyard! The nucleus of the current big cat population in the UK was from these irresponsible people."

A Room 101 Interview with Neil Arnold: Author of Monster! – The A–Z of Zooform Phenomena

Neil Arnold has written Monster! – The A-Z of Zooform Phenomena, a truly unique book with a foreword by Dr Karl Shuker. He has also done over 20 years of research into the "big cat" phenomenon. So when he volunteered to do an interview I quickly took up his offer.

Richard Thomas: First things first. Thank you very much for getting in touch and taking the time to answer these questions. I really appreciate it. How did you become interested in cryptozoology and related topics in the first place?
Neil Arnold: I first became interested in monster folklore when I was around nine. I'd always heard tales of strange local creatures and eerie stories from my dad and grandad, and so at a tender age I took it upon myself to log such reports. I was also heavily influenced by the chilling '70s movie THE LEGEND OF BOGGY CREEK and a book by Carey Miller (1974) called MONSTERS & MYSTERIOUS BEASTS and of course programmes such as

Arthur C. Clarke. I even began to collect crypto etc, documentaries and have a vast collection. I had a passing interest as a kid in UFOs and ghosts but there's nothing as exciting as a monster-hunt!

Richard Thomas: Your book is called Monster! – The A-Z of Zooform Phenomena. What exactly do you mean by "Zooform Phenomena"?
Neil Arnold: Zooform Phenomena was a term coined by Fortean researcher Jonathan Downes who runs the Centre for Fortean Zoology. It is a term which collates a void of creatures which clearly aren't flesh and blood, yet which cryptozoology and the paranormal realm attempts to file, and yet such 'monsters' fit into neither.

Richard Thomas: Black hellhounds, phantom dogs, winged humanoids...the book is an alphabetical listing of thousands of weird creatures. What are some of your favourites and why?
Neil Arnold: The book isn't that complex despite being 400 pages. It began life as a four-page article and then I realised that there's a veritable feast of info out there never before published, and these are classic campfire tales of real creatures which fit into some complex yet foggy void, i.e. black phantom dogs, winged humanoids (Mothman etc), it is difficult to pick out favourites, I just wanted to assemble the obscure info because no-one else had ever done it but creatures such as India's Monkey Man, the Highgate Vampire, Goatman and the varying phantom hounds of differing colour and purpose certainly hold my interest, but there are just so many monsters in the book, from the more known forms such as Mothman and the Jersey Devil to some very obscure stuff such as Noodleman, Sheepsquatch etc. These are creatures which have been witnessed but which clearly DO NOT lurk in the woods or the oceans despite what cryptozoologists believe.

Richard Thomas: What is the nature of this "complex void" you write about?
Neil Arnold: Zooform Phenomena is a unique study and I'm honoured that my book is the world's first on a subject. Sure, authors such as Loren Coleman have touched upon some of these creatures but they are NOT part of cryptozoology. I do not know where they are from but I believe there are connections to the

human psyche because such critters can be the product of anything from hysteria, hoax, misidentification or local dread.

The classic example of this is the Chupacabras, the 'goatsucker' of Puerto Rico. This vampyric beast has terrorised this island for centuries but only since the '90s did it take on a form resembling a small-winged, bug-eyed bloodsucker with a feathery spine and small clawed hands, however, look back into South American folklore and you'll find that the Chupacabras has always been here and has many so-called relatives, and the same can be said for the hese are manifestations that produce a snowball effect. The Jersey Devil of the New Jersey Pine Barrens has resembled everything from a large cat, a small dragon and a bat, and it has existed for centuries but it's NOT a flesh and blood creature and neither was Mothman, these are zooforms, strange entities with animal characteristics and they need to be collated together and NOT melt into the cryptozoological or paranormal void, they need their own place and that's what MONSTER! is.

Richard Thomas: Is there much overlap between "Zooform Phenomena" and UFOs or ghosts?
Neil Arnold: There are many cases in the book which mention UFOs and ghostly phenomena. Hellhounds have often been considered ghosts but clearly are something more complex. They aren't merely the spirit of someone's dog but instead guardians, or omens of misfortune which haunt old roads, graveyards, scenes where accidents have taken place, and pathways where funeral processions once marched. Naturally, some cases will melt into ghost folklore and UFOs will also be mentioned especially when involving witnesses who saw bizarre creatures in the vicinity of UFOs etc. I don't like the connections personally but maybe all this weird stuff is connected, it's us humans which have given it a label but maybe it's all part of the same jigsaw but many pieces are missing!

Richard Thomas: The idea that the Chupacabra, far from being extraterrestrial, might have a more earthly explanation appeals to me but what are your thoughts on the Chupacabra?
Neil Arnold: Although I mentioned the Chupacabra earlier, it remains one of the most baffling monster mysteries of the modern

era. Jonathan Downes is of strong opinion, after many years of research, that the beast is a porcupine, and his theories add up because it seems that many of the attacks on pets were not in fact made by an unknown predator, however, we all love a mystery and we have attempted to create a monster in the Chupacabra by connecting it to covert experiments, UFOs, the Devil etc, but every country has one of these bogeymen...that's all they are, night prowlers no different from goblins and the mythical creatures we read about when we were kids. They'll always be here in some form whether as Harpies or as vampires.

Richard Thomas: As a researcher of more than 20 years into "big cat" sightings across the world (especially in the UK) what do you think the truth behind this phenomenon is?
Neil Arnold: The 'big cat' phenomenon is NO mystery at all, not in any country. As a race we always like to add mystery to even normal situations. Crop circles, Men In Black, cattle mutilations, have always been blamed on UFOs yet without proof and the 'big cat' situation is no different. In the UK the press are to blame for the local 'beast' stories. For many the 'big cat' enigma is a modern mystery but that's because the press only became that interested the last thirty or so years, although in the UK the Surrey Puma was making a few headlines in the 1950s. The main theory as to why so many cats are out there concerns the ease such animals were obtained in the '60s and '70s. Lions, cheetahs, leopards etc, were available from local pet shops, major stores and via adverts in the newspapers and then in the '70s the Dangerous Wild Animals Act was introduced which meant any owners had to pay huge license fees for their 'pets' and so instead of paying, instead of giving them up to zoo parks, they released them into the wilds. This is a good theory but it doesn't explain the sightings on record that date back a handful of centuries.

  I have records which state that strange cat-like animals were sighted in the 1500s, and the main answer to such populations lies with many origins, 1) when the Roman's settled here they imported many wild animals, elephants, bears, and leopards, to perform in lethal combat in their amphitheatres, and I'm sure that some cats would have escaped. 2) Meanwhile, travelling menageries were very popular in the Victorian era, and not all of the exhibitions would have been up to scratch as rickety wagons took to the rough roads with their exotic cats behind bars, 3) Private collections. The Royals had their own menagerie, the Tudors used to hunt their own large cats, some cats such as Jungle Cats were used aboard boats to kill rats and once docked here such animals may have escaped/been released. There are so many reasons as to why large cats roam our woods, and in the USA it's no different except that many people believe the black cats being seen are black pumas but there has never been a black puma. In the '60s black leopards (panthers) were certainly a very symbolic pet to house and it's this animal which makes up for a majority of 'big cat' sightings in the UK and this cat is a true 'big cat' as, like the lion, jaguar and tiger it can roar.

Other cats we have in the UK are the puma which the United States can boast as a native animal, and also the lynx which we last had a few thousand years ago, but, there are too many inadequate researchers out there creating too many unnecessary complexities. These cats are NOT ghosts, NOT demons, NOT prehistoric survivors, and not mutants. Even in the US I'm convinced that most black cat sightings concern black leopards. Until someone sees a black cat scream, we must stick with the black leopard. Such animals only produce black offspring but they themselves can originally come from a mixed litter but a recessive gene means, especially in the UK, that all the leopard sightings are of black (melanistic) specimens and not normal leopards, although in the black leopard the rosettes can still be seen under the dark coat.

The British 'big cat' situation is not a complex one. We have smaller cats also such as the caracal, jungle cats (which can breed with the domestic cat) and possibly other smaller cats such as ocelots and servals which have been released. I see no need to create a bigger mystery but instead look at the facts, but all the while so many crazy theories keep on emerging these cats will eternally be relegated to folklore and put alongside UFOs etc. I could go on foreever because a lot of people out there need to be made aware that the mystery cat situation is not a mystery.

Richard Thomas: I understand you don't like your "zooform" work to influence your "big cat" research, why is this?
Neil Arnold: The mystery cats out there are flesh and blood so

there's no need to put them alongside ghosts and zooform creatures. I DO believe that Bigfoot is an unknown species of upright-walking ape so I've tried not to put many cases in the book, and I also believe a lot of sea serpent reports are of real creatures so again, anything I consider to be 'out there' in the woods, seas, rivers and skies will not be labelled a zooform. Of course, some researchers do think Bigfoot etc is supernatural, but I'm not so sure, I just think it's mankind's way of relegating an elusive creature to folklore.

Richard Thomas: Have you ever seen a "big cat" or had any other cryptozoological creature sightings yourself?
Neil Arnold: I've put many years of research into the 'big cat' situation and feel privileged that I've seen a black leopard on three occasions, possibly the same individual, in 2000 (twice) and then this year. I've also seen a lynx which took a few years to track and also two other cats, one possibly a puma the other I'm not so sure, but I just feel fortunate to see such beautiful animals, but I put a lot of time in the field and just like to monitor what's going on. I'm not interested in filming them or any financial gain, I'm only interested in the welfare of the animals.

Richard Thomas: I'm a huge Doctor Who fan and try to tie it into Room 101 whenever I can. The Loch Ness monster, yeti and even werewolves have all appeared in the series, do you have any thoughts on these creatures?
Neil Arnold: I've met a lot of researchers into Doctor Who! I've never been a great fan but it is exciting when such popular series incorporate crypto-related monsters. I've always thought that the Loch Ness Monster was a large eel or big catfish or sturgeon, certainly not a living dinosaur, and again, the media created the 'monster' that, if it was ever there, died a long time ago. As for werewolves, when you look at cases across the world there seems to be some inkling that such creatures exist, even if they are zooforms, i.e. Bray Road beast, Morbach Monster of Germany, Michigan Dogman. There are reports dating back many years of dog-headed humanoids. As for the Yeti, like Bigfoot, I think it's an undiscovered primate.

Richard Thomas: What do you think of this crossover between Doctor Who and real life myths and legends like these?

Neil Arnold: I have a massive collection of films, t.v. shows, cartoons etc that have featured/covered cryptozoological beasts and monsters so I think it's great when shows such as Doctor Who cover monsters. I'm planning a book on crypto-related movies and have a blogspot at: www.cryptomovies.blogspot.com which will eventually cover just about every tv programme/commercial and film to feature monsters which we call cryptids.

Richard Thomas: What are your plans for the future? Are you working on anything or has anything new grabbed your attention recently?

Neil Arnold: Around Halloween I should have a book out called MYSTERY ANIMALS OF KENT (www.mysteryanimalsofkent.blogspot.com), which will be unique locally, there are so many local ghost books but nothing has ever been published in regards to local sightings of creatures and my cat research. I may one day do a MONSTER! sequel but am also planning a London 'monster' nook and numerous projects out in the field.

Richard: Thanks again, I look forward to your future work.

A Room 101 Interview with Rupert Matthews

Rupert Matthews is the author of a wide range of books on the paranormal and unexplained, as well as books on more conventional history. After finding a number of these books on the shelves of my local Works bookstore, I thought it would be a good idea to track him down and ask the 20-year publishing veteran a few questions. What followed was a wide ranging conversation on everything from the British Governments controversial decision to close down their UFO desk to the British Bigfoot, Alien Big Cats and poltergeists.

Richard Thomas: First things first, thank you so much for giving us the time to answer these questions. I've read several of your paranormal books and so I really appreciate it and I'm sure our readers will enjoy your answers as well. Looking back on it now, I think my own interest in these topics first grew out of my interest in sci-fi. How did you first become interested in the paranormal and have you had any experiences yourself?

Rupert Matthews: My grandma was very interested in ghosts and the supernatural. When I was younger she used to tell me all about boggarts (we would call them poltergeists these days), white ladies, black hounds and ghosts of all kinds. I guess that is what started me off originally

Richard Thomas: In addition to books on the paranormal and the unexplained, I understand you also write history and travel books. Which came first and how did you begin your writing career?

Rupert Matthews: It was the history that came first so far as books were concerned. I always loved history and when I left school wanted to earn a living doing history somehow. I got a job at a small publishing company as an office boy, then worked my way up to staff writer at a larger company. I took the plunge and went freelance about 20 years ago now.

Back then I was doing history books, but they took me away from home to do research quite a lot. Because the archives and libraries where I was researching all close around 5pm or 6pm I often had evenings to myself with nothing much to do. I started using the time to visit any haunted hotels, pubs or open spaces in the area. Over the years I built up a large amount of photos of haunted places, interviews with witnesses and so forth. It then occurred to me that I ought to try to get it published, and one of my publishing contacts was kind enough to take the book on. It sold rather well and since then I have been doing almost as much on the paranormal and unexplained as on history. Great fun.

Richard Thomas: One of your books is called Bigfoot: True-life Encounters with Legendary Ape-Men. There seems to be two basic schools of thought on Bigfoot: the first, of course, being the conventional view that Bigfoot could be some kind of 'missing link' as the title of your book suggests. The second theory is that it might be something much stranger, perhaps even inter-dimensional, for lack of a better term. What's your opinion on both of these theories?

Rupert Matthews: Interesting stuff. If you look at the eyewitness accounts of people who claim to have seen Bigfoot there seem to be two distinct classes – though they do blur a bit. Most sightings, certainly in the forested Pacific Northwest of America, read very much like an encounter with a flesh and blood animal. The way the Bigfoot reacts is very ape-like, the way the witness reacts is very human-like. Obviously a few of these reports are fakes and others will be mistaken identity, but overall they seem to be rather mundane meetings – though the unrecognised status of the Bigfoot makes them fascinating.

The Ruby Creek case is one such, as is the Patterson movie. A typically inconsequential sighting – of which there are hundreds on record – was that of 26 June 1972. Thomas Smith was fishing from a raft in a small lake in Oregon when he saw a Bigfoot emerge from some trees and come down to the lake where it began to drink. The bigfoot then spotted Smith, turned round and walked back into the cover of the trees.

Then there are very different reports where we seem to be entering the world of the paranormal, not that of cryptozoology. On 11 May 1977 Mr & Mrs Sites were at their remote farm in New Jersey when the sensed something hostile was in the area. Mr Sites went outside to find in the farmyard a tall, hairy bigfoot with glowing red eyes. The farm dog attacked it, but was kicked violently aside and then fled. The bigfoot approached Sites with its arms raised above its head. Sites shot it four times with his .410 gauge shotgun at close range. The Bigfoot ignored the shots, then stopped before turning around and walking off. The glowing red eyes, ability to be invulnerable to being shot and the general behaviour of this bigfoot is not consistent with it being a real flesh and blood animal, but does match the behaviour of paranormal creatures across the globe.

I don't want to get all esoteric on this, but there is a case to be made for paranomal creatures taking on the form that the witness expects them to take. In England they often appear as Black Dogs, because that is what our culture has historically expected. In the US they take the form of bigfoot. In parts of South America they take the form of chupacabra and so forth.

Richard Thomas: Another Bigfoot author I've interviewed is Nick Redfern, who wrote a recent book called The British Bigfoot. What's your opinion on UK Bigfoot sightings?

Rupert Matthews: To be entirely honest I have not found the time to look into them in any great detail. From the little I have read I would put them into the paranormal category, not the flesh and blood category. I asked for the book for Christmas, but my wife bought me a pair of slippers instead.

Richard Thomas: While on the topic of British cryptozoology, my sister actually had an Alien Big Cat sighting here in Wales a few years ago. On your YouTube channel, you briefly talked about something called the "Surrey Puma." Have you ever looked into the UK ABC phenomenon at all?

Rupert Matthews: I have yes. Here we seem to be on firmer ground than with British Bigfoot. The evidence of sightings, tracks and the like seems pretty compelling to me. Again, there will have been fakes and misidentifications, but on the whole I do accept that there are big cats roaming about out there. I recall the time when farmer Ted Noble actually caught one on his land near Inverness back in 1980. He and other locals had been reporting seeing a cougar for some months, but of course nobody took the reports seriously. Then Mr Noble got lucky and actually caught the thing. Nobody could argue with him after that. where the big cats come from is, of course, another matter.

Richard Thomas: Another of your books that I've read is Poltergeists. Explain what you think differentiates poltergeist cases from more traditional hauntings and what do you think are some of the best cases you've researched that best demonstrate this?

Rupert Matthews: Put simply, poltergeists are a distinct category of paranormal manifestation. They are characterised by objects being moved, objects vanishing, objects appearing and by loud noises of various kinds. A typical ghost haunting features none of these things. Conversely a typical ghost will manifest itself in the form of a human figure – poltergeists don't do that and only in very rare cases does anyone claim to have seen one. Moreover, poltergeists will sometimes communicate with the humans – usually by means of knocking or rapping – and if they do they claim to be a ghost, a witch, a demon or something equally bizarre. But they are none of those things. I don't know what they are, but they are pretty terrifying things to encounter.

The Battersea case of 1935 is a text book example of a poltergeist visitation (I don't like the word haunting as that would imply a ghost was to blame). Pretty much everything that a poltergeist might get up to was present in that case, and was carefully recorded by the unfortunate family involved. Another well documented case was the Appleby Poltergeist of 1887. Mr Fowler, who owned the affected house, kept a detailed diary of the strange events that makes compelling reading. I also know of a case here in Surrey a couple of years ago that was very convincing, though the range of phenomena was much more limited. Having spoken to the people involved I have no doubt about what happened.

Richard Thomas: You've also written some UFO books, UFOs A History of Alien Activity from Sightings to Abductions to Global Threat being the most recent. I purchased the book becuase I was intrigued by the "Global Threat" part of the title. In your view, how serious is the threat posed by UFOs and what's your opinion on David Jacobs' theories as outlined his book: The Threat?
Rupert Matthews: I guess "not very" would sum it up. The evidence for UFOs and for the humanoid creatures linked to them can be pretty compelling. However, most of the evidence that suggests some sort of global threat is a lot less convincing. It rests on dubious testimony or simply does not mesh with the mass of evidence about UFOs available elsewhere. I have an open mind on the subject, but have yet to be convinced.

Richard Thomas: Recently, the British Ministry of Defense decided to close down their UFO desk, a strange decision perhaps given the large increase in UFO sightings we've had in the UK in recent years. What do you think were the real motives behind this action and are there any parallels to be drawn with the US Air Force's closing down of Project Bluebook back in 1969?
Rupert Matthews: I spoke to a fairly senior RAF officer about this. His view was that UFOs were not the business of the RAF. He said that the RAF was there to fly missions over Afghanistan, keep an eye on Russian spy planes and such like. He was prepared to accept that there MIGHT be an objective reality to the UFO phenomenon, but seemed to think it was a job for the intelligence services. Until we know what UFOs are and why they are here, he

did not think the RAF should be involved. The RAF has more than enough to keep itself busy. Whether that is the real reason I have no idea, but that was his view.

Richard Thomas: What's your take on the many rumours of an ultra covert British UFO group and recovered alien technology? And how much do you think the British Government know about UFOs compared to their American counterparts?
Rupert Matthews: I know that the US and UK intelligence services share a lot of information, but not everything. I would expect them to share the broad outlines about what they know about UFOs, but would maybe keep juicy details to themselves. As for alien technology, that presupposes that UFOs are alien spacecraft and that one or more has crashed and been recovered. I'm not entirely convinced by either of these suggestions. I know the alien spacecraft theory is the most popular among UFO researchers, but while it may well turn out to be the case, I think it is a case of "not proven" for now.

Richard Thomas: On your YouTube channel, I saw something about strange accounts of humanoid entities being seen in Surrey. What exactly are the details of these encounters?
Rupert Matthews: I think you mean the UFO that landed near Ash Green. Two humanoids about 4 feet tall emerged from the UFO and persuaded the witness, a Mr Burtoo, to accompany them on board the craft. After a while, the two beings told Mr Burtoo to return outside saying that he was "too old" (he was 78). Once Mr Burtoo was outside, the craft took off and flew away. Clearly the humanoids were up to something, but Mr Burtoo was not suitable so they left. There is a lot more to this incident than that, but those are the main outlines.

Richard Thomas: Before he passed away last year, Mac Tonnies completed the manuscript for his new book, The Cryptoterrestrials. As someone who has researched both UFOs and cryptozoology, what's your opinion on Tonnies' "cryptoterrestrial hypothesis" that we share this planet with another intelligent race of humanoids indigenous to Earth?
Rupert Matthews: An interesting idea, but I am not convinced.

The evidence could point in other directions just as easily. Mind you, he might be right.

Richard Thomas: We've covered a lot of ground in this interview: UFOs, ghosts, Bigfoot. Do you think it's possible that all of these mysteries might be connected in some way and maybe even have a single explanation? If so, how ?

Rupert Matthews: When I was talking about Bigfoot I mentioned that some of the sightings seem to be of paranormal entities, not real animals. There is no doubt that many sightings that would at first appear to be of entirely different things (bigfoot, aliens, ghosts, giant dogs) do in fact share some similar traits. A typical paranormal entity would be large, dark in colour, have glowing red eyes and behave in a violent or highly threatening way – but without actually inflicting any real damage. I do not mean that ALL bigfoot or alien sightings fit this pattern, but quite a lot do. This might be the case that a paranormal entity will assume the shape or form of a pre-existing real thing – thus a paranormal entity in North America would assume the guise of a bigfoot. Alternatively, however, it may be that these sightings are not objectively real, and so be more akin to hallucinations than to genuinely paranormal events – though you then have other problems cropping that mean this theory is not entirely convincing either. The evidence could fit a number of scenarios.

Richard Thomas: Where can people contact you and have you got any new books coming out soon we can look forward to?

Rupert Matthews: I am on Facebook and on Twitter. I regularly post up writings and views about the paranormal as well as mentioning new books. I would advise your readers to get in touch with me via one of these social networks. From time to time I do book signings, book launches or give talks at meetings. Those events are advertised via Facebook and Twitter if they are open to the public.

Sci-Fi Meets the Esoteric

Blade Runner: Electronic Owls and Illuminati Symbolism

One of only two science-fiction films made by Hollywood visionary Ridley Scott, (the other, of course, being Alien) Blade Runner is about far more than Harrison Ford hunting down and "retiring" rebel replicants. The first Philip K. Dick big screen adaptation the film is an undisputed cult classic and stands today as arguably the best sci-fi movie ever. Its dark, post-apocalyptic and even post-organic urban setting providing one of the few really believable sci-fi backdrops in all of cinema history.

Combined with larger questions about the nature of reality and what it really means to be human it's this convincing and well thought out sci-fi world Scott creates that invites five cuts and frequent re-watching. Almost more like a novel than a film, noticing something new with each visit. Ridley Scott's vision of a future Los Angeles couldn't be much more different to the city we know today (though it's a lot closer now than it was in 1982). With its colossal skyscrapers, heavy pollution and torrential downpours looking more like a darker New York or even DC Comics' Gotham City. Like Alien before it, the film presents a "used future" only this time it's nature itself that's falling apart not just a spaceship. Climatic change apparently wiping out most animal life to the point where artificial copies are far more common and affordable and humans (those who can afford it) are forced to retreat to the "off-world colonies."

Perhaps the strangest thing about Scott's future LA, though, is that it seems completely riddled with Illuminati imagery and symbolism. The Illuminati is the name given to a shadowy group of people who are alleged to be the power behind the scenes, steering our modern society in a New World Order. Perhaps the most obvious example of this parapolitical iconography has to be the "All Seeing Eye."

Blade Runner opens with an extreme close-up of Harrison Ford's character Rick Deckard's eye and there are numerous other eye shots throughout the film. Eyes being important to the plot because they're the only way to tell the difference between replicants (artificial humans) and real humans. Replicant eyes involuntary glowing in certain scenes. However, is this really the All Seeing Eye of the Illuminati?

Interestingly, in his DVD commentary for The Final Cut Scott did admit that the eye imagery was meant to be reminiscent of George Orwell's dystopian Nineteen Eighty-Four and that it was meant to imply that the world of Blade Runner isn't that far removed from the totalitarian regime of the classic novel. Orwell's Nineteen Eighty-Four, of course, being a favourite tool of conspiracy theorists for explaining the kind of New World Order that the Illuminati are covertly constructing around us. Some researchers even speculating that Orwell (a former officer in the Indian Imperial Police) might have based his novel largely on insider knowledge rather than being simply fiction. But let's get back to Blade Runner.

In his commentary, Scott explains that he and the writers (again echoing Orwell and Alien) envisioned Blade Runner as a future completely economically, technologically and politically dominated by three or less mega-corporations. In effect, it is a world caught in the iron grip of total corporatism: a situation disturbingly close to today but still a somewhat novel idea back in 1982 (unless you were a conspiracy buff, of course).

The largest and most powerful of these new inter-planetary superpowers, of course, is the Tyrell Corporation. Named after its founder and almost God-like creator of the Nexus-6 series replicants: Dr. Eldon Tyrell. A mega-genius with (like Dr. Frankenstein and the Illuminati before him) little or no qualms about the morality of his experiments. Creating (artificial) men and women with at least equal intelligence to their genetic designers ... only to live a mere four years max as nothing more than off-world slaves before they "retire."

Tyrell's favourite motto "More human than human" can't help but ring some alarm bells for anyone who has ever seen Alex Jones' parapolitical blockbuster Endgame. In the documentary film, Jones chronicles the secret elites plans to wipe out a staggering 80% of mankind and replace the species with what they believe is the next stage in human evolution: the post or transhuman. This "being" would be the perfect blending of man with machine, with cybernetics and genetic engineering at their zenith point, in other words, the partly organic "More human than human" replicants of Blade Runner.

However, it's the Tyrell Corporation's taste in architecture and wild life that really sounds the Illuminati alarm. The Tyrell Headquarters are a gigantic seven hundred stories tall pyramided shaped skyscraper. Perhaps resembling an Aztec or Ancient Egyptian pyramid.

A classic symbol associated with the Illuminati, the pyramid has always been an icon of authoritarianism and higher power. A meeting place between Heaven and Earth where great Kings and High Priests became gods in their peoples' eyes. Ridley Scott couldn't have picked a better design for the HQ of his replicants' post-modern father/maker and corporate dictator Tyrell.

In a documentary (Dangerous Days: The Making of Blade Runner) accompanying the DVD release of The Final Cut it's explained that a pyramid was chosen because in an older script Tyrell was exposed to be a replicant copy. The real Tyrell having died and been cryogenically preserved in a giant glass sarcophagus at the centre of the pyramided complex. Tyrell HQ, in effect, then was originally envisioned as being a kind of tomb like the pyramids of the Pharaohs. Be that as it may, perhaps there is a better reason for the strange choice of 2019 architecture.

As well as power and authority, the pyramid is also the perfect physical representation of compartmentalisation: the Illuminati system of control. It exists as a dumbed-down humanity at the base with a tiny enlightened capstone elite ruling on top, i.e. exactly the kind of Orwellian society seemingly reflected in Blade Runner.

Finally, if all this Illuminati imagery and symbolism (the All Seeing Eye, the Pyramid of Compartmentalisation, never mind the Orwellian and transhumanist overtones) wasn't enough, when Deckard (Harrison Ford) first visits Tyrell HQ he is greeted by a replicant owl. The owl (according to Ridley Scott) being Tyrell's official mascot and emblem. Yet another, be it much less well known, Illuminati symbol.

In the film that really put him on the map, Dark Secrets Inside Bohemian Grove, Alex Jones exposed how the global elite meet in secret each year to take part in a strange and bizarre ceremony called the "Cremation of Care." This is an event which, as outlandish as it sounds, involves the worship and even mock human sacrifice of an infant to a deity they call the Great Owl of Bohemia (a giant 45 foot stone owl god complete with almost demonic style horns). The horns particularly are most worrying because they're very reminiscent of the ancient Canaanite horned ideal Moloch, who, according to the Bible at least, really did have children sacrificed to it.

Did Ridley Scott really pick the owl as Tyrell's personal emblem and mascot because of its ancient association and meaning of wisdom, as most would argue? Or is there perhaps a double much darker meaning? When you put it all together: the owl, the pyramid, all the eye imagery, not to mention the fact that the only other animal replicant in the film is a snake, another Illuminati icon, it leaves little to no doubt that Scott and the writers must have done at least some research into Illuminati symbolism and imagery. Whether they believed in any of the conspiracy theories or not, is debatable and probably something we will never really know, but they must have been aware of them.

Some speculate that Philip K. Dick used remote viewing or other psycic means to write his books. Given that Hollywood celebrities like Arnold Swarchenegger are alleged to have attended the bizarre Bohemian Grove, perhaps it's just possible Scott became intrigued that way. Whatever the truth, the Illuminati imagery adds a fascinating extra layer and realism to Scott's dystopian future that most people will sadly miss but still somehow know they're missing ... pulling them back again and again ... which is the genius of Ridley Scott.

'Illuminati' Symbolism and Architecture in Sci-Fi

I have already written about 'Illuminati' or secret society symbolism in Ridley Scott's 1982 science fiction film Blade Runner, a film based loosely on Philip K. Dick's novel Do Androids Dream of Electric Sheep? In that film, there are numerous examples of symbols and ideas often associated with the 'illuminati' and other popular secret society conspiracy theories on the web. "The Owl of Bohemia," the "all-seeing eye," even David Icke's Reptilians (an extra-dimensional race of reptiles who live on Earth disguised as humans) are given a nod to in the form of a replicant snake! And all this in 1982 ... which was more than a decade before the internet gave conspiracy theorists the power to reach millions around the world with their exciting mix of in-depth research and New Age paranoia.

This was Christopher Knowles response when I asked the author of

Our Gods Wear Spandex and The Secret Sun blog about this strange aspect of Blade Runner:

"Well, we know that Dick was all over anything weird or mystical, but I don't think he had much involvement in the movie itself. Blade Runner kind of presents us with this kind of technocratic dystopia that some of these elite cult types would see as the paradise of their apotheosis. The cognitive elite in their penthouses and the poor, teeming masses huddled in the streets and the middle class a distant memory. The constant rain is kind of like the piss of the new gods in that regard. Maybe Scott incorporated some of those symbols as part of the overall social critique of this world that runs throughout the film. Maybe it was the screenwriter David Peoples, who also did similar films like Twelve Monkeys and Soldier."

A stargate or portal between Heaven and Earth, pyramids have always been an icon associated with Divine power and authoritarian rulers. So Ridley Scott and/or screenwriter David Peoples couldn't have picked a more appropriate design for the headquarters of the powerful Tyrell Corporation. The megacorporation that dominates the Earth and "off world colonies" in the year 2019, and whose motto is "More Human Than Human," a reference to the artificial beings or NEXUS-6 Replicants they create in the 'image' of their company's God-like founder, the billionaire genius and artificial human slave trader Dr. Eldon Tyrell.

In Ridley Scott's first science fiction film 1979's Alien, another "company," this time called Wyland-Yutani dominates human inhabited space in the 22nd century. Most casual fans of the Alien franchise are familiar with the company's second logo designed by James Cameron for the second film in the series, Aliens, with the interlocked W/Y, but the original logo designed for Scott's film was an Egyptian winged-sun emblem.

According to David Icke and other well known researchers in the fields of parapolitics and alternative history, "The Illuminati" (which Icke defines as a network of interlocking secret and quasi secret groups) are the "continuation of the Mystery Religions of Babylon and Egypt" in ancient times that practiced "sun worship." With this in mind maybe the title of Ridley Scott's new Alien prequel "Prometheus" shouldn't be that surprising then when you take into account the abundance of potential 'Illuminati' symbolism in Blade Runner and Alien. Prometheus was the Titan in Greek mythology who stole fire from Zeus and gave it to mankind.

But Scott's science fiction films aren't the only examples of 'Illuminati' architecture in Hollywood films. A pyramid on Mars is featured in Total Recall (another Philip K. Dick film adaptation) starring Arnold Shwarzenegger, who according to Alex Jones' 2000 documentary film, Dark Secrets Inside Bohemian Grove, has been an attendee at the mysterious summer camp event in northern California, at which the bizarre "Cremation of Care" ceremony supposedly involving the mock human sacrifice of an infant to a giant forty-plus foot stone owl deity called "Moloch" is alleged to take place.

In July 2010 it was even reported that the California "Governorator" had given a speech at the super secret rich man's retreat where political, business and Hollywood elites from the Bush's to the voice of The Simpsons' Mr. Burns, Harry Shearer, have allegedly attended.

Anti-New World Order filmmakers and secret society researchers suggest that, for the 'Illuminati' conspirators the pyramid represents the compartmentalisation of secret knowledge from mankind. But even if the conspiracy theorists are correct about this why would any secret society (whether you believe 'Them' to be the Bilderburg Group, the Skull and Bones Society at Yale University, the Freemasons, or even a conglomeration of all these and other secret and quasi secret groups) put their secret symbols in big Hollywood films for everyone to see?

"I have heard that the popular culture is used as a tool by whatever elite, business, govt, Illuminati, etc., to both gauge and control the populace. That is, the conspiracy is the conspiracy theory itself, making its way into the mainstream culture, thereby usurping the power of the populace to alter it, because one can diminish some researcher or whistleblower as someone who 'just watches too much X-Files,'" Dean Haglund, better known as Langly in the popular 1990s TV series The X-Files told me in 2010.

In a correspondence on Facebook, filmmaker and Bilderburg researcher, Timuçin Leflef, told me, "there are several facets to it – including sacred geometry." Other researchers such as Texe Marrs, author of Codex Magica, have suggested that the secret rulers of the world believe that they get paranormal powers from putting their secret signs and symbols on display, or hidden in plain sight. Hence the pyramid and all-seeing-eye on the back of the one dollar bill.

While you can't rule anything out, readers who are conspiracy-inclined should remember that there is some overlap between fans of sci-fi and the conspiracy genre. Books and films like George Orwell's 1984, H. G. Wells' Things To Come, and Aldous Huxley's Brave New World have almost become required reading and watching for anyone who wants to attempt to untangle the great conspiracy.

Might a simpler explanation be that the scriptwriters or directors of these films might have been inspired by the New Age or paranormal book section ... of course, it could all just be a coincidence too. Whatever the truth I think 'Illuminati' symbolism and architecture in films and TV shows is a subject that deserves more research.

A Sci-Fi Worlds Interview with Nick Redfern

When I interviewed Nick Redfern, he'd teased that one of his next projects was Science Fiction Secrets, a book chronicling the bizarre crossover between the non-aligned worlds of Sci-Fi and the esoteric realms of UFOs, the paranormal and conspiracy theory. When the book arrived in 2010 I knew that I had to do a fresh interview with Nick to discuss his foray into the strange connection between sci fi and esoterica.

Some of the topics delved into include Nick Pope and his UFO fiction, 9/11 and the X-Files spin-off that predicted it, Philip K. Dick, and Dennis Wheatley's UFO books to name just a few.

Richard Thomas: Just want to start by saying thanks for taking the time to do this interview. The first thing I wanted to ask you about is 9/11. I remember, a few years back, you said you were skeptical about alternatives to the official government conspiracy theory that Osama bin Laden masterminded the attacks on the Twin Towers and Pentagon. In the book, though, you dedicate a whole chapter to the pilot for The Lone Gunmen (a spin-off to the popular X-Files series) which astonishingly seemed to predict almost exactly the events of 9/11 (i.e. planes being hijacked and flown into the Twin Towers). In light of this information, and considering the time that has passed since the event, what is your current opinion on 9/11 and is "government sponsored terrorism" something you think you'll ever look more into?

Nick Redfern: I kind of liken the whole government angle and conclusions relating to 9/11 to be like their conclusions and official reports on the JFK assassination and Roswell: no conspiracy, and all very much explainable. Personally, however – and just like the Roswell and JFK reports – I think there are very big questions that still require answering about 9/11 that just don't sit well with the government's version of events. I wouldn't say I'll never do something about terrorism, but as there are so many good researchers already delving into this area, I think it would have to be something pretty substantial and ground-breaking – and that wasn't being done by anyone else – to make me get involved in that area. There are people far more knowledgeable than me digging into all this field already.

Richard Thomas: I know you now live in Texas, home of Alex Jones, Jim Marrs and the JFK assassination: what's it like to live in what many consider the heartland of "conspiracy culture"?
Nick Redfern: Yeah, me and my wife, Dana, live in the city of Arlington, Texas, which is about a 25-minute drive from Dallas. Until the summer of 2008 – when we moved to Arlington from Dallas – we actually only lived about an 8-minute drive from the Grassy Knoll! As for what it's like here, well, you obviously get a lot of tourists visiting the Grassy Knoll, Dealey Plaza etc. But, when you live here – I moved here 9 years ago – and after visiting it a couple of times, you kind of just incorporate it into your everyday life. In other words, if I drive along the stretch of road where JFK was shot, I honestly don't now give it much thought any more – I'm more concentrating on watching the traffic and the crazy drivers! That's not to sound cold-hearted, but when you've seen it once or twice, well…you've seen it. It's so small too – I was amazed. You see things like the Zapruder film and it looks like a large, sprawling area. It's actually not though.

Richard Thomas: Regarding Science Fiction Secrets, I recently researched Dennis Wheatley, someone you cover in some depth in the book. I focused more on his black magic books rather than science fiction, but how much of what Wheatley wrote about do you think was really just fiction and how much do you think might have been inspired by fact?
Nick Redfern: Well, we can never really know the answer to that question for sure. But, I would say that it's very intriguing that as

with Wheatley and several other people I mention in my book – such as Ralph Noyes and Bernard Newman – had ties to the secret world of officialdom, and then went on to write UFO novels, with cover-ups and conspiracies at their heart. So, I don't rule out the idea that some of these people may have uncovered UFO secrets during the time of their links with the government, and then went on to incorporate those same UFO secrets into a fictional setting.

Richard Thomas: One sci-fi classic surprisingly not discussed in the book is 2001: A Space Odyssey. For readers not familiar with the screenplay, it involves the discovery of a mysterious monolith on the moon, very strangely a similar "monolith" appears to be sitting on one of Mars' moons. The first chapter in your book deals with Mars mysteries, so what's your gut opinion on anomalies such as the Phobus "monolith" and famous "Face on Mars"? Do you think intelligent life could have once lived on Mars and maybe colonised Earth or perhaps vice versa?

Nick Redfern: Yes, I do think that there was more to Mars than meets the eye in the distant past. The late Mac Tonnies wrote an excellent and very balanced book on the whole Face on Mars controversy, called After the Martian Apocalypse. For me, Mac presented some very notable data suggesting that there may have been a very ancient Martian culture. And, if they developed space-travel, it's not a big leap to imagine a visitation to the Earth in the distant past.

Richard Thomas: Ridley Scott's Blade Runner is widely considered by film buffs as the definitive science fiction film, the script of which was largely based on Philip K. Dick's Do Androids Dream of Electric Sheep? If you look at the film you'll see that it is lettered with what might best be described as "Illuminati symbolism" what are your thoughts on this strange aspect of Blade Runner and why do you think the FBI were so interested in Philip K. Dick?

Nick Redfern: There's no doubt that Dick was a very paranoid man, and who saw a lot of conspiracy theories here, there and everywhere. That doesn't mean the conspiracy theories weren't valid. Rather, it means that he was so deeply into them that he quite often incorporated them into his work. As for the FBI, they watched him very closely because he claimed knowledge of a deep-underground, covert Nazi-type cabal that he believed was trying to influence people to its cause by infiltrating the world of science-fiction. In other words, he thought this group was trying to recruit science fiction authors who could spread the group's beliefs in a way that might allow impressionable people to be turned to their way of thinking.

Richard Thomas: Perhaps the film director with the most conspiracy theories surrounding them and their films, though, has to be Steven Spielberg. How much evidence do you think there is to support the rumours that Close Encounters and E.T. were both based on UFO "insider" knowledge?

Nick Redfern: There's no real, hard evidence. If there was, we wouldn't be asking the question now! But, there are a lot of rumours suggesting that elements of the US Government, military and/or intelligence world may have subtly promoted some key elements in both films.

Richard Thomas: Do you think Spielberg's UFO films or sci-fi series such as Chris Carter's X-Files might be part of some kind of official UFO Disclosure Project? If so, how old might such a project be? What are your thoughts on Bruce Rux's thesis that Orson Welles' infamous 1938 radio adaptation of the H.G. Wells classic The War of the Worlds marked the start of a UFO "education program"?

Nick Redfern: I think it's possible, and I dig into this angle quite a bit in the book. Bruce Rux's theory is definitely an interesting one that deserves more attention. I'm not sure if this is all part of some planned official disclosure – after all, the Welles production is now 72 years ago, so it would have to be a very long operation! I think more likely is the scenario that at an unofficial level, there are people in Government that may have fed ideas to influential people in the science-fiction world, to see what the public reaction is, But, this seems to have been going on for decades; so that's what makes me think that maybe it's like some sort of periodic litmus-test to try and determine where people are at in their beliefs about alien life; rather than a program gearing up to a date and an end-game scenario.

Richard Thomas: Speaking of Wells in Science Fiction Secrets you explore the idea that the Soviets were inspired by Wells' novel The Island of Doctor Moreau to create an army of human-animal hybrids, what are the chances that such creatures were ever actually born and could these experiments be responsible for Bigfoot sightings in Eurasia?

Nick Redfern: Zero! As I note, this was a crackpot project, because gorillas and humans, or chimpanzees and humans cannot successfully mate, at all. It was a strange, surreal and odd project that actually had no hope of achieving any real, meaningful success.

Richard Thomas: H.G. Wells, of course, is famous for writing the first books about alien invasion, time travel and invisibility. However there's one sci-fi concept Wells isn't credited with and that's Star Trek style teleportation or matter transport. With Donald Rumsfeld admitting back in 2001 (on September 10th strangely enough) that the Pentagon was missing $2.3 trillion anything becomes feasible, do you think that teleportation might have been developed clandestinely and if so to what extent? Also what other science fiction type technologies (for example invisibility and time travel) is there evidence to suggest might have been developed in the black?

Nick Redfern: Yes, I think with black-budgets that all sorts of unusual projects have been worked on. I wouldn't be at all surprised if there was a very black-budget alternative space-programme that is quite a bit in advance of what we know publicly about the space-programmes of various nations. I think also a lot of research has been done into invisibility and sophisticated areas of advanced camouflage. Personally, I think the idea that time-travel and teleportation have been successfully developed to where it's 100 per cent understood, functioning and controllable are still stretching things a bit.

Richard Thomas: Another figure that UFO conspiracy theories seem to follow is former member of the British Ministry of Defence Nick Pope. Back in the early 2000's, Pope, who used to work on the now defunct MoD UFO desk, wrote two fictional books (Operation Thunder Child and Operation Lighting Strike) that dealt with themes of alien invasion and UFO crashes. Do you think Nick was using his insider knowledge or is he just clever enough to make it look like he was, or might it be a case of both?

Nick Redfern: I think Nick obviously used a lot of his own personal knowledge of how the MoD works, and how the military works, to write an entertaining novel of alien invasion. I think it's fair to say that many people are split on whether the cover-up angles of the novel, and if the stories about alien bodies being taken to Porton Down etc are based on anything real, or just Nick incorporating widely-known allegations that were already prevalent in the UFO research community. I think Nick is probably very happy that people are still talking about the book, as a direct result of these scenarios and allegations!

Richard Thomas: Your follow-up book to Science Fiction Secrets is Contactees, which also came out this Fall. Tying these two subjects together, is there anything we can discern from the portrayal of contactees in science fiction?

Nick Redfern: Not really. Contactees is basically a study of the whole Space-Brothers movement from the early 50s onwards. I didn't really uncover anything to suggest a linkage between the official worlds secretly trying to infiltrate the sci-fi world in respect of Contactee cases. However, some people do believe that the 1950s film, The Day The Earth Stood Still was government-related in some way. And, admittedly, the main character in the film is very human-looking, as were the Space-Brothers. And, also as with the Space-Brothers, the alien – played by Michael Rennie – does offer warnings to the Human Race. So, maybe that's a science fiction film we should take a closer look at.

Richard Thomas: Where can people get a copy of Science Fiction Secrets and what else have you got planned for us in 2010?

Nick Redfern: People can get hold of Science Fiction Secrets at all good book-selling shops and on-line outlets too. I have 4 books coming out this year: a UFO book called Final Events; and Monsters of Texas (co-written with Ken Gerhard), Wild-Man and Mystery Animals of the British Isles: Staffordshire, which are all on my other big interest: cryptozoology.

Richard Thomas: Thanks again Nick !!

A Sci Fi Worlds Interview with Timucin Leflef: Bilderberg Researcher/Filmmaker

Recently, I got myself a copy of The New World Order, a new documentary film following people (like myself) who believe in conspiracy theories. Refreshingly, for a 'mainstream' documentary, the film was pretty fair, deciding to focus on the personalities themselves and their lives instead of trying to debunk their alternative world view. The film boasts some big names... Alex Jones, Jim Marrs and Daniel Estulin to name just a few.

The film also focused, however, on some less known researchers and activists: what might be called the next generation of conspiracy culture... names like We Are Change founder Luke Rudkowski, anti-war protester Seth Jackson, and, from my side of the Atlantic, Bilderberg researcher and filmmaker Timucin Leflef. Intrigued by a short clip from one of the director's films featured in the documentary, recently I managed to track down Timucin and had the chance to ask the Turkish-Irish filmmaker a few questions.

Richard Thomas: I think we should start with me just saying thanks for taking the time to answer these questions, I'm sure you have plenty of other projects that need your attention so it's really much appreciated.

I want to focus mainly on questions about your films in this interview but given your background it seems a little silly not to ask you how you first became interested in what the mainstream media very sadly simply dismiss as "conspiracy theories"? Also what are some of your key areas of interest: i.e. 9/11, Bilderberg etc?

Timucin Leflef: I can make time. Thanks for the opportunity.

I first became interested in this area through my desire to make science fiction films. I started writing my first Sci-Fi screenplay The Messenger in my early teens back in 1989. It was about a young alien boy sent back in time from a post-apocalyptic future Earth to "save the world" but who ironically gets caught up in a secret government project which destroys it. I guess I was a cynical teenager at the time.

The script became an ironic look at those end-of-the-world disaster movies which were so prevalent in the seventies, but it had an interesting twist at the end which I still won't reveal in case I finally do get to make it.

The funny thing is that the script predicted a totalitarian dictatorship occurring "some time in the near future", the possibility of a civil war and an "end of the world" scenario being manufactured in order to reduce world populations. I was 14 when I came up with the idea and wrote it over several years. I still have the original story which I sent to myself by registered mail and haven't opened for copyright purposes.

Then in 1993 I came across William Cooper's research paper on the Origins and Identity of MJ-12 which was circulating around university campuses at the time. Strangely, some of the things I thought I was 'making up' for my screenplay, Cooper said he had seen plans for when he was in U.S. Naval Intelligence back in the 70s, including a totalitarian dictatorship in the near future, the possibility of a stage-managed "civil war" and an end-of-the-world scenario being manufactured for the creation of something called a 'New World Order.'

I was genuinely surprised. Here I was thinking I was making up these stories and there was Cooper almost halfway around the world saying something similar had actually been in the works since the 1970s. Because of this I started investigating his work further. My key area of interest has always been the possible manufacture of a false-flag alien invasion in order to band us together under a fascist global dictatorship. This also features in the script now.

Richard Thomas: Before we go on how did you become involved with The New World Order documentary and what were your thoughts on the end result?

Timucin Leflef: The last time the Bilderberg Group met in Turkey, in 1975, it was in Cesme and happened within 2 weeks of my birth. Shortly after the country fell into political turmoil, divided between left-wing and right-wing factions. At least ten people were being killed every day on the streets of Ankara and investigative journalists who claimed that the country was being destabilised by external influences wound up dead, so it was quite obvious what was really going on. Eventually in 1980 there was a military coup d'etat and a 'new order' was established. Shortly after however the country was destabilised economically as a means, in my opinion, of keeping the population constantly preoccupied with work, in accordance with

Bilderberg policy.

When I found out this clandestine group of bankers, businessmen and society's rich elite were about to meet up again in Turkey thirty-two years later, this time in Istanbul, my city of birth, I had to investigate what their plan was for my home country this time round. Were they going to manufacture a war with Iran which has been on the cards ever since P.N.A.C. published Rebuilding America's Defenses Abroad in 2000?

Through various means I got in touch with Jim Tucker who has been following them without fail for over thirty years. I made sure he knew he was in Turkey as an invited guest and I met him at the airport just to make sure he was safe and to translate for him. He's in his 80's now, so I figured he probably needed help. Fortunately Turkish people were very supportive of him and were very clued-in to the whole Bilderberg story thanks to campaigners, websites like http://bilderberg.org/ and books like Daniel Estulin's The True Story of the Bilderberg Group. Jim is a bit of a hero now in Turkey.

There were huge protests in Taksim Square and even the Turkish Prime Minister got involved. Turkish delegates at the meeting that year told the Bilderberg warmongers that if they were indeed planning to start a war with Iran, that "Turkey would have nothing do to with it". It was the first time in history that this illegal cartel was exposed to such an extent – with huge protests and daily news reports on Turkish national TV, which fortunately isn't as censored as the western media. It appears Bilderberg were perturbed by the Turkish response and may have changed their tactics since because of it.

The crew themselves were a nice bunch, and I agreed to being involved in their documentary when they told me it was going to be about "people exposing the New World Order". However, once Alex got on board, I felt that it turned into a documentary about "Conspiracy Theorists" (his words) which is a derogatory term used to discredit genuine researchers in this field. A lot of my interview was cut and clipped. Whether they had been manipulated, or whether it was always their plan, I still don't know, but none of the information I'm presenting you with now showed up in their documentary.

I'm a filmmaker who just happens to have an interest in this area and for lack of a better term I wound up blowing the whistle on the

2007 meeting when I wrote a communique to the Turkish PM about it. Because of this I was intimidated by Bilderberg security and also received death threats as a result. (I was also assaulted because of this, but at a later time).

Again, I have nothing against the guys who made the documentary and I did everything I could to help them out as fellow filmmakers, but I still have questions about what really happened especially after attempts were made to steer their documentary. I mean, Daniel Estulin knows much more about the Bilderberg Group than I do. They followed him for almost a year, yet he was cut from the final movie. Don't you find that a little strange? Jim Tucker hardly appears in the movie and he's been following Bilderberg for 30 years! Essentially, you should never take anything at face value, even within the alternative media, as that too is susceptible to manipulation.

Richard Thomas: One of the topics I deliberately didn't ask you about was UFOs or Unidentified Flying Objects. I mention what the often misused initials stand for because I understand you're pretty sceptical about the Extraterrestrial hypothesis which has become synonymous with the abbreviation. I suppose my question is what do you think UFOs could represent and perhaps more importantly why?

Timucin Leflef: I'm sceptical about the extraterrestrial hypothesis because I know that "fear of the unknown" is a great way of motivating the masses into giving up their personal freedoms for increased security. If people are lead to believe they're being invaded by "aliens", that their own governments are powerless to defend them and that the only answer is to join a U.N.-backed global military dictatorship, then they will willingly relinquish their national sovereignty, personal freedoms and property for an alleged "greater good", especially if they believe it will save them. Pretty soon they'll find themselves slaves to an autocratic world government which will dictate their every choice – one example being the number of children they will be permitted to have, which is already being enforced in China. It will essentially be a world where they will have less rights than they were born with.

The truth is, it doesn't matter whether aliens exist or not, what really matters is what does the Global Elite want you to believe? It has been well documented that UFO technology was developed by the Nazis in order to win the Second World War. This technology was then transferred to the United States, most likely under Project Paperclip, in an attempt to take control of it before the Russians could. As fellow Sci-Fi Worlds interviewee Nick Redfern pointed out in his book Body Snatchers In The Desert, the Roswell incident was simply a military experiment that went wrong. The whole alien crash scenario was a great way of covering up the fact they used Japanese Prisoners of War in an experiment that would have eventually been deemed inhumane under the guidelines of the Geneva Convention. Stories about alien encounters have often turned out to be cover stories for military experiments or technology.

The alien invasion hoax is also another reason why so many Hollywood science fiction movies involve aliens arriving in vast armadas to destroy us and take over our planet. They were quite prevalent in the 50s and you can find modern-day examples like ID4: Independence Day, War of the Worlds and even Mars Attacks. Very few movies about extra-terrestrials actually involve aliens with peaceful intentions. E.T. certainly comes to mind, but even movies where they arrive as our benevolent "saviours" like The Day The Earth Stood Still, is still another permutation of the New World Order hoax, in which case it's about giving up our sovereignty, our "petty little differences" as Reagan put it, and joining a fascist global regime in order to achieve an alleged "world peace". It will be world peace but with a seriously heavy price on our freedoms.

Mostly, though, these movies are programming us to believe that once we see vast armadas of classified military vehicles hovering in the sky, that they will in fact be UFOs driven by "extra-terrestrials" who are here to "kill us and take over our planet." And then the only solution we'll be presented with will be a heavy reliance on a Militarised 'New World Order' to save us. That's where the real agenda lies.

Richard Thomas: In The New World Order there's a short clip from your film A.D. How did the film come about and what do you think have been some of your biggest sci-fi influences as a screenwriter?

Timucin Leflef: Back in 1991 I wrote a satirical short story for our school magazine at a time when the Catholic Church was kicking up a storm about prophylactics being sold at the Virgin Megastore. The story involved the Catholic Church taking over Ireland some time in the near future in order to restore their waning power and was a way of acknowledging the fact we had been under a Catholic Dictatorship since the 1920's. I also wrote it to acknowledge the many stories that were surfacing about some priests' predilections for young boys, which also came quite close to affecting my own life in my late teens.

When I returned from university in 1997, I rewrote the story as a 30-minute short film script entitled Totalit-Eireann, a play on the words Totalitarian and Eireann – the Irish genitive word for 'Ireland'. It was a mixture of ideas from Blade Runner to Isaac Asimov's robot stories and was about robots scapegoated by a futuristic fascist military regime. However, my attempts at getting 80k worth of film finance for it a year later failed. For budgetary reasons and for the fact that I was adamant to make it anyway, I retitled it A.D. and changed it from being a story about robot 'good guys' into alien 'bad guys'. I found that it would be easier and more cost-effective to have a man in a scary-looking alien mask than to build a convincing-looking robot.

I also changed the lead character from male to female because my sister Ayse was getting into movies at the time and I wanted to give her a dark role to scare off any potential stalkers and also to counter all the sickeningly nice 'girl-next-door' roles she was being offered at the time. Her cyborg character was rewritten as a clone, again for budgetary reasons.

However, even at a revised 10k budget, it was still difficult to get money for my movie, perhaps because most people didn't believe a special effects film could be made at that level. It eventually came to a point where in 2000 I was working as a cameraman for a Community TV station which was being closed down by the Irish Government. In the middle of all this I had the inspired idea to make the sci-fi movie on a shoestring budget, with no proper funding, no equipment and no real idea how the finished product would turn out. It was a risk, but I had to take it as I knew nobody else could make it.

Fortunately, when you get the ball rolling, providence ensues and people are more than willing to help you out. We shot most of it on a 3-chip mini-DV camera which I borrowed off a friend and edited the footage later on my computer. I also credited everyone for the actual work they did, however insignificant their contribution may have appeared. However, I also believe in the Auteur Theory – There is no 'I' in 'Team', but there is an 'I' in 'Tim', so beware.

My biggest sci-fi influences for A.D. had to be Blade Runner, The Terminator and of course The Matrix, hence the cheap experimental bullet-time effects. Add to this my biggest sci-fi influences over the years which were 2001: A Space Odyssey, Total Recall, Robocop, Aliens, The Running Man and The Time Tunnel TV Series. You could probably add Mad Max 2: The Road Warrior to this list, although like the swine flu shot, it's not quite mandatory... yet.

Richard Thomas: The trailer for Project Bluebeam, your other film, seems to be heavily based on the old 1950s sci-fi and horror trailers: are you a fan of those kind of films at all and, if so, what are some of your favourites? I'm a big fan of the old Hammer and Universal horror films myself so I don't know if they were an influence or not.

Timucin Leflef: Well, I do love movies from that era, especially the ones that are visually stylish, thrilling and funny. That's why I've always liked Hitchcock movies, especially North By Northwest and also the early Bond movies from the 60s, like Goldfinger and From Russia With Love. Dr. Strangelove is also a personal favourite of mine for these reasons. It has to do with finding a certain type of tone, style and humour.

With the UFO B-movies of the 50's, I essentially like them for their unintentional humour, which I find is often funnier than the gross-out comedies you see nowadays. I like Earth Versus The Flying Saucers mainly for Ray Harryhausen's work and just to see how they did their special effects back then. Project Bluebeam itself is a way of harking back to those movies from the 1940s and 50s with their film noir style, quaint-looking effects, and their naïve outlook on 'the future'. I like the idea of making a sci-fi film noir done very much like Sin City, except funny, in colour and hopefully – if I can get the budget for it – in 3D.

Richard Thomas: One of the things I love about A.D. and from the look of it Project Bluebeam too is that they seem to be borrowing heavily from conspiracy culture and blending it together with sci-fi. Looking back on it maybe that's exactly what George Orwell did with Nineteen Eighty-Four, although, you're doing it in a much more tongue in cheek style. Do you think this might be a more successful formula for waking the general public up?

Timucin Leflef: Well, yes. The plan is to wake people up to certain possibilities and the best way of reaching them would be through popular culture. Books are certainly one way of achieving this goal and both George Orwell and Aldous Huxley were quite successful in alerting people to the Elite's fascist global agenda.

Documentaries are another way, but over the years I have noticed how several researchers, writers and documentary makers have either been murdered or have died under suspicious circumstances, including Bill Cooper, Rik Clay, Jim Keith, Stephen Knight and allegedly Hunter S. Thompson who was making a documentary.

However, mainstream features are most likely the best choice in my view. Not only are they a means of reaching a mass audience, but primarily because you're telling a story to entertain people. And what better a way to enlighten than through entertainment? This is what I think Stanley Kubrick was attempting to do with some of his movies, like Dr. Strangelove, which in my opinion is a perfect satire on Dr. Henry Kissinger and his cra-haaaa-zy pro-nuclear foreign policy. You just gotta hand it to Old Heinz! Anthony Burgess admitted that A Clockwork Orange was based on rumours about the British Government's use of mind control techniques on prisoners in the 1970s. And of course Eyes Wide Shut – just Google the Elite's interest in Satanic ritual and I'll say no more.

Feature films therefore may be a safer alternative as they can give you a degree of artistic license. I find comedies tend to be popular, and sci-fi is certainly one genre that allows people to suspend their disbelief to the point where they're open to accepting fresh ideas, which is useful if you're attempting to cause a shift in people's consciousness. This is why a movie like The Matrix could only have worked as Sci-Fi. Try doing it as a musical – "Hey Dude, Where's My Gun? I just found out I'm The One" – and it may not have been as effective.

Richard Thomas: What was your favourite performance in A.D. and will any of the same actors be in Project Bluebeam?

Timucin Leflef: Well, I really admire John Collins's ability to pull off dead-pan humour and keep such a straight face. We were laughing so much shooting his scenes. He has a knack when it comes to comedy and reminds me of a younger, leaner Leslie Nielsen, so I was quite lucky to have him on board. Owen Callaghan ('The Cleaner') was also quite good even though he was a non-actor. Considering the fact we had very little money and hardly any time for rehearsal, I was quite happy with the way a lot of the performances turned out. And although I'd prefer more rehearsal time in future, I find it's usually better just to cast the right people in the right roles and let them be themselves. That way their performances come across as being more genuine on screen which is perfect for the implicit nature of film acting as opposed to stage acting where you need to project more.

It was also a matter of pride for me to have friends and family in the movie. Luckily, my sister Ayse proved perfect for the main role. So much so, I wrote the feature-length version with her in mind, although she's married now and has a young kid which means acting is on the back burner with her for a while. So definitely, I have no doubt I will work with them all again. Except maybe Lord Gator. He's moved onto bigger things now.

Richard Thomas: The opening voice over and CGI in A.D. was particularly impressive, what do you think were the biggest obstacles to realising your vision for the film and how did you get around them?

Timucin Leflef: The biggest obstacle for me was getting funding for the movie. After a few initial rejections, I finally gave up trying which was probably the best decision I made. Once I decided to go no budget and produce the movie myself "no matter what", the second biggest obstacle then was getting the actors to take time out from their schedules and commit to working on a specific day. I had to shoot around their conflicting schedules because I couldn't afford to pay them proper wages or could only pay them partial wages at best. This is why a lot of A.D. was shot over weekends.

Another problem was that the original story was about robots, which would have been prohibitively expensive, so I figured if I changed the story into one about aliens, it would be easier to make. Just get a guy in a scary mask and hey presto!

Additionally, another major obstacle in my mind was the audience's high expectations regarding special effects in movies these days. When you're shooting a movie like that on a shoe-string budget, something has got to give. I therefore figured if I made it as a comedy the audience would be more forgiving of its rough edges, hence the tongue-in-cheek humour which developed during the rewrite. Fortunately, people who see it often think it's funnier and in ways better than many of the short films funded here to the tune of 80k by the Irish Film Board. That gives me a real sense of achievement.

Richard Thomas: Given your Irish background people might be a little surprised that Roman Catholicism instead of British imperialism is presented as the capstone of the New World Order in A.D. Why did you make this choice and does it reflect your own research or upbringing at all? How important do you think the Vatican might be in this New World Order?

Timucin Leflef: Again, it was another of those cases where I had written a story which turned out to be more accurate than I had initially realised. I wrote it originally to poke fun at Catholic Imperialism. Fortunately, after doing further research, I was pleasantly surprised I had hit the nail on the head, albeit through sheer dumb luck on my part. Legally speaking, the U.S. is still a colony of the British Empire, but Britain itself was colonised by Rome.

As the Vatican is a continuation of the Roman Empire which itself has been around for over two millennia, you'll find they have accumulated a vast amount of wealth over that period. Some think they funded Hitler and then created the Bilderberg Group to continue Hitler's plan for a New World Order. And I say that the Vatican is a military order, much like in my movie, which is why some of their members have titles such as 'Knights' or 'Generals'.

Essentially, if you follow the money, you'll find the Vatican is a major player in the scheme of things and that the old adage "All Roads Lead To Rome" is still applicable to this day.

Richard Thomas: In A.D. we follow Malice 101 a genetically engineered assassin "perfect in every way" and programmed to kill. Given this do you share my concerns about what is called the "Transhumanist" movement?

Timucin Leflef: Wow, you make her sound like she's Mary Poppins on steroids. I've never heard that actual term being used before, although I do know that mind control experiments have been around since the 1950s when MK-ULTRA was formed as a research programme into chemical control of the human mind. Then in the 1960s, Dr. Jose Delgado's pioneering research lead to the development of the 'stimoceiver', a radio receiver which could be implanted into the brain to create what would have eventually lead to, in Delgado's view, the creation of a "Psychocivilized Society". He demonstrated this device by implanting it into a bull's brain and managed to stop it from charging at him simply by pressing a button. This transmitted a radio frequency to the bull which stopped it in its tracks. The demonstration was filmed, is well documented and lead to further research being done through a covert military operation in the1970s known as Project MILAB. Again, the idea of 'alien abduction' and 'alien implants' was used as a clever way of covering the fact they were conducting military mind control experiments on an unsuspecting public. A documentary was even shown on Irish national television in the late 1990s in which European MEPs were attempting to get these experiments stopped.

Richard Thomas: If you were to write a sequel or spin-off to A.D. taking place outside Ireland where do you think you'd set it and what would be the opening?

Timucin Leflef: I wrote a feature-length version of the movie on a Masters Degree course back in 2006. It was also set in Ireland and probably has one of the most exciting opening sequences in sci-fi film history. I'd like to think so anyway. However, the Irish Film Board told me they don't like making 'genre movies' which came as a bit of a surprise to me seeing as cringe-inducing movies about miserable people living boring little lives is a whole genre unto itself at which the Irish Film Board excel. I've therefore set my film in the States now, but still won't reveal the opening sequence until the movie has been released.

Richard Thomas: Are you working on or have any ideas for any other sci-fi films right now? Also if you could write for any sci-fi series past or present, film or TV what would it be and what do you think you'd do different?

Timucin Leflef: Well, I've been developing A.D. and Project Bluebeam, both of which are features, over the last few years. I was also making my own documentary on the New World Order, but was whacked on the back of the head last year in a suspicious assault, so I guess I may have to back out of that now. The funny thing is Jim Tucker predicted something like that would happen.

I'm primarily a writer-director. Because of this, I only write scripts I would direct myself. Writing scripts for someone else to direct is like giving away your best work to make someone else look good. Besides, they're only going to change your vision of it anyway. So no, I wouldn't write for any series or film unless I was also given the freedom to direct it, turn it completely on its head and make it more interesting. As regards remakes, I don't think I'd ever remake someone else's movie as they seldom turn out as good as the original, unless I were making a spoof or approaching the material from a totally different angle. With this in mind, I was quite impressed by the latest Star Trek offering in that they brought a fresh perspective to the franchise and also harked back to the colour, style and the sense of fun of the original series. That would be more my style of filmmaking.

Richard Thomas: Thanks again Tim, maybe we can do this again sometime. Where can our readers watch your films and maybe find any websites or blogs you might have?

Timucin Leflef: Most certainly. You can check out my site lightfilms.com and also see my short films at vimeo.com/lightfilms and youtube.com/lightfilms1 I've also started my own personal blog at www.timucin.com And of course you can add me on the alleged CIA data-mining site ... Facebook.

Interview with Bryce Zabel: Co-Author of A.D. After Disclosure

What if the secrecy and ridicule surrounding the UFO topic vanished overnight? That's the premise of the new book A.D. After Disclosure by creator of the Dark Skies TV series, Bryce Zabel, and author of UFOs and National Security State, volumes I and II, Richard Dolan. What follows is an interview with Bryce Zabel about their new book.

Richard Thomas: How did you first become interested in the UFO subject, I know you've been involved with sci-fi series like Dark Skies and Taken, did your interest result from your research for those shows and similar projects, or were you already interested?

Bryce Zabel: I think everybody — even skeptics — is at least casually interested in the topic of UFOs. If it's real, then it's the biggest story ever. If it's not, then what has caused so many people for so long to see things that aren't real? What's up with that? I remember as a kid reading The Interrupted Journey and Flying Saucers Serious Business but that was about it. I think I read them more as sci-fi than admitting in my mind they could be true. But in the 1980s I started to write about them dramatically — starting with a spec script called Progenitor that became the SyFy Channel's (was Sci-Fi) first original film, Official Denial. I wanted to write an authentic script and so I started reading: Missing Time, Communion, Clear Intent, Above Top Secret and I begin to realize this wasn't science fiction. Underneath all the hoaxes, the liars, the bullshit artists, there was still a core truth. Some of those objects flying around in our skies, objects that aren't supposed to exist, actually are real and, based on their performance characteristics, they are probably from somewhere that isn't here. I guess I started reading and just kept reading. And I've kept writing about it, too.

Richard Thomas: How did you first start working with UFO historian Richard Dolan?

Bryce Zabel: Among the two books I felt are the best of the best are Richard Dolan's first two installments in his trilogy, UFOs and the National Security State. In late 2009, I called Rich to reach out to him about optioning his books.

Richard Thomas: I'm sure the fact that you've written this book will have the conspiracy theorists talking. As someone who has worked in television on shows like Dark Skies and Taken, what do you think of the widespread belief among UFO researchers that such series are part of some kind of official Disclosure project?

Bryce Zabel: How do you know we weren't? Okay, nobody can see me smiling in a print interview so, no, we were not a part of that. However, there is no doubt that Dark Skies is all about Disclosure. John Loengard represents the "people have a right to know" wing and Frank Bach represents the "people can't handle the truth" wing. This is all laid out in a lot of detail in the new extras on the DVD set and I urge fans to give a listen. Plus, there are lots of easter eggs in there that also shed some light on this.

Richard Thomas: There have been many books about the history of the alleged UFO cover-up, but this is the first UFO book to my knowledge to look into the future and ask what happens "After Disclosure," why do think the time is right for this book now and how soon do you expect UFO Disclosure?

Bryce Zabel: I've made a living in television where timing is everything. You need a great idea and you need to be first out with it. Rich Dolan and I simply knew that this book had to come out now. He set aside the third part of his trilogy and I set aside a feature script to get it done. The time is right because, as we all know, the center simply cannot hold on this secret forever.

Richard Thomas: In the book you refer to the UFO occupants as the "Others," instead of extraterrestrials, aliens etc. Why did you use this term and do you have any opinions about what these "others" are or where they might be from, outer space, another dimension, inner Earth etc?

Bryce Zabel: We call them "Others" because it is a more neutral term than extraterrestrial. All we know, for sure, is that they are not us, therefore they are Others. My own opinion? I'm thinking that there are several groups and that they may not all be from the same neighborhood of reality.

Richard Thomas: In the book a mass UFO sighting is the trigger for Disclosure. Given we've already had the Phoenix Lights and other more recent high profile sightings, what sort of incident do you envision would bring about Disclosure, and do you think another sighting is really necessary when we've had so many over the last 60 years?

Bryce Zabel: Well, Phoenix was mass, but it didn't yield the across the board recognition for a variety of reasons. And, yes, another sighting is necessary in that it needs to be one that provides a modern media tipping point. Photos, videos, thousands of witnesses, radar, media observation, etc., all triggering whistleblowers, deathbed confessions, etc.

Richard Thomas: There have been a lot of rumours about UFO information to be released on Wikileak recently, is this the kind of rumour you would expect on the eve of Disclosure, and what other signs might we expect?

Bryce Zabel: Wikileaks is not apt to be the sole inciting incident, no matter what they have. I'm not sure I am looking for "signs" as much as recognizing that conditions are moving in the direction of Disclosure. What has been impossible is now inevitable but, as I said previously, timing is everything.

Richard Thomas: I'm one of the ones that would be very sceptical about what the US or any other government would disclose about UFOs, but if Disclosure does come, what kind of Disclosure do you think it will be, in the book you right about three different types of Disclosure, full, partial and false?

Bryce Zabel: Nobody is going to disclose out of the goodness of their heart. It will be a symphony of events, or more of an avalanche. I believe that the first act of Disclosure will be partial, and there will be years after where the details are pried out one at a time.

Richard Thomas: Be careful what you ask for, you might just get it. Do you sympathise with the concerns of people who think UFO Disclosure might be abused to create a global police state at all, in other words, do you think nation-states can survive the news that humankind isn't alone in the Universe, and what other potential dangers do you think Disclosure might pose?

Bryce Zabel: I think we can survive Disclosure with our liberties intact. It will be destablizing, at least in the short term, but it may also lead to a new birth of freedom as people take charge of their lives. The jury is out.

Richard Thomas: What do you think the positives could be?

Bryce Zabel: The single powerful positive is as simple as can be. Whatever the truth is about our lives and realities, good or bad, it should be ours to deal with as best we can, and it is not up to elites to make that judgment for us. Truth is positive. However, whether the overall experience will be positive, depends on how it is handled and, even more importantly, by who these Others are and what their agenda really is.

Richard Thomas: Thanks for answering my questions Bryce. Where can readers find the book, and have you got a website or something else you'd like to plug?

Bryce Zabel: Our book can be found at Keyhole Publishing if you want it autographed and it comes with a free copy of the "Need-to-Know" song I produced with Cherish Alexander last year. A lot of people will get it from Amazon (UK and US) as a hardcover, and it's available as a Kindle and iBook. Alternatively you can visit www.afterdisclosure.com.

Interview with Christopher Knowles: Author of Our Gods Wear Spandex

Are The Lone Gunmen pilot and the Doctor Who serial "The Pyramids of Mars" examples of "Precog fiction"? Did the writers of Ridley Scott's Blade Runner incorporate "Illuminati symbolism" into that film? Is there a secret government program to gradually acclimatise the public to the reality of extraterrestrial life? What follows is an exclusive interview with the author of The Secret Sun blog Christopher Knowles about all this and more.

Richard Thomas: Thanks for agreeing to this interview Christopher, I know my own interest in the paranormal, UFOs and conspiracy theories etc. was largely an offshoot of my interest in sci-fi, was your own interest in comic books the spark for your interest in Fortean type subjects?

Christopher Knowles: I don't know if one follows the other. I'm a child of the 70s and weirdness was mainstream entertainment, certainly in the first half of the decade. I remember UFO and paranormal stuff being everywhere, and certainly stuff like Chariots of the Gods was very popular. Comics definitely picked up on all of that, particularly a lot of the occult and cosmic themes that a lot of the hippies who entered the business brought with them from the fanzines and undergrounds.

Richard Thomas: Do have any thoughts on why so many people in the paranormal and conspiracy fields seem to start out with an interest in sci-fi, comics etc first? Is it just that the two parallel somewhat, the only difference being one is presented as fiction and the other as reality? Or, is it something more like the kind of people who enjoy sci-fi tend to be the kind of people who also enjoy to ask questions and speculate about the world around them?

Christopher Knowles: Do they? In my experience, most sci-fi and comics fans look down on paranormal and conspiracy stuff, since a lot of your arch-skeptic types like Issac Asimov and Harlan Ellison were so aggressive in their attempts to denigrate and ridicule anything they decided was "irrational," quote-unquote. You see a lot of sci-fi fans who fetishize conventional government/corporate science, even though none of them really understand it. On the flipside of that, you have a lot of the conspiracy types who think sci-fi is all government brainwashing. But again, I'm a child of the 70s when things weren't so polarized and people were a bit more curious and open-minded, which was a byproduct of the Sixties counterculture.

Richard Thomas: How did your blog first come about and is their any reason in particular you chose the name "The Secret Sun," I thought it might be a comic book reference or something like that perhaps?

Christopher Knowles: The blog came about because I was promoting my book Our Gods Wear Spandex and wanted to field test some ideas I'd developed in a manuscript on sci-fi movies. The name itself comes from a recurring dream of mine in which the sun comes out in the middle of the night, but only certain people know about it.

Richard Thomas: I know like me you're a Doctor Who fan, do you have a particular favourite story and/or writer, and why do you think the writers seemed to borrow so heavily from the paranormal genre, for instance most notably in serials like "The Abominable Snowmen" and "The Daemons", and in the new series there was even a reference to the Roswell crash and another one to the bees disappearing?

Christopher Knowles: I watched Doctor Who in the 70s in the Tom Baker days, but kind of lost touch with it for a very long time. Then my wife and I watched the William Hartnell pilot at a convention and got hooked all over again. We love those early Hartnell serials, but we're both really big fans of the new series. I could never get into the Eccleston or Tennant stuff.

As to your second question, I think writers will borrow from anything since story ideas are hard to come by, especially with a long-running series like that. But here's the deal — most sci-fi has nothing to do with science. It's really about magic, so any kind of paranormal or occult theme is going to fit right in. Radioactive spider bites and warp drives are as magical as anything you read in a Harry Potter book.

Richard Thomas: A poster on the Fortean Times forum actually pointed out to me that the 1975 Doctor Who serial "The Pyramids of Mars" pre-dated the famous 1976 Viking 1 photos. Of course, there's also the pilot episode of The X-Files spin-off series The Lone Gunmen broadcast in 2000, which seemingly predicted the events of 9/11. Do you think this kind of thing is just coincidental or might there be something more to it than that perhaps? Some kind of remote viewing maybe?

Christopher Knowles: Oh yeah, I cover a lot of examples of precog fiction on The Secret Sun, including both of those examples you cite there. The mind is magic, and the creative mind all the more so. I do believe that the same part of the brain that pulls these kinds of stories out of the ether has something to do with remote viewing. It's about entering into a state of consciousness in which time and space are relative in the extreme.

Richard Thomas: What are your thoughts on Bruce Rux's theory as outlined in his book Hollywood vs. The Aliens: The Motion Picture Industry's Participation in UFO Disinformation that the US Government are using sci-fi TV shows and films to gradually acclimatise the public to the existence of extraterrestrial life?

Christopher Knowles: I do think there are elements within the government involved in doing so, but by no means the government as a whole. There are probably a lot more people within the government who want the issue to go away entirely. But it's hard to argue that there isn't some program going out there, seeing that articles on alien contact are running in The Guardian, of all places. A lot of this might have to do with the rise of countries like China and India, who don't see the issue in the same light that the conservative and religious elements within the US do.

Richard Thomas: You're also a fan of Nigel Kneale's third Quatermass story, "Quatermass and the Pit," what do you think it is that makes Quatermass and the Pit stand out from The Quatermass Experiment and Quatermass II, and why do you think so many sci-fi and UFO authors have borrowed from Kneale's third Quatermass script?

Christopher Knowles: It's a classic initiation narrative, at least the version that most people are familiar with. You have an underground cavern where you go to discover who you really are and it changes everything. You find out that you're the descendant of heavenly beings who came to earth and created men in their own image. You have Quatermass as the hierophant and Barbara as the oracle and Roney as the self-sacrificing savior. You have mystical visions, you have the authorities-slash-archons who seek to prevent the alien gnosis from spreading and then to top it all off, you have an apocalypse. It's classic stuff, straight out of the Mystery cults of Alexandria.

Richard Thomas: Nothing to do with UFOs per se but have you ever noticed the abundance of "Illuminati Symbolism" in Blade Runner and what, if anything, do you think it could mean? I know Philip K. Dick had an interest in paranormal type subjects, did he have much input into the film? (You can read my column here.)

Christopher Knowles: Well, we know that Dick was all over anything weird or mystical, but I don't think he had much involvement in the movie itself. Blade Runner kind of presents us with this kind of technocratic dystopia that some of these elite cult types would see as the paradise of their apotheosis. The cognitive elite in their penthouses and the poor, teeming masses huddled in the streets and the middle class a distant memory. The constant rain is kind of like the piss of the new gods in that regard. Maybe Scott incorporated some of those symbols as part of the overall social critique of this world that runs throughout the film. Maybe it was the screenwriter David Peoples, who also did similar films like Twelve Monkeys and Soldier.

Richard Thomas: Thanks for answering my questions Christopher. How can readers purchase your books and get in touch with you?
Christopher Knowles: The best way to get the books is on Amazon (UK and US). You can find my blog at www.secretsun.blogspot.com.

Sci-Fi Worlds Interview with Nick Pope

I love the BBC TV seris Doctor Who, so when I had a chance to interview Nick Pope, about his UFO work for the MoD, I was delighted to discover that he shared my love for this epic series and sci-fi in general. The icing on the cake, though, was when the two-time sci-fi author quickly agreed to do an interview where we get his thoughts on Doctor Who and touch on some other classics.

So what does a real life Brigadier Lethbridge-Stewart (though I'm not sure about Nick's rank) have to say on the Whoniverse and other sci-fi worlds?

Richard Thomas: First things first. Thanks for agreeing to do this so soon after my last interview with you. In that interview we centred on your UFO work for the MoD, so here it will be interesting to do a sci-fi focused interview. As a successful sci-fi author yourself I'm sure you will be able to answer my questions and no doubt intrigue our readers too.

You've written two excellent sci-fi novels, Operation Thunder Child and Operation Lightning Strike. In our Room 101 interview you said: "As a successful sci-fi author myself I've been greatly influenced by Doctor Who." Which stories in particular do you think have influenced your sci-fi work the most?
Nick Pope: Although my two sci-fi novels are – on the face of it – about alien invasion, I wanted to get away from a one-dimensional good versus evil conflict. I wanted to blur the lines and make people think about the moral issues. While it's difficult to nail down particular Doctor Who stories as an influence, a central theme of

morality run through the show as a whole. I guess the idea of the military being in the frontline is common to my novels and to any of the stories featuring UNIT.

Richard Thomas: In our other interview you also said that: "I'll always look back on Genesis of the Daleks as the all-time classic story. I'd love to see this remade or revisited in some way." I'm a big Genesis fan myself, why do you think so many fans continually pick this as their all-time favourite Doctor Who story?

Nick Pope: A number of reasons. Tom Baker was one of the greatest Doctors and the three way dynamic between the Doctor, Sarah-Jane and Harry worked very well. The Daleks have always been popular villains, so the story was bound to appeal. But Genesis was more than just another Dalek story – it was the story of the creation of the Daleks and the central question of whether the Daleks could be instilled with a sense of morality, or destroyed, made this a 'high stakes' story. Other highlights included the introduction of Davros and the Doctor's moralizing over his right to destroy the Daleks. Finally, I think people enjoyed the parallels with the Nazis: a brutal, militaristic society in a total war. Genetic experiments. Genocide. The uniforms and the salutes. All this and more was present, with Davros as Hitler and Nyder as his Himmler.

Richard Thomas: Season four of the new series saw the return of the Daleks and their evil genius creator Davros. Why do you think they continue to be so popular with younger audiences?

Nick Pope: With CGI and a bigger budget, we can have more sophisticated-looking Daleks and more of them. And now we have the fix to the 'they can't get up the stairs' issue. But again, I think the popularity reflects the fact that they are the ultimate Doctor Who villains: aggesive, ruthless, persistant and without any pity.

Richard Thomas: I think the first four Doctors will always be iconic. Whose your favourite Doctor and why?

Nick Pope: People often ask this and ask the same question about James Bond. Popular wisdom is that the answer is usually "the first one you saw". I started watching when it was Jon Pertwee, but eventually I came to prefer Tom Baker, who until recently was my favourite. But Doctor Who is now so polished that Christopher

Eccleston took over the top slot … until David Tennant joined. David, to me, is the best Doctor. I just think his acting is brilliant. He perfectly portrays the sadness, the loneliness and the detachment that are so central to the Doctor's character, but also the strength and sense of purpose. He brilliantly shows the audience the quiet "fury of the Time Lord".

Richard Thomas: Personally my favourite Doctor Who adversary has always been the Cybermen. The Moonbase, Tomb of the Cybermen and The Invasion are easily some of the best black and white stories, which is loudly echoed in the new series. With the Cybermen returning again what do you think it is about them that still scares children so much? Why do you think the Cybermen have survived in the age of CGI special effects?
Nick Pope: I think there are parallels with the Daleks. People like the continuity of villains that return again and again. It gives the writers a chance to develop themes that couldn't really be included in a one-off story, such as the wider evolution of a race. But the idea that they were once humanoid, but transformed themselves into these cyborgs is scary. It's a case of "they're like us … but not like us". Something green with tentacles is obviously alien, but maybe the Cybermen are a little 'too close to home'.

Richard Thomas: After Genesis of the Daleks, The Daemons is often said to be the best of the classic Doctor Who adventures. The way this and other classic stories like The Pyramids of Mars tied Erich von Däniken's theories into Doctor Who makes for an interesting mix of mythologies. What do you think of this?
Nick Pope: I think it's very clever. It was tapping into the popularity of such ancient mystery books in the Seventies, largely started by von Daniken. The Nazca lines get a mention in Death to the Daleks, as I recall. And we can't have mention of The Daemons without quoting the Brigadier's classic "Jenkins, chap with the wings there, five rounds rapid" line.

Richard Thomas: Curiously, Doctor Who and the Silurians came out in 1970 the same year as Ivan T. Sanderson's Invisible Residents: The Reality of Underwater UFOs was first published. Do you think it might just be possible that another intelligent species like the Silurians or Sea Devils could have evolved right here on Earth? (ala the cryptoterrestrial hypothesis.)

Nick Pope: Well, I reference the cryptoterrestrial hypothesis a fair bit in my first sci-fi novel, Operation Thunder Child. There are plenty of USO (Unidentified Submerged Object) reports and many UFO sightings where an object is seen over water, so who knows? I'm not hugely attracted to the cryptoterrestrial hypothesis, but I certainly can't rule it out. And as the saying goes, we arguably know less about the deep ocean than we do about the Moon or Mars.

Richard Thomas: Doctor Who and the Silurians ends tragically with the Brigadier blowing up the Silurian base. As someone who used to work for them, hypothetically how do you think the MoD would deal with a species like the Silurians or Sea Devils in the real world?

Nick Pope: Obviously I can't discuss specific details of Rules of Engagement, but in general terms I think I can say that if attacked, we would respond with proportionate force. However, in any contact with an extraterrestrial (or cryptoterrestrial) civilisation the key strategic objective would be to open lines of communication and facilitate peaceful contact. Secondary objectives would include information exchange, with a particular emphasis on science and technology.

Richard Thomas: In the following Jon Pertwee story, The Ambassadors of Death, Great Britain not only has a manned space program but also already sent men to Mars. As someone with an interest in space how far away do you think this was from reality at the time?

Nick Pope: This story was broadcast fairly shortly after the Apollo 11 moon landing, so there was immense public fascination in anything to do with space, coupled with a feeling that we'd all be holidaying on the moon by the end of the century. Those within government, however, would have been well aware that a manned space programme was quite beyond the UK at the time, both in terms of technical capability and, critically, finance. We still spend far too little on space, given the huge benefits to be reaped in terms of resources and knowledge.

Richard Thomas: Jon Pertwee's best enemy was easily the Master.

CHAPTER 5

What did you think of Derek Jacobi's and John Simm's portrayals of the character in season three of the new series?

Nick Pope: Both are brilliant actors and both were excellent in different but complementary roles that brought out that mixture of charisma and menace that defines the character of the Master. The scene where John Simms dances to the Scissor Sisters song "I Can't Decide" was outstanding.

Richard Thomas: I think Robert Holmes (who wrote the first Master story Terror of the Autons, as well as Pyramids of Mars and many other classics) will always be thought of as the best of all the Doctor Who writers but its starting to look like Steven Moffat might well give him a run for his money. I'm very much looking forward to his time as lead writer and executive producer beginning in 2010. What do you think?

Nick Pope: Russell T Davies will be a hard act to follow, but Steven Moffat can do it. The Empty Child/The Doctor Dances, The Girl in the Fireplace and Blink were some of the best stories since the relaunch of Doctor Who, as was Silence in the Library/Forest of the Dead, so this all bodes well for the future. There's a darkness and a poignancy about his stories that I like (e.g. the "she's ghosting" scene from Silence in the Library) and another thing that appeals is that he's a writer who deals really thoughtfully with the philosophy of time travel.

Richard Thomas: Stories like Spearhead from Space, Ark in Space and The Lazarus Experiment seem to have been heavily influenced by Nigel Kneale's Quatermass serials. Interestingly, David Tennant also appeared in the BBC's 2005 remake of The Quatermass Experiment just before he became the new Doctor. What do you think of this mix? Why do you think Nigel Kneale's fiction continues to inspire writers even today?

Nick Pope: I agree that some of the Doctor Who stories have been influenced by Quatermass, probably because some of the Doctor Who writers watched Quatermass when they were younger. Quatermass and his British Rocket Group even get namechecked in a couple of Doctor Who stories. There are clear parallels between the two shows and in particular the idea of a clever, moral but quirky character facing down all manner of alien threats, despite the odds being stacked against him. Sci-fi is arguably dominated by big budget Hollywood movies, so Kneale's work (like Doctor Who) appeals to us because there's something very British about it.

Richard Thomas: I grew up in the 1990s when Doctor Who was sadly trapped in the void known as UK Gold. However, there was another show on the BBC that sent me running to "hide behind the sofa." That, of course, was The X-files. What did you think of the way the series incorporated the UFO mythology into its own storylines? For instance, Roswell, Area 51, abductions, MJ-12 and even the Face on Mars are all worked into the series.

Nick Pope: Skeptics often say UFO witnesses and abductees may be influenced by sci-fi, but if anything, the reverse is true. The X-Files is the classic example and the writers clearly did their research and borrowed freely from the UFO/abduction literature. I was hired by 20th Century Fox to do some of the PR for the new X-Files movie, I Want to Believe. As well as giving a number of media interviews I was commissioned to write material on real life mysteries and conspiracy theories, which was then used in various newspaper and magazine features that came out in the run up to the movie's release. I met David Duchovny and Chris Carter at the UK premiere and Chris already knew about my government work on UFOs. The X-Files is a brilliant creation and when they 'do' UFOs, they do it really well.

Richard Thomas: Do you foresee any new esoteric mysteries becoming a part of the sci-fi canon, much like abductions and Face on Mars have?

Nick Pope: Well, the disappearing bees got a mention in Doctor Who recently and all sci-fi writers will keep an eye out for real life mysteries. I think the big one to watch is 2012 and the associated mysteries and theories that surround the Mayan calendar. The sci-fi movie 2012 will be released next year and I'm sure the whole 2012 issue will crop up in other sci-fi books, movies and TV series.

Richard Thomas: Would you like to write more sci-fi yourself? Perhaps your sci-fi books might make interesting audio books. Any plans or thoughts?

Nick Pope: I'd love to write more sci-fi and at some stage, a third novel to follow the previous two. But I'm too busy with TV and promotional work at present to write another book. Operation Thunder Child was previously optioned by Carnival Films and a screenplay was written, but the project stalled. Operation Thunder Child and Operation Lightning Strike are currently being looked at by a major Hollywood studio, with a view to making them into a blockbuster sci-fi movie.

Richard Thomas: What do you think of Steven Moffat era of the Dr Who sci-fi programme so far and how do you think it compares with the RTD era?
Nick Pope: Steven Moffat is building on RTD's excellent work, while not being afraid to take some big decisions of his own (e.g. resting the Daleks) and move the show forward in his own vision. The key to this has been the development of River Song – a character he created – who is fast becoming one of the best-loved characters in the history of Doctor Who.

Richard Thomas: What have you thought about Matt Smith's portrayal of the Doctor? Where do you think he ranks with the other Doctors?
Nick Pope: David Tennant was always going to be an extremely hard act to follow, but I think Matt Smith is excellent. His Doctor is among the best portrayals yet. He captures the essence of the Doctor very well: part eccentric, part misfit, part warrior, part adventurer – someone with companions, who is always alone; someone moral, but responsible for so many deaths. Someone with secrets, some of which will probably never be revealed. The only difficulty with a good portrayal of such an iconic character is that the actor will be snapped up for even bigger roles, and/or won't want to stay long, to avoid being typecast.

Richard Thomas: Last year we saw the return of the Silurians in two-parter The Hungry Earth / Cold Blood. They were changed quite a lot, do you think they were still the same "Earth Reptiles" we first met in 1970?
Nick Pope: I think they were different, but I think it worked. In a sense, this is exactly what happened with the Cybermen; the appearance had changed – as had the back-story – but while purists

may have taken offence, most people were either unaware of the change (in the case of younger audiences unfamiliar with the original) or weren't bothered by it. It's OK to be nostalgic, but one shouldn't be wedded to the past. Doctor Who is often at its best when reinventing itself.

Richard Thomas: Perhaps the most controversial redesign has to be that of the Daleks. Do you think that after nearly 50 years it was about time for a change or do you think they should be changed back?

Nick Pope: Following on from the previous answer, I'm not resistant to change, and in many cases it's a good thing, but in this instance, I don't think it works. The new multi-coloured Daleks just don't look as threatening as when they're grey or black. To my mind, these 'Habitat Daleks' lack menace and perhaps it's no coincidence that Steven Moffat has decided to rest the Daleks for a while. The official reason is that he thinks they've been over-used and that people won't be scared of them if they see them defeated time after time. Maybe so (though the answer to that is to give them some victories), but one wonders whether the reaction to the redesign was a factor as well.

Richard Thomas: If you were ever approached by either the BBC or Big Finish to write a Doctor Who story what do you think you would suggest?

Nick Pope: Having had two sci-fi novels published and being currently involved in creating and developing a series for the BBC, I'd jump at the chance to write a Doctor Who story, or to have some creative input in the show. I don't want to be too specific in my answer here, as it's something I've thought about seriously, so I'm not going to give much away. Suffice to say, I'd push a few boundaries, break a few taboos, push the darker themes and up the fear factor as much as I could, pre-watershed.

The Esoteric Worlds of Doctor Who

Dr Who is the longest running science fiction television series in the world and, in my opinion, also the best. For those people that do not own a television set and haven't had the time to read the novelisations, Doctor Who is about the adventures of a mysterious alien known simply as "the Doctor." With his companions, the Doctor explores time and space in his travel machine the TARDIS (Time And Relative Dimension In Space), encountering danger, solving problems and righting wrongs wherever he goes.

I first became a fan of Doctor Who when my father bought me a video of Genesis of the Daleks, written by Terry Nation. It tells the story of how the Doctor's greatest enemies, the Daleks, were created millennia ago on the war devastated planet Skaro by the evil genius Davros. To this day, it is my favourite Doctor Who story and, as a child, it triggered my first major interest in science fiction and the possibility of intelligent life elsewhere in the Cosmos.

If I had to narrow it down to one single thing that got me interested in esoteric subjects in the first place, it would have to be watching repeats of Doctor Who while I was growing up. The writers of the series would often take inspiration from the realms of the esoteric and, in its original 26 season run, everything from bug eyed aliens to the lost city of Atlantis and the Loch Ness Monster would make an appearance. There are far too many examples of how esoteric subjects were tied into Doctor Who to write about them all, so here are just some of my favourites.

Death to the Daleks, again by Terry Nation, is an excellent example of how the esoteric was tied into Doctor Who. In this story, the Doctor is drawn to the planet Exxilon, where he must outwit the native savage Exxilons and a crew of stranded Daleks in order to survive.

It looks like the description of the Greys, short with grey skin and big black eyes, might have played a big part in the design of the Exxilons costumes. This is interesting because the story was first broadcast back in 1974, three years before that image of what an alien should look like was made so popular by the release of Steven Spielberg's Close Encounters of the Third Kind in 1977.

Also the writers seem to have taken a lot of inspiration from Erich von Däniken's Chariots of the Gods and the ancient astronaut theory. At one point in Death to the Daleks, the Doctor goes as far as stating that he believes that the ancient Exxilons, who we learn were far more advanced, travelled to Earth and taught the Peruvian Incas how to build their great temples. In an earlier story, The Dæmons, the Doctor tells us that another advanced race of aliens, the Dæmons from the planet Dæmos, came to Earth 100,000 years ago in order to help mankind's development as part of some scientific experiment.

As well as the ancient astronaut theory, Mars anomalies also seem to have inspired the writers of Doctor Who. One story, written by Robert Holmes, is even called Pyramids of Mars. In this story, it is revealed that the ancient Egyptian Gods were inspired by a race of powerful aliens called the Osirans, the last of whom, Sutekh the Destroyer, is imprisoned in the Great Pyramid of Mars.

The lost city of Atlantis is another major esoteric subject that is tied into a number of Doctor Who stories. In The Dæmons, after learning about the many wars and atrocities mankind has committed against their own people, Azal, last of the Dæmons, warns the Doctor that: "My race destroys its failures. Remember Atlantis."

In two other stories, the Doctor even visits the lost city itself. In The Time Monster, the Doctor travels back in time before Atlantis was struck by disaster and we learn that Atlantis was part of the Minoan civilisation (which is a real life theory still advocated by some today). This is another sign that the writers were very much inspired by the esoteric and the ideas circling it. In an earlier story, The Underwater Menace, the Doctor discovered that some Atlanteans had survived the sinking of Atlantis and had continued to live beneath the waves in isolation from the rest of humanity into modern times (perhaps, in a small way, echoing some of the ideas that would evolve into Mac Tonnies' cryptoterrestrial hypothesis).

However, by far the best two examples of Doctor Who stories that incorporate elements of what would become the cryptoterrestrial hypothesis are Doctor Who and the Silurians and its sequel The Sea Devils, both by Malcolm Hulke. Both stories centre on an ancient super intelligent race of reptiles that evolved on and dominated the Earth when man was nothing more than a primitive ape. After resting in hibernation deep underground and beneath the sea for millions of years, they awake only to discover that the apes have evolved into man and now rule their world. Very interestingly, Doctor Who and the Silurians was first broadcast in 1970 the same year Ivan T. Sanderson's Invisible Residents: The Reality of Underwater UFOs was first published. This book hypothesised that perhaps an advanced aquatic non-human civilisation may have evolved right here on the Earth, much in the same way as the Silurians and Sea Devils of Doctor Who did.

Ivan T. Sanderson was also well known for his books on cryptozoology (a word Sanderson himself coined in the early 1940s), in particular, books on Lake Monsters, Sea Serpents, Mokèlé-mbèmbé, Yeti, and Sasquatch. All of these creatures, in some form or other, would make an appearance in Doctor Who. For instance, in Terror of the Zygons, the Doctor encountered the Zygon Skarasen at Loch Ness, Scotland, the creature was clearly the Loch Ness Monster. In Invasion of the Dinosaurs, we saw a number of prehistoric beasts in modern London, among them a Brontosaurus, perhaps an ancestor of Mokèlé-mbèmbé. Finally in The Abominable Snowmen and its sequel The Web of Fear, both written by the team of Mervyn Haisman and Henry Lincoln (one of the co-authors of the controversial 1982 bestseller The Holy Blood and the Holy Grail), the Doctor is threatened by a small army of alien robots disguised as Yeti.

So clearly the writers of Doctor Who were inspired by and tied a lot of esoteric type subjects into the stories. So what?

Well, one of the big question issues Tim Binnall keeps raising in BoA: Audio is the lack of young people in Ufology and some other esoteric subjects. Perhaps the best way to solve this problem is to get children interested in science fiction first. Let them learn about these esoteric mysterious through fiction, then, as they grow up, they will come looking for the truth behind the fiction. The first documentaries about UFOs and the Yeti that I probably watched were episodes of Arthur C. Clarke's Mysterious World and the reason I watched them was because I had heard about UFOs and the Yeti on Doctor Who!

If this theory is correct then Ufology and other esoteric subjects have nothing to fear, the new series of Doctor Who is going strong with millions of very young fans. With that growing fanbase, we can be hopeful that in a few years they, too, will discover our esoteric world.

Welsh UFOs – The Real Torchwood

For those left wondering about the title, Torchwood is a Doctor Who spin-off series about a covert group who research and combat alien threats in Wales. Here I want to reflect on some key UFO cases in the principality, including the recent UFO sightings here and in neighbouring England. Interestingly, I had a possible UFO sighting in Wales, which I mention earlier in this book.

Looking at UFO cases in Wales, we'll begin with what has been called the "Welsh Roswell," the Berwyn Mountain UFO incident of 1974. The Berwyn range is an isolated and sparsely-populated area of moorland located in the north-east of Wales. Basically, on the 23rd of

January 1974 it is alleged that a UFO crashed there and that it, complete with dead alien bodies, were secretly recovered by the British military soon thereafter. It was the typical UFO crash scenario or, to put it another way, the Roswell incident all over again, in all but name, date and place.

However, what makes the Berwyn crash particularly interesting, and all the more real, is the immediate reaction of the local residents. To begin with, no one was talking of UFOs and aliens, far from it. People thought that a plane had crashed on the mountain and were chiefly concerned about trying to save the lives of any survivors. The police were called in and set up a search team that was later even joined by an RAF Mountain Rescue Team. Apparently, after a long search, nothing was found. But with such a legitimate reaction, it would seem likely that something equally real must have crashed.

Whatever this was, though, we still don't know. Astronomers believed that it might have been a meteorite landing, but no impact crater was ever found. Adding to the intrigue, in May 2008 the British MOD released a number of its classified UFO files to the public. There had been a lot of speculation that we might, at last, get to the bottom of the Berwyn mystery. But, strangely, no files relating to the Berwyn event were even released. If the whole case can be, as the sceptics suggest, explained away by natural phenomena (the combined misinterpretation of a meteor shower and an earthquake) perhaps we should ask why nothing about the case has been released in the MOD UFO files.

Maybe something was found on the Berwyn Mountains after all. Of course this wouldn't have to be alien, it could have been some kind of black aircraft or other secret weapon. The remote area would make for an ideal location for Britain or perhaps even its primary ally, the US, to test their secret aircraft.

The West Wales flap of 1977 is another major part of Welsh UFO history. Focused upon a strip of rugged coastline within the Pembroke National Park, the series of strange encounters made national headlines at the time, beginning with an exceptionally strange sighting near Broad Haven Primary School on the 4th of February.

During their lunch break that day, as many as 15 schoolchildren said they saw a silver cigar-shaped UFO land in the fields behind the school. Fantastically, some of the nine to 11 year olds even went as far as to claim that they saw a silver man with pointed ears come out of the craft. Of course, people put this down to simple make believe but the children were so adamant they saw something real that they handed in a petition to the police. Further, their head teacher later asked them to draw the UFO and was amazed at how alike their pictures turned out.

After this, UFOs soon became the talk of the nation and by May of that year, as well as odd lights, people were also reporting strange sightings of mysterious humanoid figures wearing Nasa-like spacesuits, prowling the remote Welsh countryside late at night. Stranger still, though, is the fortilla of Fortean phenomena that allegedly engulfed the Coombs family at Ripperston Farm.

The family reported repeated close encounters with strange craft and their occupants. For instance, on one occasion they were allegedly pursued along a country lane by a fiery object shaped like a rugby ball. Perhaps their scariest alleged encounter, though, was with a 7ft figure in a spacesuit, who suddenly appeared at their sitting room window late one night. This may well have been the work of a hoaxer. But whatever it was, the family's terror was certainly very real. Many years later, in 1996, the police officer that dealt with the incident went as far as saying that: "that was the most frightened family I have ever been to see."

Interestingly, the Coombs family also made the weird claim that a herd of cows were somehow transported from a locked field into to an adjacent farmyard. If this is in any way true, perhaps it could in somehow be related to the famous cattle mutilation phenomenon? Exactly how we could only guess at, however, some suspect that the US military may be behind many of the cattle mutilations in the American Southwest. Could they or the British military be behind the strange phenomena in Wales? It might explain the NASA-esque spacesuits.

Then there are the odd happenings at Ripperston Farm, best documented in Peter Paget's 1979 book The Welsh Triangle. Including most of the southeast corner of St Bride's Bay, along with the towns of Milford Haven and Haverfordwest, Paget claimed that aliens had indeed established an underground base in this Welsh equivalent to the Bermuda Triangle. It is certainly true that the area does seem to have been the focus of the 1977 wave. However, perhaps the range of military bases that were nearby (including a top secret rocket testing station) might offer a more down to earth explanation for the UFO activity.

More recently we've been having something of a new UFO flap in Wales and England. First, on the 8 June 2008, a South Wales Police helicopter was apparently forced to swerve sharply to avoid being hit by what they termed an "unusual aircraft" near RAF St Athan, a military base outside Cardiff. Then, only a matter of weeks later, we learned that a soldier (with three others) had in fact seen several "craft" spinning in the skies above his military barracks near Market Drayton, Shropshire. What more, the sighting took place only two hours before the helicopter incident. Ultra careful UFO reasearcher Nick Pope (who ran the British Government's UFO project at the MOD for three years) was so impressed by the sighting that he went as far as saying: "Now there has to be an official inquiry ... the military tend to make good witnesses ... it's not something an ordinary aircraft or satellite would do."

Since then, UFO sceptics have tried to debunk the sightings as nothing more than wedding party sky lanterns. Which, if true, means the British public should be very concerned that both their police and military don't know the difference between nuts and bolts craft and sky lanterns. True, a strong case can be made for the lantern explanation. In both cases, lanterns were realised in the right place at the right time. But, use a bit of common sense, would a sky lantern really move so fast that an experienced police helicopter crew could not capture any images before it vanished out of sight?

Whatever the truth about these key Welsh cases is, perhaps we'll never know. Although I strongly suspect that there is probably some kind of military explanation for many of them, for all I know there could be an 'alien' base somewhere in Wales. It could be argued that dotingly believing in what might be called the "lantern hypothesis" is probably equally as bad a dotingly believing in the Extraterrestrial hypothesis. However we can be sure of one thing, as we've seen the recent UFO activity in Wales is by no means new and no doubt there will be more to come in the future.

Ghosts, Aliens, Yeti And The Late Great Nigel Kneale

Who was Nigel Kneale? This is the question some readers are probably asking themselves right now, which is a real shame, because without the work of this great television pioneer, there probably would have never been a Doctor Who or X-Files and science fiction, on television at least, would in all likelihood still only be Saturday morning nonsense for little children.

Born on the Isle of Man, Nigel Kneale was a writer active in television, film, radio drama and prose fiction. He wrote professionally for over fifty years and was, in many ways, the father of serious science fiction drama on television. Kneale's most famous creation being the legendary Professor Bernard Quatermass, a heroic rocket scientist who saved humanity from a range of very different alien menaces in a trilogy of stories written by the Manx writer in the 1950s.

The trilogy began with The Quatermass Experiment, in which the first-ever manned space rocket returns to Earth with two of the three astronauts on board missing and the third possessed by some kind of hostile alien organism. In time, this organism consumes and changes the last astronaut into something horrific: a creature that threatens to possess and consume all other life on Earth. However, Quatermass confronts the monster and, with a moving speech, reaches what is left of his friends humanity, persuading him to sacrifice himself to save the rest of mankind.

In the next story, Quatermass II, the professor is asked to examine strange meteorite showers falling in rural England. His investigations lead to him discovering a vast conspiracy involving alien infiltration at the highest levels of the British Government. Somehow these aliens, who have a group consciousness similar to the Borg in Star Trek, can control the minds of people exposed to an alien parasite concealed in their meteorite like projectiles. The aliens plan to colonise the Earth, but Quatermass manages to stop them by destroying their asteroid base in orbit, very sadly losing his close friend and colleague Dr. Pugh in the process.

Finally, in the best and last story of the 1950s trilogy, Quatermass and the Pit, Quatermass becomes involved in the discovery of a strange object near some ape men remains, millions of years old, at an archaeological dig in Knightsbridge, London. The odd object is first thought to be an unexploded World War II bomb, but then more ape men remains are found mysteriously inside the back of the object and later, more disturbingly, the decaying bodies of dead insect like creatures are found inside the front. The object turns out to be a nuclear powered spaceship, five million years old, the creatures: Martians and the ape men: their creations ... us ... the human race.

In the story we learn that when Mars was dying, the ancient

Martians had tried to create a colony on Earth by proxy. They altered mankind's early ancestors, giving them minds and abilities like their own, but with a body adapted to Earth. More worryingly, they also passed on to mankind their genocidal instincts to destroy anyone different from themselves. In effect, making us the Martians now. Fortunately the Martians died out before completing their plan and, as mankind bred and further evolved, most outgrew their darker Martian inheritance.

Unfortunately, somehow the spaceship reawakens the old Martian instincts, transforming more and more people into genocidal Martians on a race purge, destroying anyone unaffected by the ship's evil influence. However, Quatermass finds a way to stop the ethnic cleansing before the Martians turn the Earth into a second dead planet. He also tragically loses another friend in doing so.

In each of the three Quatermass stories Kneale managed to tap into the popular interests and, more importantly, anxieties of the time. In The Quatermass Experiment, he played on the mass interest in the early space race and the new threat of nuclear war. The UK conducted the earliest post war tests of captured Nazi V-2 rockets in Operation Backfire, less than six months after the war in Europe ended, and the development of a British launch system to carry a nuclear device started in 1950. So there was a real fear that one of these rockets could come falling out of the sky bringing with it destruction, as one does in The Quatermass Experiment. Then, in Quatermass II, before Invasion of the Body Snatchers, Kneale exploited the popular paranoia about the threat of communist infiltration and subversion of the West. Like nuclear war, this was a real fear at the time. For instance, in 1951, two members of British establishment, Burgess and Maclean, had made international headlines by very publicly defecting to the Soviet Union. And, finally, with the Notting Hill race riots of 1958 still very much fresh in peoples minds, Kneale wrote Quatermass and the Pit admittedly as a fable about race hate.

Kneale's Quatermass trilogy clearly had a huge impact that continues to be felt even today, influencing everyone from Chris Carter to Gene Roddenberry. The Quatermass Experiment (1953) was the very first science fiction production to be written especially for an adult television audience and cleared the way for the many others that followed it. Also, the three basic alien invasion storylines were first pioneered on television by Kneale in the Quatermass stories. In The Quatermass Experiment, we go to the aliens and bring them back, in Quatermass II the aliens come to us, and in Quatermass and the Pit we discover that the aliens were here all along.

But it would be a mistake to think that Nigel Kneale only wrote stories involving alien possession and invasion. An excellent example of this is The Abominable Snowman, a 1957 Hammer horror film based on Kneale's own BBC television play The Creature. Again tapping into popular interest at the time, the film follows the exploits of an English anthropologist with an American expedition as they search the Himalayas for the legendary Yeti, the ape man of Tibet. In the real world, speculation about the existence of an unidentified creature living in the Himalayas had been sparked off in November 1951, when Eric Shipton and Michael Ward of the Everest Reconnaissance Expedition found several large footprints as they traversed the Menlung Glacier, and, two years later, Edmund Hillary made a similar discovery during his historic conquest of Mount Everest.

In the film, Kneale turns perceptions on their head by suggesting that the so called Abominable Snowman is not so abominable at all and, perhaps, even a great deal better than mankind who turn out to be the real monsters. The central idea being that the Yeti are our collateral descendants from the apes and are patiently and peacefully waiting for mankind to destroy himself, either quickly through war or slowly through pollution, before descending from the mountains to inherit the Earth.

Another excellent example is The Stone Tape, a Christmas ghost story from 1972 and Kneale's last major original work for the BBC. Like Quatermass and the Pit before it (which suggested that poltergeist activity could be explained by the psychic abilities left to us by the Martians), The Stone Tape combined science fiction with the supernatural. The television play revolves around a group of scientists who move into a new research facility: an allegedly haunted Victorian mansion. Curious, they investigate the alleged ghost but soon determine that it is really just some kind of recording of a past event somehow stored by stone in one of the rooms (the stone tape of the title). Believing that this discovery may lead to the development of a whole new recording medium, which they were originally brought together to find in the first place, they throw all their knowledge and high tech equipment into trying to find a means of playing back the stone tape recording at will. However, their investigations only serve to unleash a far older and more malevolent force, with tragic consequences. Of course, The Stone Tape is where "the stone tape theory" familiar to many paranormal researchers today originates.

Kneale also wrote three excellent dystopian texts, a fourth Quatermass story The Quatermass Conclusion, a 1954 television adaptation of George Orwell's Nineteen Eighty Four for the BBC, and The Year of the Sex Olympics.

It is the last of these that proved to be the most prophetic. Broadcast in 1968 The Year of the Sex Olympics seemed to accurately predicted the creation of reality TV in the 1990s.

Set "sooner than you think" in the TV play society is divided between "low-drives" that receive no education and "hi-drives" who control the government and media. The low-drives are controlled by a constant broadcast of pornography that the hi-drives believe will pacify them. But after the accidental death of a protester during the Sex Olympics gets a massive audience response, the authorities create new TV programme, The Live Life Show. In the new show a family are moved to a remote Scottish island while the low-drive audience watches.

Hopefully, this goes some way to answering the question of who Nigel Kneale was. Of all the great science fiction writers to emerge from these islands since World War II, including the likes of Arthur C. Clarke, perhaps only Nigel Kneale comes anywhere close to matching H G. Wells in terms of lasting public impact and sheer brilliance. Both successfully tapped into the mass anxieties of their time and placed them at the centre of their stories, making science fiction accessible to the general public. In short, what Wells did for science fiction in print, Kneale did on television, clearing the way for intelligent science fiction drama on the small screen.

We Are the Martians Now!

Back in 1959, British scriptwriter Nigel Kneale turned H.G. Wells' classic 'Martian Invasion' novel The War of the Worlds on its head with the concluding instalment of his landmark Quatermass trilogy: the hugely influential Quatermass and the Pit.

Back then, all science fiction about Martians or similar alien invaders could be broken down into essentially two basic storylines: either we go to them or else they come to us. And in his previous two outings for Professor Quatermass (The Quatermass Experiment and Quatermass II), Kneale had already exhausted both these avenues. However in Quatermass and the Pit, Kneale smashed both these molds and crafted a new third alien invasion scenario: they were here all along!

A full decade before Erich von Däniken's Chariots of the Gods, it was really Kneale who was the first to introduce a mass audience to the concept of "ancient astronauts" that visited Earth in the remote past and might have played a significant hand in mankind's genetic and cultural evolution. The plot in Quatermass and the Pit, basically revolved around a five million year old plan to transform the Earth into a "colony by proxy" for a dying Mars.

In the tale, the Martians were facing a situation not at all that dissimilar to what many fear the Earth may be facing today: the imminent destruction of the Martian biosphere and the total extinction of all life on the planet. In Kneale's screenplay, the ancient inhabitants of Mars attempt to cheat this fate by using their advanced knowledge of genetics.

Realising their fragile insectoid bodies could never survive very long in Earth's dense atmosphere and gravity, the Martians instead choose to infuse their genes into the most advanced life forms on their neighboring world: a race of primitive Pliocene apes. The result was a new hybrid subspecies armed with all the advantages of Martian intelligence but perfectly adapted to the conditions on Earth. In other words "that we owe our human condition here (on Earth) to the intervention of insects."

Kneale's Quatermass stories were just that, stories. But few students of the unexplained could fail to see the parallels not only with von Däniken's "ancient astronauts" but the alien abduction literature too. Referring, of course, to the concept of small insect-eyed creatures experimenting with human DNA and cross human-alien hybridisation.

One of the most important factors that seems to separate good science fiction writers from the truly great, seems to be their almost prophetic knack to somehow accurately predict future events or developments. Perhaps the best example of this being Jules Verne's 1865 novel From the Earth to the Moon that accurately predicted an American expedition to the Moon more than a century before the

Apollo 11 landing. Another good example would be H.G. Wells' 1936 film Things to Come that much more disturbingly foresaw the blitz of London in World War II . And, of course, Arthur C. Clarke is often credited as being the inventor of the communications satellite.

Although less well known many would put Nigel Kneale in the same league as these sci-fi visionaries. So given this might there be more to the hypothesis posited by Professor Quatermass in The Pit than most people would dare consider?

In his first non-fiction book, After the Martian Apocalypse, the late Mac Tonnies theorised about the possibility that an ancient Martian civilisation might have been responsible for anomalies on the red planet, most notably the so-called "pyramids" and "face on Mars." Given certain similarities between these alleged "monuments" on Mars and those of Ancient Egypt and the Americas: could it be possible that a prehistoric Martian colonisation might have indeed taken place? Also, given the reported three million Americans who believe themselves to be victims of alien abduction, might this colonisation effort still be underway in someway?

Such a scenario – or any involving Martians for that matter – might sound crazy but it would at least go some way to explaining mankind's preoccupation with the pyramids and Mars. The ancient Pharaohs could have chosen any shape for their tombs but they choose a pyramid design, why? Might this fascination with the pyramid shape have been programmed into our DNA, a racial memory of Mars?

Further, the famous Martian rocks that got huge press back in 1996 because they might contain fossilised evidence of extraterrestrial life, has led to the increasing popularity among mainstream scientists that life might have originated elsewhere in the universe (perhaps Mars) and caught a ride via meteorite (or other means?) to Earth. So perhaps the Quatermass hypothesis isn't so outlandish after all.

Before he sadly passed away, Tonnies completed his second book, The Cryptoterrestrials, a book detailing his theories about the possibility that mankind might be sharing the planet with another indigenous race of humanoids. If he had lived, I had planned to ask Tonnies if he thought his Mars ideas and his cryptoterrestrial hypotheses might be compatible in some way, in other words, if Tonnies' cryptoterrestrials might indeed be a Martian proxy colony. Sadly I'll never get the chance now.

Ultimately, as with any paranormal thought experiment, we're left with more questions than answers. And it goes without saying that there is nowhere near the kind of proof that Professor Quatermass is confronted with, i.e. crashed Martian spaceships and dead alien bodies. Well not admitted to anyway. However, if the so-called "face on Mars" really is a face – instead of just a pile of rocks – then it appears to be a human face. Which would mean there would have to be a connection between ancient Mars and humankind. Maybe this is it.

In his recent appearance on BoA: Audio, Christopher Knowles speculated about the link between creativity and shamanism. Maybe in Quatermass and the Pit, Nigel Kneale managed to somehow cross this divide. Then again, maybe Kneale was just what he seemed to be: a damn good storyteller way ahead of his time with science fiction and speculation running through his vanes.

Either way, though, until mankind finally leaves the cradle of Earth orbit and takes their first tentative steps on the Martian surface (circa 2030), the Red Planet will continue to hold onto its secrets ... whatever they may be.

A Sci-Fi Worlds Interview with Richard Holland

Richard Holland is former editor of Paranormal Magazine. We begin by talking about the great BBC series Dr Who.

Richard Thomas: Growing up in the 1990s, I didn't really have my own Doctor (unless you count the Paul McGann TV movie in 1996) but if I had to pick a personal favourite I would have to pick Jon Pertwee's incarnation. Watching him Sunday mornings on UK Gold, I really believed he was a mega genius scientist from another world. Who was your Doctor growing up and which one would you say is your all-time favourite?

Richard Holland: For those of us who were lucky enough to grow up with Who on the air, it seems common that the first Doctor you remember is the one who remains your favourite. For me, then, it's Patrick Troughton, despite only having the very vaguest memories of watching him (I'd have been only 4 when his tenure ended). Nevertheless, reading all the Target books in the 70s reaffirmed my love for his character (and the few surviving stories I've seen on video since confirming it). I like Pertwee a lot but he was a much more archetypal hero, a show-off even, but Troughton's Doctor was so self-effacing, often pottering about in the background making things happen.

Small, fragile, yet possessing this enormous courage and unswerving sense of justice. He's a totally British hero: I cannot imagine a hero like him originating in any other country. And he was very funny and likeable, too, of course. Having said all that, the Philip Hinchliffe era Tom Baker runs a very close second. Alas, I think the character became a tosser from about '77 onwards.

Richard Thomas: Other than Genesis of the Daleks (everyone's favourite) do you have a particular favourite story?
Richard Holland: Well, that's an assumption. I admire Genesis but it's not my favourite. I prefer Seeds of Doom and Weng Chiang and Pyramids of Mars and Ark in Space (if we're talking about Tom Baker). Tomb of the Cybermen, The Web of Fear and Fury From The Deep would have to be included. Also, The Daemons, Terror of the Autons and Green Death. The opening episode of The Daleks remains one of the finest Who moments in TV history and The Daleks Invasion of Earth is classy as hell. And The Empty Child still has me gawping at its genius and effrontery. Sorry, I've lived and breathed Dr Who from birth: it's impossible to name an absolute favourite.

Richard Thomas: Robert Holmes' Terror of the Autons, The Ark in Space, Pyramids of Mars and The Caves of Androzani are just some of my favourites. Why do you think Holmes' stories are so popular with fans and do you think Steven Moffat (Silence in the Library/Forest of the Dead) might be the writer to finally give Holmes a run for his money?
Richard Holland: It's no surprise to find you've mentioned a couple of my own faves. There's no secret to Robert Holmes's and Steven Moffat's success and popularity: they're both bloody good writers, imaginative, able to tightly plot a story and capable of creating memorable, believable characters. They get the balance between horror/fear and humour just right. Moffat as the new Holmes? Yes, that seems fair.

Richard Thomas: As a Doctor Who fan and Paranormal researcher if you were ever asked to come up with an idea for a new

Who story and/or monster what would it be?

Richard Holland: I do have a few ideas bubbling away in my subconscious, including one based on Welsh fairylore, but nothing mind-blowing. If I had the chance, I'd ask permission to write a new Yeti yarn. I like the idea of some dotty old lady clairvoyant, trying to get in touch with 'the other side' and finding herself possessed by the Great Intelligence instead. The next thing you know, she's got glowing red eyes, the room has become full of a mysterious fog and all the Yetis stashed away at UNIT suddenly come to life...

Richard Thomas: My other favourite Doctor Who writer has to be Terry Nation, creator of the Daleks. How do you think he would have responded to the way the Daleks have been used in the new series?

I have one complaint myself and that's that the Daleks are now pretty much extinct. I miss the old series idea of a vast interstellar Dalek Empire that threatens all intelligent creation. You never used to know whether the TARDIS had materialised on one of the countless worlds the Daleks had conquered or not and that scared me a little when I was a younger viewer.

Richard Holland: Frankly, I don't think Terry Nation would care less what they did so long as he was getting the royalties. I do feel some of the new stories have pulled the Daleks' teeth somewhat, despite the reminders in the script about how invincible they supposedly are. That one in Manhattan was ludicrous but I loved the mad, religious maniac Emperor in the Eccleston season and the big send-off last season had a feel of the old Dalek Empire about it.

Richard Thomas: I'm also a big fan of Terry Nation's Blake's 7. Living during the 21st century Terror Wars, the series (about a group of freedom fighters battling an evil totalitarian government) probably resonates more now than ever. My favourite episodes have to be the first episode The Way Back where Blake rediscovers he is really a political dissident and is sentenced to life imprisonment on Cygnus Alpha; Trial where Blake's nemesis Travis is finally put on trial for the massacres of political groups; and the final episode Blake, of course, where everyone is finally hunted down and eliminated by the Federation.

Do you have any favourite moments or episodes of the series?

Richard Holland: I have mixed feelings about Blake's 7. I was a fan of the first two series or so and even contributed to an old Who/Blake fanzine called Frontier Worlds back in the day but watching them again more recently I found them rather uninspiring, even episodes I remembered fondly like Orac. There were some great characters, though, with Servalan and the original Travis actor, and Avon and Vila, making two great double-acts.

Richard Thomas: Which vision of the future do you think Mankind is closer to someday realising, Nation's Orwellian interstellar police state in Blake's 7 or Gene Rodenberry's utopian United Federation of Planets in Star Trek?

Personally I think it's sadly Blake's 7. Though if the series was ever revived like Battlestar Galactica it might remind people that DNA databases, anti-depressant drugs, surveillance cameras and even torture are not supposed to be the products of a free and open society. Then maybe we could avoid the "third century of the second calendar" and the authoritarian Earth Federation.

Richard Holland: I would tend to agree that an approach of commonsense and even-handedness never seems to thrive. But that's because we've become too used to a technology-based, patriarchal social system. Earlier cultures were mellow and happy. I think if technology takes a different direction, opening up our minds to the truth about ourselves and about the universe around us, the technocrat bullies mind find themselves in for a big surprise. Suddenly the Many might not allow the bullying Few to rule.

Richard Thomas: I know you're a big Hammer Horror fan like me. My top ten Hammer films have to be:

The Quatermass trilogy,
The Abominable Snowman,
Horror of Dracula,
Brides of Dracula,
Dracula: Prince of Darkness,
Curse of Frankenstein,
Revenge of Frankenstein,
The Devil Rides Out,

The Mummy,

Twins of Evil.

As you can tell by the list I'm a big Nigel Kneale fan too. Do you have a top ten you would like to share ?

Richard Holland: Isn't it cheating having a trilogy counting as one? I'd include The Quatermass Xperiment because the original series doesn't survive (and because Richard Wordsworth's performance as the monster is superb) but I wouldn't include the other two because the TV versions were so much better. Quatermass and the Pit was a decent attempt, with Kneale adapting it himself, but couldn't match the original. I'm amazed to see Twins of Evil in a top 10 but then a few of mine might have you raising your eyebrows. In chronological order:

The Quatermass Xperiment,

X the Unknown,

Curse of Frankenstein,

Horror of Dracula,

The Mummy,

Curse of the Werewolf,

Plague of the Zombies,

The Devil Rides Out,

Frankenstein and the Monster from Hell,

Captain Kronos Vampire Hunter.

I'd like to include Horror Express as well – what a fantastic romp – but of course it's not a Hammer film.

Richard Thomas: Thanks mate, hope we can do something together again sometime. Twins of Evil might not be the best film ever but I love Peter Cushing's performance in it as fanatical Puritan witch hunter Gustav: "Seek out the Devil worshipers ... by burning them!"

Don't forget to remind people about where they can find Paranormal Magazine and your other projects.

Richard Holland: Cheers, Richard. Paranormal Magazine is available in UK newsagents and in Barnes & Noble in the States. You can buy copies direct from paranormalmagazine.co.uk (postage is free within the UK), or download digital copies from zinio.com. You might also like to check out my blog site, a bunch of articles I've written on British ghosts and folklore (with a few guest writers): www.uncannyuk.co.uk

Sci-Fi and Parapolitics

The New Doctor Who

After 26 seasons, the original series was axed in 1989, leaving a whole generation of children without their own Doctor and only video releases and UK Gold repeats to fill the void. Then in 2003 (the 40th anniversary year of the classic series) came the exciting news that the BBC were going to revive Doctor Who. So, how has the new series done?

When fans first heard that Doctor Who was coming back, many were worried that the series would either make the silly mistake of changing too much and alienating the fandom or, more dangerously, changing too little and confusing new viewers. It is often argued that the reason the old series was cancelled in the first place was because it became a fan show bogged down in its own continuity, instead of a family show for everyone. Fortunately, it looks like the new series has somehow managed to walk this tightrope incredibly well, resurrecting old favourites, inventing new ones and adding to the epic mythology of the program instead of becoming trapped by it.

Over the last four years, we've witnessed the return of legendary monsters like the Autons, Daleks and Cybermen; as well as the Doctor's nemesis the Master; and old allies UNIT, Sarah Jane Smith and robot dog K-9. But each time the new series has revived popular elements like these from the Doctor's past, it has done so in a way that both changes them enough to make them relevant to today, while at the same time staying true to the original concept. The program has successfully recycled old Cold War creations for a post 9/11 world and much more technological age.

Perhaps the most obvious example of how the new series has done this has been the reintroduction of the Doctor's greatest foes, the Daleks, to the series. The new metallic bronze design of the Dalek machines stayed true to what a Dalek is and built upon it, when the temptation must have been to totally redesign them. More significantly though, who and what the Daleks are meant to represent seems to have been updated in a similar way.

In the original series, Dalek creator Terry Nation made it clear what his steel creations represented. When the Daleks first appeared in 1963, WWII had only been over for 18 years and the memory of the Nazis and their crimes was still very much fresh in people's minds. The links between the Daleks and Hitler's Third Reich were made particularly obvious in the 1964 story The Dalek Invasion of Earth, where the Daleks occupy mid-22nd century Earth. In the story, the Daleks organise (like the Nazis had) slave labour camps, use Nazi terminology like "extermination" and are even seen giving their own version of the Hitler salute. Also, later in the 1975 story Genesis of the Daleks Nation introduced a very Fuhrer-like Davros as their leader.

When they returned in the new series, it was made equally clear what the Daleks were now meant to represent. In a move that both updated the Daleks for modern audiences but also echoed what were probably Nation's original intentions, the Daleks were changed from Nazis to symbols for the new evil fresh in peoples minds: radical religious fundamentalism and terrorism.

This change is probably most prevalent in season one of the new series. For instance, in Dalek we encounter a lone Dalek soldier, who after being tortured by its American captors (in an attempt to quite literally make it talk) escapes and exterminates most of them. And, if the parallels here with the War on Terror and Guantanamo Bay weren't already strong enough, the story ends with the escaped Dalek "terrorist", in effect, committing suicide by blowing itself up.

Further, in The Parting of the Ways, the Daleks are even openly shown as religious fanatics, not only talking of "blasphemy" for the first time but also showing religious devotion to their Dalek Emperor, going as far as worshiping the mutant monstrosity as the "God of all Daleks."

Much like the Daleks, the Doctor's second most popular enemies, the Cybermen, were similarly updated when they returned in season two of the new series. Originally created in 1966 by the writing team of Dr Kit Pedler and Gerry Davis, the Cybermen made their first appearance in William Hartnell's last story as the Doctor, The Tenth Planet. They went on to make numerous returns in the series, with a decapitated Cyber head even appearing on display in Dalek.

Interestingly though, the Cybermen we meet in the new series come from a parallel Earth and have nothing to do with the old series'

Cybermen: who originally came from Earth's long lost twin planet Mondas. Despite this change, the new series' Cybermen probably reflect the original premise of their creators better than the old ones ever did. Making it graphically clear who and what they are meant to be ... humans who had had their humanity surgically removed and replaced with cold technology.

In the age of the Internet, mobile phones and iPods, where we're all becoming increasingly dependant on technology, this fact is probably more relevant now than ever. It could even be argued that because of our growing obsession with technology, that we're all, in a way, becoming Cybermen ourselves. A point not missed by the new series in Rise of the Cybermen and The Age of Steel, where we see how a parallel Earth's obsession with the latest upgrade eventually leads to the mass conversion of the population into Cybermen.

It would be a big mistake to think the new series writers are afraid to add to the Cyber mythos though. In the 2008 Christmas special, The Next Doctor, they not only continued to stay loyal to the original vision (for instance, having the Cybermen invade London again) but also introduce two new variants of Cybermen: the wraith like Cybershades and the powerful Cyber-King, a Cyberman Dreadnought style battleship with the capability to convert millions into Cybermen as the steel giant strides through the streets of London.

Another good example, of course, is the Master, who was brought back in season three of the new series. Out of all the Doctor's old enemies to return in the new series, probably none have changed more than the Master. Which is perfectly acceptable, because, like the Doctor, every incarnation of the Master (a fellow Time Lord with 12 regenerations) should be unique. All the key characteristics of the Master are still there, he is still an evil genius and psychopath with dreams of universal dominion, only now instead of simply being a renegade Time Lord ... he's the British Prime Minister and dictator of Earth. Perhaps we should ask if the Master has regenerated into Tony Blair?

Perhaps the most interesting change to the Master though has been the character's new sense of humour. Mirroring Tennant's Doctor the new Master jokes and makes light of tense situations, turning one of the Doctor's greatest strengths against him as well as making the parallels between the two more clear. Not only making the Master more accessible to new audiences but also tying in well with the old series, where the Master was often shown to be the Doctor's parallel and where it was even sometimes hinted that the two are somehow mutually dependent on each other. In the old series the Doctor even went as far as saying: "He's a Time Lord. In many ways, we have the same mind". Interestingly, the Daleks also seem to go back to their roots in this story. Behaving more like Nazis again instead of terrorists: conquering planets, experimenting on prisoners and even going as far as speaking German for the first time.

In the last episode of the Russell T. Davies era, The End of Time, the Time Lords make their return, lead by a resurrected Rassilon who was last seen in 20th anniversary special The Five Doctors.

In season five and six the new head writer Steven Moffat would continue to use this formula, brining back not only the Earth reptiles or Silurians but other favourites the Autons, Sontarans, Daleks and Cybermen ... as well as his own creations the Weeping Angels. And for the first time ever, all these enemies (with the exception of the Weeping Angels) finally put their differences aside and unite against their common enemy: the Doctor.

So six seasons on, the new series has managed to walk the difficult line between pleasing new audiences and fandom incredibly well. Resurrecting and reinventing old series favourites for modern times, making them more relevant to today but in a respectful way that echoes the intentions of their original creators.

Battlestar Galactica – Sci-Fi and the Terror Wars

Very sadly Stuart Miller's Alien Worlds magazine "will not be published again." Although short lived, I really enjoyed my time working with Stuart and am very proud to say I wrote for AW. In a field largely trapped in the 1990s (if not the 1950s), it was fresh, young and innovative, not afraid to seek new answers to old questions or even ask new ones. Perhaps the best evidence of this is the fact that Stuart was prepared to take a gamble and give new writers like me the chance to show what they can do. For those who don't know, I wrote a sci-fi/TV related column called Sci-Fi Worlds, and my first piece was on Doctor Who. Anyway, before I got the sad news about the magazine I had already written a second piece on Battlestar Galactica so I thought it might be a good idea to publish it here instead. Hopefully you'll find it thought provoking, even if you disagree with some of my views.

In particular, though, we'll be considering how the new series, right from the beginning, has reflected the events of 9/11 and their aftermath, what might be remembered as the Terror Wars of the 21st century: Afghanistan, Iraq and Lebanon, as well as 7/7 and a series of other terrorist attacks.

Unlike the new series of Doctor Who, the resurrected Battlestar Galactica is not a continuation of the classic story but rather a total re-imagining of it. Like its counterpart, the new series begins with 12 colonies of humanity getting savagely attacked and ruthlessly wiped out by the Cylons. A relentless and calculating race of war machines that appear hell-bent on the complete annihilation of all mankind. The Cylons' holocaust leaves only a handful of survivors. A ragtag fugitive fleet, 41, 402 people desperately trying to escape their cybernetic hunters and clinging to the hope of finding the legendary 13th colony called Earth.

But other than this shared back story, the two series have surprisingly very little in common. This is a good thing, because the original descended into little more than a childish action adventure, especially when compared to the more serious, adult drama and post 9/11 allegory which is the new series.

The parallels with 9/11 and the War on Terror were made particularly clear in the three-hour miniseries that relaunched Galactica in 2003. The Cylons' sneak attack on the 12 colonies directly mirrored the surprise attacks on the Twin Towers and Pentagon. What's more, the Colonial Fleet in Battlestar completely fail to protect their home worlds from the attacks, just as NORAD completely failed to defend the United States on 9/11. Probably the most emotional and direct reference to the 9/11 attacks, though, is the Memorial Hallway: a shrine onboard the Galactica, walled with hundreds of photos, newspaper clippings, drawings and other mementoes of lost loved ones. It is a haunting reminder of the events that begin the series but, more importantly, also the victims of that black September day.

Perhaps the most interesting and, by far, the most disturbing parallel with 9/11, however, is how the survivors behave in the wake of the tragedy. Of course, just as in the wake of 9/11 in the real world, we witness incredible courage, as well as a stubborn determination to continue in the face of terrible adversity. But, we also sadly see how fear, fueled with a legitimate need for revenge, can bring out the worst in people, changing victims into criminals, the terrorized into terrorists, and moving society closer to the evil it is meant to be opposed.

The best example of this, both in Battlestar and the real world, has been the disturbing maltreatment and even torture of prisoners of war. Mirroring Guantanamo Bay and the Abu Ghraib scandal, Cylon captives (models that look and feel entirely human), are cruelly beaten, raped and even murdered by colonials in various episodes of the new series. Humanity's favourite method of execution being "spacing," or put simply throwing Cylons out the airlock.

Interestingly, the post-9/11 parallels are completely turned on their head in the third season. In the miniseries, as well as season one and two, the Cylons are clearly meant to represent Al Quada and fundamentalist Islam, whereas the humans clearly parallel America. However, in the shadow of the Anglo-American invasion and occupation of Iraq, these roles seem to have been somewhat reversed during season three. The bad guy Cylons become the invading westerners and the humans take the place of the Iraqi insurgency.

Much of season three takes place on what the colonials name "New Caprica": a cold, remote and hostile world that most humans decide to settle on after abandoning their vain search for Earth. However, they are eventually found and, strongly echoing real world events in Iraq, invaded and occupied by the Cylons one year later.

The Cylon invasion and occupation of New Caprica is an obvious mirror for the Iraq war, directly reflecting the conflict in several key ways. For instance, the human resistance is continually referred to as "the insurgence" by the Cylons. Also, again echoing Guantanamo Bay and Abu Ghraib, the Cylon-occupiers use torture against captured insurgents. Saul, the leader of the resistance, is so badly beaten by his Cylon captures that he even loses his right eye.

Moreover, strongly paralleling the Iraqi Police Service created in the immediate aftermath of the 2003 invasion, the Cylons establish the New Caprica Police: a group of human volunteers who work for the Cylon authority to establish law and order within the settlement. The NCP are considered nothing more than Cylon collaborators and traitors by the resistance who, again like their counterparts in Iraq, even go to the extremes of using suicide bombers in their campaign against the Cylons.

Another interesting parallel with Iraq, of course, is the role religion plays in the conflict on New Caprica. The Cylons worship what they call the "one true God," whereas the colonials have many different gods. This is perhaps an echo of the religious differences between a predominantly Christian America and Muslim Iraq.

Chiefly though, perhaps the greatest parallel is that both nightmares, Iraq and New Caprica, are largely born out of a lethal cocktail of misguided good intentions mixed with fear. Initially, the Cylons invade New Caprica under the sincere intention of finally finding some way to live in peace with their human creators and former masters. However, when the humans obviously fight back they soon give in to the fears of the more militant Cylon models and, far from living in peace, become a brutal occupation force.

Similarly, many people sadly supported the 2003 invasion because they were beguiled into believing our troops were fighting to free Iraq from an evil dictator before he could develop weapons of mass destruction and threaten, paradoxically, international peace. Sadly, though, the invasion led to civil unrest, bloodshed and opportunities for undesirable elements.

Perhaps we should give the Cylons some credit though. Unlike Bush and Blair, at least the Cylon leadership didn't have to rely on what turned out to be a false story about WMDs to take their people to war. Likewise, despite everything they go through, the humans still give arch traitor Gaius Balter, who had been the Cylons' puppet president on New Caprica, a fair trial. Which, whether he deserved it or not, is far more than Saddam appeared to get.

Four seasons on from its relaunch, the writers of the re-imagined Galactica have to be congratulated. It would have been easy to write a more simplistic series with, like the original, everything presented in distinct black and white terms of good vs evil and no shades of grey. Instead, they created a highly compelling post 9/11 allegory, a mirror for our troubled times that shows the Terror Wars, warts and all. Hopefully, the rest of the series and the planed spin-off Caprica will be equally brave and thought provoking.

Outbreak! Predictive Programming and Sci-Fi Pandemics

Listening to the Alex Jones Show can sometimes be a scary ride for someone who has listened long enough to see more than a few of the filmmaker's controversial and, more often than not, dark and even disturbing prophesies come true. Most notable, of course, being 9/11 and the Terror Wars without end in the Middle East, the new Great Depression and now the global flu pandemic: like a good weatherman Jones (and his guests) forecast them all months, sometimes even years, before they went down.

It's this alarming accuracy and almost prophetic track record that should have even the most casual or sceptical of listeners more than just a little concerned about what Jones is now predicting for the next decade or so ... a series of staged global pandemics and compulsory vaccinations. Each designer outbreak, and accompanying jab in the arm, deadlier than the last with the ultimate Illuminati Endgame of a worldwide population reduction of between 80 to 90%. This gigantic, almost pagan-like, sacrifice to Mother Earth that would put even Christopher Lee's Lord Summerisle (The Wicker Man, 1973) to shame.

What more ... as if this apocalyptic future wasn't nightmarish enough already ... Jones goes further, suggesting that we've all been secretly conditioned already, practically since birth, to accept this 21st century mass culling through predictive programming in sci-fi films and television shows. The idea being, of course, that if the species is pre-programmed via fiction to sub-consciously associate apocalyptic plagues, Third World Wars and yes European or even Global police-states with the future, then when these things finally do occur the masses will be more inclined to just accept them as the natural course of history and so fail to resist them. Absurd you say ... maybe but that doesn't make it wrong, people would have said the same thing about planes being deliberately flown into buildings ... perhaps only time will tell one way or another.

However, given Jones' past successess ... not to mention the swine flu hype that dominated the mainstream corporate media in 2009 and the push to forcibly vaccinate everyone in the US, Britain and other countries ... only a fool wouldn't at least consider that the documentary film maker could be right about this one too. There certainly isn't any shortage of disturbing government/medical precedents that should give people reason for concern: the infamous Tuskegee Syphilis Experiment being perhaps the most damning, not to mention forcing US pilots to fly through radioactive mushroom clouds in the early Cold War and even contaminating New York City's subway system with dangerous anthrax simulant in 1966.

Whatever the truth, though, global pandemics definitely seem to have been a regular stable of science fiction going right back to when the genre was first conceived. Remember, in H G Wells' ever popular novel The War of the Worlds (first published in 1898) it's a virus that, perhaps suspiciously, finally defeats the Martian invaders.

Lethal viruses, of course, were also a major element of another famous British sci-fi writer, Terry Nation, the creator of the Daleks and the cult series Blake's 7. Several of Nation's scripts for television centered around the idea of a deadly new virus bringing civilization to its knees. Most notably, in Nation's 1964 Doctor Who serial, The Dalek Invasion of Earth, it's a mysterious space plague brought to Earth by meteorites that paves the way for the Dalek conquest of a severally weakened mankind.

Also, maybe a little disturbingly, despite the six part Dalek epic taking place sometime after 2164 the narration on the BBC trailer suggested the story took place in the year 2000! Oddly enough Tom Baker's incarnation of the Doctor later reaffirmed this date when interrogated by the evil Dalek creator Davros in 1975's Genesis of the Daleks. Further, in a classic scene between Baker and Davros the mad scientist even threatens to create a virus capable of destroying all life in the Cosmos. Cold and calculatingly whispering then madly ranting of the God-like power over life and death that would give him: "Yes. Yes. To hold in my hand, a capsule that contained such power. To know that life and death on such a scale was my choice. To know that the tiny pressure on my thumb, enough to break the glass, would end everything. Yes. I would do it. That power would set me up above the gods!"

It might sound a little ridiculous to suggest all this might have been an attempt to prepare the generation growing-up in the 1960s and 70s for a series of global pandemics today, but it certainly doesn't contradict the idea and, in an age where there were still only three channels in Britain, most of the country would be watching.

In 1975, the same year Genesis of the Daleks was first broadcast, Nation also revised the super pandemic idea for his popular series Survivors. As the series title might suggest, the cult classic followed the struggles of a small band of survivors in the wake of a mysterious pandemic that annihilates almost all of the world's population. Interestingly, if not even a little alarmingly, Survivors was remade by the BBC in 2008 which might lend some extra weight to the idea that we're all being prepared for something big coming down very soon.

In Hollywood, too, we certainly haven't seen any shortage of apocalyptic type films involving the outbreak of a killer virus or global pandemic these last few years. 28 Days Later and its sequel 28 Weeks Later, of course, being two of the most blatant examples. In fact you could include most, if not all, of the zombie and vampire sub-genre films. You might even include Children of Men. While the reason why humanity has become sterile by 2028 might never be explained, it ties in perfectly with the theme of population reduction.

It's Will Smith's 2007 film I Am Legend which has to take the prize for being the most worrisome though. Directly mirroring the dark warnings of the conspiracy theorists, in the film it's a new experimental vaccine that's responsible for the pandemic and resultant collapse of civilization in the first place. More troubling still, the Batman vs. Superman publicity poster seems to strongly hint at the film taking place in our real world in the not too distant future.

Perhaps we're just seeing patterns in things that aren't really there ... it's still too early to know one way or another. Regardless, though, people need to take the concerns of researchers like Alex Jones very seriously and do their own research before taking any vaccine rushed through by any government. Particularly in the case of here in Britain, where this is the same Labour government that lied to us about weapons of mass destruction. A lie that has killed over a million people now in Iraq, do we really want to let them stick a needle in our arm because they say it's safe?

Transhumanism in Doomwatch

Transhumanism or Post-humanism is a global movement that advocates advancing human evolution via artificial means such as genetic engineering, cloning and other newly emerging technologies. Made up of academics and enthusiasts alike Transhumanists see certain aspects of the human condition such as old age, sickness and mortality as unnecessary and therefore undesirable. The central premise of the movement being that by merging with technology humans will be able to evolve into a new race of Transhumans free of all forms of human suffering. As so often these real-life developments were foreshadowed in sci-fi.

Back in 1966 Doctor Who was facing a major crisis. After three years as leading man William Hartnell was leaving the series due to ill health and to make matters worse Terry Nation wanted to take his Dalek creations to America to star in their own spin-off series without the Doctor. Thus leaving Doctor Who without its two biggest icons.

It was decided then that Hartnell would be succeeded by Patrick Troughton as the Doctor and that this transition would be helped via the introduction of new star monsters to the series: but who or what exactly could possibly even come close to replacing the Daleks? That was the difficult conundrum then script editor Gerry Davis approached the unofficial scientific advisor to the series Kit Pedler with as Doctor Who approached its fourth season.

Reflecting on his own fears as a medical Doctor of "dehumanising medicine" Pedler delivered in spades. Pedler imagined a race of human beings who had been forced by circumstances beyond their control to slowly replace most – if not all – of their vital organs and limbs with steel and plastic replacements. Ultimately even replacing large parts of their brains with computers and neurochemically programming out their emotions altogether. In effect, surgically erasing all traces of their humanity and transplanting it with cold technology and relentless, uncompromising logic. Pedler and Davis called these new nightmarish life forms Cybermen.

In the 1974 Target Book adaptation of the first Cyber-story The Tenth Planet (which introduced Troughton's Doctor) Gerry Davis described the fictional origins of the Cybermen:

"Centuries ago by our Earth time, a race of men on the far distant planet Telos sought immortality. They perfected the art of cybernetics, the reproduction of machine functions in human beings. As bodies became old and diseased, they were replaced limb by limb, with plastic and steel. Finally, even the human circulation and nervous system were recreated, and brains replaced by computers. The first Cybermen were born."

Somewhat ironically, though, despite this apparent great evolutionary leap forward Pedler reasoned that such beings would be driven solely by the most primitive of biological instincts ... the will to survive whatever the cost no matter what. A frightening contradiction that made itself felt much more prevalently later on when Pedler and Davis decided to revisit the initial concept behind the Cybermen for the entirely separate sci-fi drama sereis Doomwatch in the 1970s, oddly enough in an episode starring Patrick Troughton. Far from battling the Cybermen, though, on this occasion Troughton does everything he can to become one of them! In Troughton's own words: "I keep trying to tell them machines can't catch diseases!"

In the season two episode In The Dark a terminally ill man Alan McArthur (played by Troughton) desperately tries to prolong his life artificially by replacing his dieing body piece by piece with experimental life support systems. Although the experiment is successful it has a terrible price. McArthur begins to think of himself as well as other human beings (if you can still call him human at this point?) as nothing more than bio-chemical machines: ultimately planning on cheating death completely by becoming nothing more than a living brain attached to a dead machine. A procedure that would leave him utterly alone and unable to communicate with the outside world forever, with only his thoughts to keep him company in the endless darkness. Fortunately, though, Professor Quist and his daughter manage to persuade McArthur that this would be a fate worse than death and he decides instead to finally switch off the machinery and die a human being.

Such a scenario might sound fantastic but even back in the 1960s and 70s there would have been signs that such a hypothetical hybridisation between man and machine might become a reality sooner rather than later. In 1960, Belding Scribner invented the Scribner shunt a breakthrough kidney dialysis machine that later saved the lives of countless people with end-stage kidney disease around the globe. More substantially, though, in December 1967 (only a matter of months after The Tenth Planet was broadcast) the first successful human heart transplant took place at Groote Schuur Hospital in Cape Town, South Africa.

It is difficult to appreciate this today but the spare-part surgery envisioned in Mary Shelley's novel Frankenstein and by Pedler was becoming a part of everyday life and was causing a great stir. In Doomwatch Professor Quist essentially offered his friend McArthur a simple choice: live forever as a machine or die a human being? It might sound absurd now but to people living in the 60s and 70s new developments in medicine such as heart transplants would have signalled that many of us might face this kind of difficult decision ourselves someday. Something which might have been premature back then but maybe not so much so today.

Runaway spare-part surgery, however, was only one of Pedler's concerns when he invented the Cybermen. Replacing the human body is one thing but trying to replace or subvert the human mind (and by extension the human soul) is something far more serious. As discussed the Cybermen had altered their brain chemistry, in effect, deleting the last vestige of their biological past: human emotions. And this concept of suppressing or controlling the mind chemically also made itself felt more strongly later on in Doomwatch.

In the season one episode The Devil's Sweets, for instance, chocolates laced with a new drug are used to increase cigarette sales. It is in the season three episode Hair Trigger where the idea is explored best though. In it a violent psychopath and convicted murderer of his family undergoes a revolutionary form of therapy aimed at totally rehabilitating violent offenders and returning them to normal society. Unfortunately, although having a 100% success rate, this "therapy" is nothing short of turning people into remote controlled men and women. As Professor Hetherington explains in the episode: "Electrodes are planted in the patient's pleasure centre, in the cepstral region of the brain, by stimulating this pleasure centre we can counter act severe states of anxiety and depression." And as if turning people into de facto robots wasn't enough this "treatment" is also dangerously addictive. In the words of one of the patients (or victims) "better than sex."

Pacifying people at the push of a button and suppressing human emotions chemically might sound like the stuff of pure science fiction but the latter had already become a serious problem by the 1970s. Directly mirroring the "treatment" seen in Doomwatch so-called 60s "wonder drugs" such as Valium had been prescribed prodigiously – and have latterly been shown to have some serious side effects. The solution, of course, more drugs! A problem Kit Pedler as a medical doctor would have been acutely aware of and exactly the kind of "dehumanising medicine" that inspired the original concept behind the Cybermen.

Anti-anxiety drugs and spare-part surgery are one thing but lets fast forward to today. While the Cybermen might have made interesting food for thought back in the 60s and 70s, today the human race really is close to possessing the kind of technology necessary for reinventing ourselves. Not just limb by limb as Pedler envisioned but gene by gene. Like heart transplants and dialyses machines such technology will no doubt save the lives of countless people but we must be cautious that in saving lives we do not rob people of their humanity.

As Professor Quist points out in In The Dark human beings are separated from animals by two factors: knowledge of our own mortality and human emotion. To become a race of emotionless immortals isn't a step forward it is a step back. Maybe then Prehumanism might be a better name for the so-called Transhumanist movement.

The Devil Rides Out

By the late 1960's the once cutting edge Hammer Films was falling quickly behind the times. Back in the 1950's, the small British studio had been the leader in horror. It was the innovator that bravely treaded where others were afraid to go. Meanwhile, American studios were making mostly bad science fiction films about alien invaders from the Red Planet and giant radioactive monsters (obvious stand-ins for Communists and the bomb). Hammer, on the other hand, were busy remaking the classic Universal gothic horrors that first launched the talkie era back in the 1930s (Dracula, Frankenstein and The Mummy) in glorious techno colour. This time round, though, adding the "dangerous cocktail" of blood and nudity to the horror mix. This might sound rather tame by today's standards but was genuinely shocking to 1950's audiences.

Sadly, however, the studio that dripped blood was unable to stay ahead of the horror game indefinitely. Between the 1957 release of their first gothic horror The Curse of Frankenstein and their last film to date To the Devil a Daughter in 1976, the basic Hammer product for the most part failed to evolve at all. There's only so many Dracula and Frankenstein sequels a studio can make before audiences get bored. By the time Hammer made The Legend of the Seven Golden Vampires in 1974 (kind of a mad mix between a Dracula and a Bruce Lee film), the writing was already well and clearly on the wall. Night of the Living Dead, Rosemary's Baby, The Texas Chainsaw Massacre, The Exorcist ... these are the films that Hammer should have been making a year before their transatlantic competitors did, not an eighth Dracula sequel without the franchise's biggest star Christopher Lee as Seven Golden Vampires was!

There was one film, though, that could have changed the fortunes of the troubled studio and bought them the extra time they needed to regain lost ground. However, the film makers failed to adequately capitalise on the picture's success early enough. That film was The

Devil Rides Out: an adaptation of Dennis Wheatley's bestselling but disturbing 1934 novel about the Occult and widespread practice of Satanism at the highest levels of modern society. It's worth noting that Wheatley's black magic books sold in their millions, even outselling James Bond creator Ian Fleming. Though, they were never popular in America due to Wheatley's VERY British style of writing and imperialistic heroes.

Upon its 1968 release, the film adaptation of The Devil Rides Out was immediately hailed as a return to form by impressed critics. Today, the film is widely considered by fans as perhaps the best of the Hammer Horrors. In 1976, Hammer adapted another of Dennis Wheatley's bestselling black magic adventures: To the Devil a Daughter. But despite doing the best business Hammer had seen in years, it was already too late for the collapsing company ... if they had only released it sooner.

Old British horror films starring Christopher Lee might be interesting to film buffs and might even make fun late night viewing, but what does any of this history lesson have to do with the unexplained, paranormal or even parapolitics?

Well consider this, what if it wasn't all fiction? Both Dennis Wheatley and Christopher Lee (who was instrumental in getting the film rights for Hammer) had at least been somewhat associated with Britain's elite ruling class. Wheatley spending much of WWII in Churchill's basement fortress as part of the Joint Planning Staff with the rank of Wing Commander. And Christopher Lee even claiming (via his mother Contessa Estelle Marie) to be a descendent of Charlemagne, the famous European monarch who through his conquests effectively recreated the Roman Empire in the middle ages. The question must be asked then did this pair know things the general public didn't?

At this point, it's important to point out that by "Satanism" we're definitely not talking about the very limited Christian fundamentalist definition of anything they don't understand but, more seriously, any attempt to use the Occult sciences for selfish, destructive or evil ends. The secretive Sith religion practiced by the evil Emperor of the Galaxy and Darth Vader in the popular Star Wars films (which oddly enough also star Christopher Lee) would definitely qualify, but the Wicca faith, which emphasises a "rule of three," most certainly would not.

That said, the answer to all of the above, as weird as it might sound, is an alarming but definite "yes." Dennis Wheatley was famous for saying, when asked about the supernatural and occult, "don't meddle!" More substantially, though, in a recent documentary titled To the Devil ... The Death of Hammer, made to accompany the DVD release of To the Devil a Daughter, Christopher Lee goes into some detail about how he and Wheatley originally intended the Hammer adaptations of The Devil Rides Out and To the Devil a Daughter to be a kind of "propaganda" warning about the serious dangers of Satanic worship and belief.

Also in the same documentary, filmmaker David Wickes goes into detail about how Wheatley was an "authority" on Satanism and the Occult. Wheatley didn't just make stuff up, he actually knew the meaning of all the different symbols and based his black magic books strongly in real Occult lore and fact. This might explain why the Satanic worship scenes and certain plot elements from The Devil Rides Out seem to mirror, bizarrely, events and oddities in the real world.

The most obvious example, of course, being the "Cremation of Care" ceremony which is alleged to mark the beginning of the annual (and very weird) three week long 'encampment' each summer at Bohemian Grove. A secluded 2,700 acre redwood grove located in northern California. It is widely reported in esoteric cirles that the ceremony involves the mock human sacrifice of an infant to a giant 45 foot stone owl god, and what's more, many of America's and even the world's most elite names in politics, business and the media attend the annual gathering dressed in outlandish but expensive Ku Klux Klan style robes. Which, rather suspiciously, are just like the robes worn at the black magic ceremony to call the "Goat of Mendes" in The Devil Rides Out. It's worth pointing out, too, that the "Great Owl of Bohemia" (which may or may not be meant to represent the Canaanite idol Moloch) has horns.

Then there's the Skull and Bones Society at Yale University, of which President George H. W. Bush, his son President George W. Bush, and the latter's 2004 presidential opponent, Senator John Kerry, are all admitted members. The secret societies headquarters, ominously known as "The Tomb," have become famous on the university campus for their own bizarre rituals (which allegedly involve members dressing up as the Devil, getting in and out of coffins, oh and more mock human sacrifice) as well as the malevolent screams and chants of "Devil equals death!" and "death equals death!" emanating from the building. The windowless "Tomb" is also allegedly decorated with pentagrams and other Occult type imagery. And this is where America's political class have spent their college years since 1832 ... maybe American policies suddenly make a lot more sense.

Perhaps the creepiest and definitely the strangest parallel, though, is that just as in The Devil Rides Out (and again the Star Wars films, strangely enough), after being initiated into The Order of Skull and Bones members are given new Satanic sounding names. George Bush senior's Skull and Bones name allegedly being "Gog" or perhaps "Magog."

How seriously anyone in Skull and Bones or the Bohemian Club take these strange rituals is anyone's guess. However, the elite have certainly put a lot of time, money and research into something they claim is just a bit of harmless recreational fun. Whether Dennis Wheatley knew about either of these secret societies and their rituals isn't known but one things for sure: what they appear to be is exactly the sort of obscene practices he was writing about in his books and, with Christopher Lee, wanted to warn the world about in the Hammer adaptations.

Alternative 3 and the Secret Space Program

In this edition of Room 101, we are venturing to a place where conspiracy theory, UFOs and cult sci-fi meet and merge into one. We are going to discuss Alternative 3, the controversial 1977 spoof documentary that caused uproar in the UK when it was first broadcast.

Originally shown as part of the Science Report documentary series, the spoof suggested an incredible link between Great Britain's "brain drain" of disappearing experts leaving the UK for the US, climate change and a secret space program. The Orson Welles, War of the Worlds, style hoax was so convincing that it actually managed to fool many of the millions that saw it originally into thinking that the world was about to end.

Perhaps the major reason why so many Britons were fooled by the hoax was because it retained the same format and same presenter as the serious programme Science Report. However, as we will discuss later, perhaps there were other reasons why so many people were taken in by Alternative 3.

Beginning as a documentary about Great Britain's then contemporary "brain drain," Alternative 3 soon evolves into an investigation into the mysterious disappearances of a number of different space experts. The research presented over the course of the programme leads to the fantastic hypothesis that the missing experts have been taken off world as part of some secret American/Soviet space program. Further, it is suggested that space travel is far more advanced and has been a reality for much longer than most people believe. The programme even featured a fictional Apollo astronaut, who claimed to have stumbled upon a mysterious Lunar base during his moonwalk.

It is claimed on the programme that scientists had determined that the Earth's surface would soon become uninhabitable, due to pollution causing catastrophic climate change, and that three Alternatives to this problem were suggested. The first two Alternatives were considered too crazy to work and were quickly abandoned. Leaving only the third Alternative, the "Alternative 3" of the title, to colonise Mars via a base on the Moon.

Alternative 3 ends with a video of an alleged manned landing on Mars in 1962, seven years before Neil Armstrong stepped onto the Moon. The video even goes as far as showing something moving beneath the Martian soil, strongly suggesting the presence of life on the red planet.

So how much of Alternative 3 is true and how much is fiction?

Alternative 3 is clearly a fake documentary, the fictitious astronaut makes that obvious. However, the writers do seem to have stumbled upon something in Alternative 3. Themes such as climate change and even the possibility of space settlement have been getting a lot more attention in recent years.

In 2004, President Bush unveiled a new vision for the US space program. He proposed an ambitious plan to return Americans to the moon by 2020 and use the Moon, like in Alternative 3, as a steppingstone for future manned missions to Mars and beyond. Then, in 2006 Nasa announced plans to build a solar-powered outpost at one the Moon's poles, expected to be permanently staffed by 2024.

More recently, Stephen Hawking called for a massive investment in establishing colonies on the Moon and Mars in a lecture to mark NASA's 50th anniversary. Hawking argued that the world should devote about 10 times as much as NASA's current budget to space.

The renowned physicist had previously spoken in favour of colonising space, just like in Alternative 3, as an insurance policy against the possibility of humanity being wiped out by catastrophic climate change: "Life on Earth is at an ever-increasing risk of being wiped out by a disaster such as sudden global warming... I therefore want to encourage public interest in space."

Also, in The Case for Mars: The Plan to Settle the Red Planet and Why We Must, aerospace engineer Robert Zubrin made a strong case for his Mars Direct plan for a manned mission to Mars using only current technology. The ultimate goal being the eventual colonisation and even terraforming of Mars.

It is clear then that Moon bases and Mars colonies, much like the ones alleged to secretly exist in Alternative 3, could well become a reality in the near future. However, what about now, is there any suggestion that there could be a secret space program of any kind?

The answer is an astonishing yes.

Gary McKinnon, the famous UFO computer hacker who was arrested for allegedly hacking into NASA and the US military computer networks, claims that he spent two years looking for evidence of UFOs and suppressed free energy technology. During which, he says that he found a list of officers' names under the mysterious heading "Non-Terrestrial Officers," as well as a list of "fleet-to-fleet transfers" and ship names.

Further, McKinnon claims he checked the ship names and discovered that they definitely weren't US Navy ships. Leading him to suspect that the US have some kind of secret space program: "What I saw made me believe they have some kind of spaceship, off-planet."

Interestingly, McKinnon also says he saw pictures of what looked like cigar-shaped UFOs on a NASA computer. Perhaps these and other NASA UFOs could be part of such a secret space program. With the Pentagon missing $2.3 trillion in transactions (according to Donald Rumsfeld), almost anything becomes feasible.

However there is much harder evidence than this of a secret US space program. On August 7, 1989, a very interesting article called Pentagon Leaves the Shuttle Program appeared in The New York Times. Amazingly, the article openly discussed the existence of a secret US military astronaut program in the late 1970s and 1980s: "In 1979, the Air Force Space Division in Los Angeles founded the

Manned Spaceflight Engineer Program, an elite corps of military astronauts that was to specialize in deploying top-secret payloads. Mr. Cassutt said corps members were told they would fly in space at least once. The secret program, he added, eventually trained 32 engineers and had an annual budget of about $4 million." Admittedly this is no where near the scale of the scenario in Alternative 3, but it is real, a little glimpse into the secret space program.

Many people look at the night's sky and wonder whether mankind will ever reach the stars, perhaps we're a lot closer than we might think.

About the Author:

RICHARD THOMAS is a freelance feature writer specialising in Fortean subjects living in Swansea, South Wales. Richard has written feature articles for high street magazines, including Alien Worlds Magazine, Paranormal Magazine and UFO Matrix Magazine.

He is also a blogger for UFOMystic (www.ufomystic.com) and columnist for Binnall of America (www.binnallofamerica.com).

In addition to writing about the paranormal and unexplained, Richard also writes a column entitled "Grand day out" for the weekend section of the South Wales Evening Post, Wales' largest circulation newspaper. He also writes a lot about sci-fi and TV, and has written features for The Doomwatch Fanzine (www.doomwatch.org) and The Doctor Who Appreciation Society's official magazine – The Celestial Toyroom. You can visit his website at www.richardthomas.eu.

Disclaimer
The views expressed by the author and interviewees are theirs and theirs alone.

Bretwalda Books Ltd